A BENEDICTINE LEGACY OF PEACE

the life of Abbot Leo A. Rudloff

by Brother John Hammond
Monk of Weston Priory

Forword by Eugene J. Fisher Ph.D.
Afterword by Rabbi Arthur Green

Weston Priory, Weston, Vermont

Weston Priory
58 Priory Hill Rd.
Weston, VT 05161-6400 USA

http://www.westonpriory.org

ISBN 0-9763005-0-8

Photos: Weston Priory, unless otherwise noted.

Printed in USA.

Contents

Foreword
by Dr. Eugene J. Fisher

It is impossible to put into words how honored I am to have been asked to write a preface for this wonderfully readable and deeply moving book about my friend, Abbot Leo Rudloff. I knew Abbot Leo for only a half a decade, from the late 1970s until his death in the early 1980s. He influenced me profoundly in that short period. But it was not until later, when researching the history of the Second Vatican Council, that I was to learn how significantly he had influenced my life and, indeed, the lives of my whole generation of, to put it mildly, serious American Catholics. My life as an active lay Catholic has intersected personally with that of many who should be, someday, counted among the saints of the Church: Dorothy Day, Philip and Daniel Berrigan, Archbishop Rembert Weakland, Monsignor George Higgins, Cardinals Willebrands, Bernardin, Keeler and Koenig, Eva Fleischner, Sargent Shriver, and Abbot Leo.

I write, of course, a generation after the good abbot's death. I write as one who has spent his life trying to implement in the life of the Church the fifteen Latin sentences he and Monsignor

Oesterreicher and Cardinal Augustin Bea wrote for the consideration of the Fathers of the Church, words that would become the fourth paragraph of the Conciliar declaration, *Nostra Aetate,* words that he and Bea and Oesterreicher were not totally happy with (as this book notes), but which nonetheless were sufficient to give my generation a mandate to move forward toward the great goal of Catholic-Jewish reconciliation that Abbot Leo had been inspired by God to envision.

I first met Abbot Leo in the fall of 1977 when I attended my first meeting of the Israel Study Group (now called the Christian Scholars Group on Jews and Judaism) at LaGuardia Airport in New York City. This was and is a very eminent group of Protestant and Catholic scholars formed shortly after the Second Vatican Council to work together on common theological issues arising for Christians from their dialogues with Jews. Having just turned 35, I was definitely the new kid on the block amidst a group whose names I had revered since my graduate school days at New York University's Institute for Hebrew Studies.[1] I was immediately drawn to Abbot Leo's calm wisdom and deep passion for Christian-Jewish relations. It would not be until some years later that I learned of his involvement with Monsignor John Oesterreicher and Gregory Baum in drafting the text of the Council's declaration, *Nostra Aetate, no. 4.*

Brother John's wonderful biography mentions Abbot Leo's deep disappointment with the final version of the text. It was a sentiment shared by many, among them his friend, Rabbi Abraham Joshua Heschel. Unlike Abbot Leo, Heschel felt no inhibition about sharing his views with the world (but I am sure Abbot Leo found a way to express his views privately to the Holy See). Most of the criticisms of the text were actually responded to in subsequent statements of the Holy See's

Commission for Religious Relations with the Jews, such as their 1974 "Guidelines and Suggestions for Implementing *Nostra Aetate, no. 4*," which summarized the Council's "deploring" of anti-Semitism using the word "condemn," as well as their 1985 and 1998 statements.[2] So in a very real sense, although it took another three decades for the Church to catch up with Abbot Leo's pioneering vision, it finally has, which I think would please him.

Abbot Leo's pamphlet on why Christians should support the State of Israel, I recall, was the subject of one of the LaGuardia meetings, and was very well received. It did precipitate a heated discussion between my predecessor, Father Edward Flannery, and a Protestant colleague on whether there could be such a thing as a "Christian Zionist," with Flannery holding the position that there could not be since one had to be Jewish to be any kind of Zionist. In my own view, a Christian such as Abbot Leo, who is willing to live in Israel and thus tie his or her fate to it, can indeed be a Christian Zionist (in the best sense of that now much-abused term).

Abbot Leo always wanted the Israel Study Group to come to Weston Priory to hold one of its meetings and to meet the community there. At our meeting of March, 1982, a meeting in which I was elected chair of the group, we accepted his invitation. He had arranged for us to come when the colors of autumn would be at their peak in the mountains. They were, and we came. But instead of being there physically to greet us, he joined us spiritually when, with the brothers, we held a moving memorial service for him. The weather for the meeting itself was all that he would have hoped for—a magnificently sunny autumn day—although the night before I had flown in a thunderstorm through the mountains buffeted by high winds and lightning in a one-engine, 5-seat airplane to get there! It was the only time I have been close to being sick in an airplane.

Abbot Leo was one of the greatest spiritual leaders of my time, and I was very privileged to have known him.

Dr. Eugene J. Fisher
Associate Director
Secretariat for Ecumenical and Interreligious Affairs
U.S. Conference of Catholic Bishops

1. Autobiographical essays by eleven members of this pioneering group can be found in John C. Merkle, ed., *Faith Transformed: Christian Encounters with Jews and Judaism* (Collegeville, Minn.: The Liturgical Press, A Michael Glazier Book, 2003). Further information on the group can be found on the website of Boston College's Center for Christian-Jewish Learning under "Partner Organizations": http://www.bc.edu/research/cjl.

2. The Council had been instructed by Pope John XXIII not to use the word "condemn," so it would not be perceived as an "anathematizing Council" like Trent. The word was only used once, with reference to nuclear war. The Vatican documents and commentaries on them can be found in Eugene Fisher and Leon Klenicki, *In Our Time: The Flowering of Catholic-Jewish Dialogue* (Mahwah, N.J.: Paulist Stimulus, 1990) and Eugene J. Fisher, ed., *Catholic-Jewish Relations: Documents from the Holy See* (Washington, D.C.: US Conference of Catholic Bishops, 1999). The statements and numerous other useful resources in Catholic-Jewish relations can also be found on the Boston College website.

Introduction

It is primarily with my community of brothers at Weston Priory in mind that I have undertaken this writing. For the present community and for future generations, the living memory of brother Leo—his vision, his values, and his person—is the source of inspiration and challenge for the constant renewal and deepening of our monastic life. With the passing of time, there is the inevitable temptation to replace reality with myth in remembering significant persons. While mythic memories have a place in our human stories, I think nothing is richer, though less idealized, than "the sublimity of reality" to borrow a phrase from Abraham Joshua Heschel.[1]

Because brother Leo also profoundly influenced so many events and people far beyond the limits of the Weston Priory community, I am happy to share this rather intimate account with a wider audience. For those of us who shared life and home with brother Leo, this is a gift to be extended to others.

It is my hope that something of the humanity of brother Leo shines through this writing. He was truly a noble person who loved faithfully and inspired many in his rich life spanning eighty years. Ultimately he saw himself as a monastic Christian with a Jewish heart as well as the mother who conceived and nourished Weston Priory through its youthful years. His teaching and the example of his life bear these things out.

In recounting the story of brother Leo in the pages that follow, I have relied principally on his "Reminiscences," written at Weston in the years 1974-76 and "A Bird's-Eye View of the Reminiscences," that he wrote in the following year. In the text all references that are not otherwise identified are taken from those sources. His teaching on monastic issues and on Christian-Jewish relations are largely taken from articles that he wrote for the benefit of the Priory community, oblates and friends, and published in the Weston Priory Bulletin.

Correspondence from brother Leo's files and the Priory archives has been utilized to fill in the gaps and to complete the story. In some instances I have resorted to personal memories.

Myriad persons were significant in brother Leo's life—not least of all, the monastic brothers with whom he lived. For the sake of simplicity and in order to let brother Leo tell his own story I have generally named in this writing only (but not all) the individuals mentioned by him in his "Reminiscences" or correspondence.

In successive stages of this story reference is made to *Frater, Father, and Abbot Leo.* To make the reading less cumbersome for the reader, these titles have been used sparingly. In the final period of his life, Leo was known as *brother Leo.* The designation, *brother,* is not capitalized indicating that it is neither a title nor a role, but is a reminder of fraternal relationships among the members. The Weston Community adopted this practice in the mid-1960s following reflection on St. Benedict's injunction, "When they address one another, no one should be allowed to do so simply by name..." (Rule of Benedict, Chapter 63).

Brother Leo frequently used images to illustrate and to give 'feeling' to his message. I can think of no better image for capturing the inheritance our founder left to his brothers of Weston Priory than the picture evoked by Pope John XXIII in his "Moonlight Address" delivered on the eve of the Second Vatican Council:

> When you return home you will find your children: Caress them and tell them, "This is a caress from the Pope." You will find some tears to dry. Speak words of comfort to the afflicted. Let the afflicted know the Pope is with his sons and daughters, especially in hours of sadness and bitterness.... It is a brother who speaks to you, a brother who, by the will of our Lord, has become a father. But fatherhood and brotherhood are both of them gifts of God. Everything is.—Everything.

John Hammond
Weston Priory

1. *God in Search of Man,* Abraham Joshua Heschel, Jewish Publication Society and Meridian Books, 1960, p.39

"A great influence on me in my youth was my first visit to Wildshausen, the estate of my aunt Else, my father's sister...There was an atmosphere of noble living in Wildshausen, into which I settled as if into my natural right."

1

From Düren to Rome with a Touch of Nobility

Foreboding Skies and a Happy Youth

> The place that first emerges clearly and distinctly in my consciousness is surmounted by an uncanny sky. The horizon is overshadowed; the air is as if filled with smoke. The sun shines, but it gives only a bleak light; it stands in the pale dome like a cold dreary disk. The sky is cloudless, but without friendly blue radiance. It is colorless, and as if swept by sinister storms, which do not reach us. Here, down on earth, it is oppressive, without breeze and as if the sun were in eclipse. The people live here as if in the grasp of a dull pain: they are either under the burden of suffering, or they themselves are the foes who inflict that suffering, hard and to be feared.

In the first entry to his "Reminiscences," written at Weston Priory when he was about seventy-four years old, brother Leo gave an English translation of a text he composed more than fifty years previously when he was known as Frater Leo von Rudloff, a young monk in the monastery of St. Joseph in

Gerleve, Germany. In vivid imagery he paints a grim picture of "the place which first emerges clearly and distinctly" in his consciousness. That foreboding picture may well be a premonition of his stormy and adventurous life's journey through darkness, pain, and confusion to a place of reconciliation and peace.

Leo's "first clear and distinct" memory doesn't come from the place of his birth—Düren, a thriving Prussian industrial city.[1] At the start of the twentieth century, Düren was home to some 25,000 inhabitants, among them a family headed by Otto von Rudloff, a civil servant. Fastidious in dress and taciturn in speech, Otto was entitled to call himself Baron. He and his wife, Zoë, already parents of six sons and a daughter, welcomed their youngest child on January 31, 1902. Christened Alfred Felix von Rudloff, he grew up as Fred, and would eventually become Abbot Leo.

The *von* prefix in his surname at birth signaled a family of the lower German nobility, although his father's title had by that time lost much of its aura of prestige. As a government bureaucrat, Fred's father was to a great extent discontented in his work. His persistent dissatisfaction led to several family moves, including relocation to Bromberg. It is that city, to which his family moved when he was two years old, that the young monk of Gerleve saw so bleakly in his earliest memory. In fact, turn-of-the-century postcards show Bromberg to be a classic European enclave with attractive streetscapes, handsome churches and squares, and rows of townhouses bordering both sides of the canal that flowed through the city. With the perspective of time, brother Leo saw more clearly the basis for his childhood memory:

> I see things now a little different. There was much sunshine, and not only shadow, in those early days. The truth of the matter may be that a feeling which was prevailing

> in my mother at that particular time had affected me. The place described above was the city of Bromberg in the Prussian Province of Posen to which we moved when I was two years old. It is now Bydgoszcz in Poznan (Poland).

The mother's 'depression' left a lasting impression with her youngest sensitive child.

> My mother, a native of the beautiful Rhineland, had grown up in the lovely spa of Neuenahr...[she] was always terribly homesick in that East German city. In Bromberg there was a sharp dividing line between the upper crust of society, made up of Prussian officers and Government officials like my father, and the lower stratum which was almost exclusively Polish. All of our servants were Polish.... My mother felt foreign in that surrounding.

Although the youngest son sometimes wondered if his father's apparent banishment to the east represented disciplinary action, his brothers insisted it was a promotion. Still, another stark scene observed by a six-year-old, who couldn't grasp its meaning, would remain with him all his life.

> My memory of our departure from Bromberg is even more poignant. I see myself with my mother and sister in the horse-drawn coach that was to take us to the railroad station. Then I see Herr Schattschneider, the landlord and director of a conservatory of music which he had installed in the same building, come up to the carriage and extend his hand to my mother. My mother refuses to take it, which was totally contrary to her nature. Then I hear Mr. S. say: *Wollen Sie denn so von mir scheiden, Gnaedige*

> *Frau?* ("Do you really want to depart from me that way, Madam?") My brother Kurt tells me that, alas, my father in his weakness for drink, had financial troubles. He had been unable to pay the last outstanding rent on the apartment and Mr. S. had become unpleasant about it. It was my Aunt Else, my father's sister, who bailed us out. This is the background to the scene so vividly imprinted in my childhood memory.

Otto von Rudloff was likened by his son to the archetypal hunter of the Book of Genesis. "He was quite a Nimrod. He liked to get his deer or boar." Of his father's personality and background, the son wrote:

> He was by nature meant to be a country squire, the lord of a manor. He was thoroughly happy when he visited his sister on her estate, Wildshausen. But alas, for him, there was no manor and no beautiful estate; the family fortunes had dwindled. My father had been raised in luxury, several servants always at his beck and call. No doubt he was spoiled, and when he was condemned to the drudgery of office work, although he performed his duties conscientiously, he was quite unhappy. So there was a time when he found escape in drink. Thank God he was able later on to pull out of it. He voluntarily submitted to treatment that had the hoped-for success, but in the meantime, he made my mother, who loved him, quite unhappy.

After departing Bromberg and government service, the elder von Rudloff retained his title of government counselor. That allowed him, back in Westphalia, to take up the practice of advocacy, which, his son reported, "proved to be an unfortunate step."

> He was a shy, retiring man, a real introvert, and to argue a case before the court went against the grain. He won some and was highly praised, and some clients retained a great attachment and admiration for him. He lost others, and soon found that his office was rather empty. Again he turned to alcohol for solace, and this, of course, made his work less satisfactory. Except for his government pension, we could soon have starved. Even with it, and despite my mother's frugality, my parents just about made ends meet.

The family's return to their native Westphalia brought them to Münster, the place where Fred grew up, the place he thought of as home. An administrative center with a university dating from the eighteenth century, Münster had splendid Baroque architecture and still older landmarks. The name means a monastery church; the city grew up around a twelfth-century *münster.*

Still at an impressionable age, Fred's visits to his aunt Else's estate in the Sauerland marked his emerging personality with a touch of nobility that lasted throughout his lifetime. He acknowledged the influence of that early experience in his "Reminiscences":

> One thing which had a great influence on me in my youth was my first visit to Wildshausen, the estate of my aunt Else, my father's sister. It was my first visit of many.... There was also an atmosphere of noble living in Wildshausen, into which I settled as if into my natural right. It is a most beautiful estate, with over a thousand acres of lovely hills and well attended forests. The family, not titled, by the name of Cosack, lived in the baronial style introduced by my aunt.... There were the butler, the coachman, the private forester, and several maids.

During his Münster years, the future monk delighted in the walks he took with his father at Wildshausen in the Sauerland mountains of southern Westphalia. Those walks were among his fondest memories. Decades later in the Green Mountains of Vermont, he would express his feelings for the forest that sprang from those father-son excursions.

> It was there that I fell deeply in love with the woods, so much so that it sometimes frightened me. The woods sort of accepted me and sucked me in. I felt an almost mystical oneness with them, and I felt a real relationship with their inhabitants, especially the deer.
>
> I can still feel that deep yearning in my soul for the forests, and there is still hardly anything I enjoy more than a silent, lonely walk in the woods. My father, too, enjoyed the quiet walks. Often we went together over the paths, which were kept free of twigs that could make a noise and warn the deer. We hardly spoke a word on those walks, but we shared an inner communication there that needed no words. You have to be quiet in the woods. Noise and loud talking in a forest still disturb me.

When a young monk at Gerleve, he had tried to capture his experience of nature in a poem originally written in German. Later at Weston, he translated it:

Now has the wood's embrace, so full of comfort,
slip't from me almost like a dream,
the woods through which I strolled
as through a wonder of an intimate fulfillment.
The forest's silence, full of mystery enveloping,
is still resounding in my inmost being.
My ear harkens to the tender leaning of the blades
when the deer walks over them to feed.

Now the poor walls of my cell surround me.
Into their fastness hurls itself that echo
like a water-jet into my hollow hands.
It breaks in pearls. But a mighty song
grows in the bosom of my heart:
The prototype is speaking when silent are the symbols.

As the youngest of eight children in the von Rudloff family (seven boys: Kurt, Ernst, Walther, Otto, Werner, Hans, Alfred, and one girl, Zoë), Fred was a favorite and later viewed himself as spoiled by the attentions of his mother and siblings. His mother was a sensitive and frail woman, pious and devoted to her Catholic religion. Abbot Leo noted that, though she was born in Cologne, Germany, "she came from the well-established burgher's family of Lenné, which had emigrated from Liège in Belgium to the Rhineland," and that her first language was French. Of her, Abbot Leo would write,

> Her face was a wonderful blend of love and devotion, of openness, joy of living and cheerfulness and goodness. She was a very devout woman, a most convinced Catholic, but far from pietism and bigotry....
>
> She loved growing things, beautiful flowers and useful vegetables, and she could always laugh and play with the eight children to whom she gave birth. The lightness, flexibility, optimism, and trust, which in all of us counteracts a certain heaviness and perhaps indolence, comes from her side.

During World War I, the family suffered material deprivation. All the young men in the family with the exception of Alfred, who was too young, served in the military. One brother, Walther, died on the battlefield. Fred's mother, Zoë, died

above: “There has always been a close relationship between all of us.” Fred, left of his sister, Zoë. *center left:* “My mother Zoë was a very devout woman.” *center and right:* Father “was by nature meant to be a country squire, the lord of a manor.” *below left:* Fred with Zoë. *below center:* With older brother Johannes, future Bishop of Hamburg.

when Fred was in his teens. His only sister, named Zoë after her mother, took over the mother's role in the family and became very close to her youngest brother. Her health, too, was poor, and she died while still in her twenties.

In spite of the difficult moments of family problems, Fred's youth was a happy time. He enjoyed school and was a good student. He attended public schools and enrolled in dance classes. Though not especially athletic, he liked track and the outdoors. He was popular among his schoolmates, but already sensed uneasiness because of class distinctions:

> Before World War I, the *von* before a name had a magical power. The Weimar Republic did not change that very much. Although titles were officially abolished then, they could still be used as part of a name. I must confess that as a boy I gloated somewhat on that fact, although even then I saw the questionable validity of that state of affairs. I realized the unfairness of giving advantages to anyone because he had an inherited title of nobility.

Fred's eldest brother, Kurt, eventually a musician and composer, introduced him to the classical music he took pleasure in throughout his life. Another brother, Hans, went to the seminary; eventually he became the Auxiliary Bishop of Osnabrueck and Episcopal Vicar of Hamburg and the surrounding country.

By the time Fred graduated from the *Gymnasium,* or High School, the war had ended. He entertained the possibility of becoming a Franciscan friar. Later he wrote sparingly of his "calling to the monastery."

> It is very difficult for me to talk or write about this and I must needs be much shorter and more reticent than the thing deserves. I feel a great reluctance to manifest

> something which is so intimate to me that it can hardly be expressed.... It was, at the beginning, childlike and simple and unshakable.... Religion was for me a joyful affair. God was good and loving. Of that I had always been convinced. That again was probably due to a great extent to my mother's childlike relation to God. I must confess that a very personal relationship to Christ, and through him to God the Father, developed then and grew and grew. Later, through theological studies, it was intimately linked with a lively feeling of God's indwelling in us through the Holy Spirit...and it was not really a call to a distant, transcendent God somewhere up in heaven. It was rather an intimate conversation as with a lover.

As he pondered his future, he was invited by a priest friend to visit the Benedictine Monastery of Saint Joseph in Gerleve, not far from his home in Münster. "There and then it happened. It was a new and more concrete falling in love. I knew from that moment that it was there that I belonged and that I could realize my dedication concretely." Immediately he felt an attraction to the flourishing monastic community. He was drawn to the peacefulness of monastic prayer and the harmony of study, work, and communal life.

A visit to another Benedictine monastery, Maria Laach in the Rhineland, served to further his resolve to enter the community at Gerleve. In the aftermath of World War I both Gerleve and Maria Laach had attracted many young men eager to embrace the monastic life. Maria Laach enjoyed prominence among the monasteries of Europe as a center for liturgy, art, and theological studies. Ildefons Herwegen, known for his erudition and influence in the social and political world, ruled the monastery in the manner of a prince-abbot. In contrast, Fred saw in the community of Gerleve a certain humble simplicity that appealed to him. The abbot there, Raphael Mollitor, while authoritarian in the same Beuronese monastic tradition that governed Maria Laach, was a more paternal figure. Fred also sensed a friendlier, more familial spirit within the community. Without further delay, at eighteen years of age, he applied to enter Saint Joseph's Abbey at Gerleve and was accepted as a postulant.

Life in the monastery turned out to be all that Fred had hoped for: he found joy in the studies, the prayer and the quiet. When he became a novice after a year as postulant, he received the name Leo and was called Frater Leo. His first two years at Gerleve passed quickly and he was soon ready to make a lifetime commitment to monastic life.

As in other Benedictine monasteries, the first monastic commitment is for a period of three years after which the monk is free to depart or to commit himself for life. On making his first monastic profession, Frater Leo considered it to be a life commitment: he placed no conditions on his love for the community at Gerleve.

While happy, and content with the monastic observance in the monastery, Leo did hope for growth and change. He and several other monks "felt the lack of genuineness and spontaneity of brotherly relations between the monks." The received wisdom was that "private friendship was dangerous, almost evil." Early on, he and a confrere suggested that there should be more opportunity for fraternal exchange and personal friendship among the monks. They observed that relationships were too formal and that personal communication was restricted to abbot, novice master, spiritual director, or other officials of the community. Their suggestion was met with a cold and rigid rebuff. The strict Beuronese Constitutions of the time that the Gerleve monks were to follow left no room for satisfying such human needs.

Besides the absence of personal friendships, Leo also experienced painfully the separation between the lay brothers and the priest-monks. Manual labor and menial tasks were the domain of the lay brothers. They did not join the priest-monks in choir for the prayer of the monastic office, but sat separately and prayed the rosary and other devotions together. Nor could the lay brothers vote in the monastic chapter. They were not even present for community recreation. The priest-monks and those training for the priesthood, on the other hand, devoted their time to study, prayer, and classes. They also preached retreats and assisted in parish work in nearby towns.

A glimpse of the chasm between the monastic classes at Maria Laach comes from another priest-monk of a monastery of the same Congregation in Germany in the 1920s. "Even the lay brothers whose hair had grown gray looked at the youngest novice as a future priest and met the newcomer with much of the reverence which they felt for an ordained priest."[2] While such a two-tier system was common in Benedictine monasteries of the period, it seemed to Leo to be at variance with the Rule of Saint Benedict that called for equality among the members regardless of their previous status in society.

Throughout this period and later, Leo always spoke highly of his original monastic home, the community at Gerleve. Yet he refused to idealize it, as he wrote in the 1970s:

> Gerleve was—and is—a good monastery. There was a good discipline, true fervor and also brotherly love.... At the time I left (1938), there were about ninety members, almost equally divided into the two groups—choir monks, who all were or became priests, and lay brothers. Here we see already the elements that militated against an intense communication and closeness of fraternal relationship. Among so many, it is impossible to establish brotherly

exchange and intimate relationship. And the two classes mentioned above were quite sharply distinguished: training was separate; novitiate was separate; recreation, as a rule, was held separately. The brothers inhabited separate parts of the monastery, having no single cells, but dormitory-like bedrooms. They did all the manual work, except for a few items.

Sojourn in the Eternal City

In 1923, Leo was sent by Abbot Raphael to pursue studies for the priesthood at the Benedictine College of Sant'Anselmo in Rome. Recognizing the intellectual and monastic potential of the young monk, the abbot directed him to earn a doctorate in theology so that he could teach his confreres on his return to Gerleve.

In the mid-1920s the College of Sant'Anselmo was barely twenty-five years old. Intended by the abbots of the Benedictine Confederation as a center of learning for Benedictines from every nation, it was also the home of the Abbot Primate of the Benedictine Confederation. His task was to facilitate relations between the Holy See and the independent Benedictine monasteries all over the globe and to preside as Abbot over the diverse College community.

In the early years of Sant'Anselmo, both the student body and the faculty were predominantly European. While Latin was the language spoken in classes, students tended to stay together within their respective modern language groups: Germans with Germans, French with French, English with English. Although there was a degree of diversity represented by the different observances and thinking of far-flung home communities, all students were uniform in appearance, wearing the traditional black tunic and scapular of Benedictine monks.

Sant'Anselmo was the place where Frater Leo first encountered the church and the world in a somewhat wider context. All the while maintaining his usual serious focus on studies, he met two men who were to influence his monastic future profoundly. One was a student, the other a professor. Damasus Winzen was a young monk of Maria Laach, who combined a sparkling sense of fun with an avid taste for art, the classics, theology, and monastic spirituality. A magnetic personality, Damasus was a natural leader. In contrast to Leo—tall, thin, pale, reserved, sedate, and proper—Damasus was a stocky figure with ruddy complexion, reddish brown hair, and mischievous eyes, who was gregarious and impetuous.

The friendship between these two young German students, begun on the Aventine Hill—one of the seven that surround the ancient city of Rome, the center of early Christianity—was to become the seedbed of an innovative, contemporary approach to monastic life in the middle of the twentieth century. Damasus, taking the lead, introduced Leo to the wonders and historical sites of Rome and to occasional raucous partying with fellow German students. Spontaneously, Damasus would joke about the eccentricities of their professors. He delighted in conjuring up for the benefit of his comrades the nightly ritual of Pater Josephus Gredt, their philosophy professor. With great detail, he told how each night the professor would meticulously fold down his bed covers, and then proceed to crawl under them from foot to head, until he reached his pillow where he would contentedly drift off into the dream world of scholastic Thomism.

Leo had his own tales to tell of the illustrious professor of Thomistic philosophy whose dense Latin text books were still widely used in Catholic seminaries throughout the western world in the 1950s:

> Father Gredt, a Rhinelander by birth, was a monk of Seckau in Austria and later of Trier when the old Abbey of St. Matthias in Trier was revived. He was quite a character.... He was very fond of sweets, and his colleagues were wont to push an additional dessert to him at dinner. He chewed garlic, which was supposed to counteract hardening of the arteries. For a long time he maintained that no one could smell it. When at last he was convinced that one could smell it at a distance of a mile, one of his students asked him: "Are you now giving it up, Father Joseph?" and he answered with supreme logic: "What is the use? One smells it anyway."

These two very different personalities, Damasus and Leo, entered into a lifelong dialogue. Leo, thoughtful, rational, steady, was attached to the land wherever he found himself. Damasus came out of the Maria Laach tradition of Odo Casel, who had elaborated "the theology of mystery" in the liturgy and sacraments. Adventurous, exploring, brooding, at times Damasus seemed lost in the clouds of mystical thought. Years later, Leo characterized their poles-apart personalities:

> Were we on an ocean voyage, I would be standing at the prow of the ship, feeling the wind and the splash of the raging waves, watching, leaning into the weather and the vastness ahead. He would be below decks in his cabin, reading the Psalms and brooding over the meaning of what was happening overhead.

A Maverick Professor "Under a Cloud"[3]

The second significant figure at Sant'Anselmo for the future of Leo was a monk-professor from the Belgian monastery of Mont César. Amid an otherwise bland and colorless faculty, Lambert Beauduin stood out, a disconcerting teacher and a maverick monk constantly in conflict with ecclesiastical authorities in Rome. Only the frequent interventions of his friend, Cardinal Désiré Joseph Mercier, the progressive archbishop of Malines, Belgium, assured his survival as a Benedictine in good standing.

In the first decade of the twentieth century, a time of powerful reaction by church authority to both anti-clericalism and innovation, Lambert had introduced the first daily missal to give the laity active participation in Eucharist and the public prayer of the church. In a time of isolationism and of defensiveness by the Roman Church, he actively engaged in ecumenical dialogue with Protestant and Orthodox churches. In a time when monastic revival meant reverting to the "golden age" of the medieval Church, Lambert called for a radical renewal of monastic life rooted in the original inspiration of the earliest monks while at the same time responding to contemporary needs and issues.

Beauduin's approach to ecclesial and monastic life was far from theoretical. His thinking was immersed in experience. During World War I he went underground in an effort to hamper the German occupation. Posing as a wine merchant, he crossed back and forth between Belgium and Holland, helping people escape to England. Arrested by the Germans in 1915, he eluded his captors and made his way to Holland. After the war he returned to the monastery of Mont César and, in 1921, was sent to teach at Sant'Anselmo. He taught in Rome for four years, exerting his influence on a large group of young Benedictine students. While there he formulated a plan for a new experiment in monasticism with a special emphasis on ecumenical dialogue. Pope Pius XI approved the experiment in the brief, *Equidem verba,* addressed to the Abbot Primate. Thus commissioned, Lambert left Sant'Anselmo in 1925.

In March of that year he also met with Angelo Giuseppe Roncalli, the newly appointed Apostolic Delegate in Bulgaria (later Pope John XXIII), who would publicly attribute to Beauduin his own understanding of the importance of ecumenism. Nine months later, Beauduin birthed his new monastic experiment in a vacated Carmelite monastery at Amay-sur-Meuse in Belgium.

During his research in Rome, Beauduin's discovery of the ecclesiology of the Eastern churches had led him to a deeper understanding of the Catholic church. At Amay, the life was one of genuine poverty, the accent on prayer, manual labor, and study. All monks had a role in work, Beauduin himself performing the most menial tasks. Matins, Lauds, and Vespers were sung. Prime and Compline were recited in choir. Terce, Sext, and None were recited privately or with a companion. Most remarkable, the community Mass was celebrated in the Eastern-rite liturgy. Eventually the community consisted of two choirs, each using a different liturgy, one in the Latin rite, the other, the Byzantine rite.

As he pioneered in ecumenical activity, Beauduin reached beyond the limits of authoritarian monastic restrictions. This led to his exile in the early 1930s from the very monastery he had founded. Not until the papacy of John XXIII was Beauduin restored to his bi-ritual community, relocated in Chevetogne, Belgium. Only then was his vision vindicated and the importance of ecumenism acknowledged by the Second Vatican Council.

Lambert Beauduin's teachings had far-reaching effects on Benedictine monasticism in the mid-twentieth century. Gregory Lemercier, a contemporary of Beauduin at Mont César founded Our Lady of the Resurrection monastery in Cuernavaca, Mexico, in 1947. Damasus Winzen, one of the founders of Mount Savior Monastery in Elmira, New York, in 1951, acknowledged Lambert's inspiration in his monastic development. Abbot Leo's own monastic vision, promoted at both the Dormition Abbey in Jerusalem and Weston Priory in Vermont, was profoundly influenced by the Belgian monk's insight.

Recalling "one of my most inspiring professors," and commenting on his exile from Amay, Leo said, "For a time, Father Lambert was under a cloud. His was a pioneering mind, way ahead of his time, in ecumenical matters, often bold in his teaching, extremely lively and interesting." Comparing Ivan Illich to his mentor, he observed, "Alas, such men all too often get into trouble with the Roman 'establishment' in our days."

Leo completed his theological studies and earned his doctorate with a thesis on Saint John of the Cross and the Rule of Benedict. Before leaving Sant'Anselmo, he was ordained to the priesthood, a step considered by monks of that era the crown of monastic life. Armed with ordination and doctorates, Leo and Damasus bade farewell to their student companions in Rome in 1928 and returned to their respective monasteries in Germany.

June 22, 1941, Fifty members of the German Gestapo occupied the monastery of St. Joseph in Gerleve. "Some monks fled; others were conscripted." Nazi garrison stationed at St. Joseph Abbey in Gerleve, World War II. *Archiv der Benediktinerabtei Gerleve*

2

Germany in the Thirties: Gathering Storm

Little had changed at the Abbey of Saint Joseph in Gerleve since Leo's departure for studies five years earlier. The community was peaceful in its rural setting: the lay brothers efficiently operated the dairy farm; the ordained choir monks chanted the monastic hours of prayer in Latin. The orderly rhythm of life was all that Father Leo had hoped for.

Not yet thirty years old, Leo was entrusted with teaching philosophy and theology to the young monks in the community. He also enjoyed preaching retreats and conducting discussions with guests who came to the monastery's youth hostel. Over a three-year period, he lectured in religious studies at the College of Social Workers in nearby Münster.

> On the whole I was much occupied at Gerleve with lecturing and preaching. One confrere once counted the talks I had given in a week, and it came to a staggering number. These were in addition to my regular classes.

Scholarly research and writing further busied Leo. His first book, *Das zeugnis der Vater*—a book on the Patristic period of the Church—was written at that time.

> It was absorbing, pleasant work. At one period I had up to twenty volumes of Migne's Latin and Greek editions of the Church Fathers in my room, working in them simultaneously. Many articles in magazines as well as book reviews were done at that time and my doctor's dissertation was published in a series of articles in *Divus Thomas*.

His most popular book, *Kleine Laidendogmatik,* subsequently translated into fourteen languages, was written at Gerleve. Herder & Herder published the English edition under the title, *A Layman's Theology*. Leo credited Joseph Pieper, the distinguished German philosopher, with providing "great stimulation and very constructive criticism" for his work on the book. At that time in the 1930s, when theological writing was limited to the sphere of the professional, putting the teachings of Thomas Aquinas into the hands of the laity was a radical departure. His book on the Church Fathers was less popular and received less acclaim.

The Third Reich Threatens

While life inside Saint Joseph's Abbey moved gently with the calm rhythms of intellectual work and rural activity, troubling forces were stirring the Abbey of Maria Laach, home of Father Damasus. These years bracket the ascendance of Adolph Hitler and his Nazi Party, fueled by promises to create social reforms that would free Germany from the economic straits that followed World War I for years, through the dire inflation of the 1920s (4 million Deutsche Marks to one U.S. dollar) and into the 1930s when as much as 43 percent of the German labor force was unemployed.

The community of Maria Laach and its abbot, both enjoying a large public following, were influential in church circles in Germany. In recognition of the need for social change, the monastery at first backed Hitler's proposal for a renewed German nation. In a public address the abbot spoke favorably of the emerging socialist party. Leo's friend and classmate, Damasus Winzen, was actively involved as a chaplain in the Catholic youth movement. Soon, however, it became evident that Hitler intended to infiltrate all youth movements in the country in order to inculcate Nazi hatred and anti-Semitism.

Meanwhile, inside his monastic community, Damasus had come into conflict with his superior. Abbot Ildefons, who had supported and encouraged Damasus in his monastic life and studies, now objected to new ideas that the professor was advancing to younger monks. Damasus argued that the role of the abbot was to be the spiritual father of the community, not a prince-abbot or hierarch in the ruling style of Maria Laach. He also held that priesthood was not the culmination of monastic life; to become an authentic monk, it was not necessary to be ordained. The abbot perceived these ideas as an attempted revolution against the prevailing understanding of monastic life.

Prosper Guéranger, founder of Solesme Abbey in France, and Maurus and Placidus Wolters, founders of Beuron Abbey in Germany, major reformers of the mid-nineteenth century, had initiated a revival of Benedictine monastic life. They took as their model and inspiration the monasticism of the Middle Ages. The highly developed institutional and clerical model that was theirs would prevail well into the twentieth century.

In taking positions contrary to Abbot Ildefons Herwegen's regarding the abbatial role, priesthood, and monastic life, Damasus, young and daring, was pressing beyond the limits of that prestigious reform movement. Abbot Ildefons was directly in the line of those illustrious predecessors, and his role as prince-abbot was quite faithful to their vision. The more enduring work of Guéranger and the Wolters was in liturgy: what they began led to a shift in the Catholic Church that would culminate in the liturgical reforms of Vatican Council II.

Their vision of monasticism, however, called for a return to what was seen as the golden age of church worship in the feudal times. At a very early date, Damasus challenged the validity of that vision. He saw that what was needed was not reform, but renewal—a return to the spirit at the source of Christian worship and monastic life, rather than a revival that imitated an idealized past.

The situation of economic and political crisis in Germany provided Abbot Ildefons with an opportunity to put some distance between Damasus and the community of Maria Laach. It was against this backdrop that Father Damasus arrived one day in 1937 at the door of Saint Joseph's Abbey in Gerleve, asking to speak with Abbot Raphael Mollitor. The abbot listened as the young monk poured out the story of mounting Nazi pressure on Maria Laach. Recalling at Weston the German experience of that period, Leo wrote, "Pressure from the Nazis grew worse and worse. One felt the strangling clutch around one's neck and gasped for air. Often they tried to implicate us in some crime, either national or moral."

There was fear that Benedictine monasteries would be suppressed and the monks sent into exile. As Leo explained:

> The community of Maria Laach decided to send some monks to America to be of some help, if possible, in pre-

> serving our traditions and, later on, coming to the aid of our monasteries. Prior Albert Hammenstede of Maria Laach had already gone to the United States in search of an opportunity to initiate some sort of foundation. He was in touch with Archbishop Walsh of Newark, New Jersey, who needed professors for his seminary quickly and on a temporary basis, until some of his younger clergy returned from their studies in Rome and Louvain. So he asked Father Albert to get two more monks with degrees to fill those posts. Father Albert asked for Father Damasus, and Father Damasus asked for me.

The abbot summoned Leo who, during their conversation, had no inkling of dramatic, imminent change:

> At that time I was the subprior at Gerleve. Abbot Raphael asked me what I thought of the idea of sending a monk with Father Damasus to America. He did not mention me, and I thought of one individual who could be sent. So I spoke strongly in favor of the idea. Only then did Abbot Raphael say, "I meant to send you."
>
> Quite honestly, I was not too happy about that decision at the time, or, at least, I received it with very mixed feelings. I was very happy and settled at Gerleve. America frightened me. I thought about it as so many Europeans still think. They identify America with New York, perhaps, or with Chicago and its gangsters, skyscrapers, busy streets, technical know-how, but no culture, no poetry, no beauty. That was the image of America I had in mind. But then the spirit of adventure seized me, especially after talking to Father Damasus. It also became clear that beyond the need of the moment, namely escaping the Nazi menace, there were deeper reasons and loftier aims which we hoped to accomplish in America.

In her story of the Mount Savior monastery, besides addressing with candor the involvement of Maria Laach with the Nazi movement, J. Madeleva Roarke explores the underlying reason for the dispatch of Father Damasus to America. After extensive research, she observes about the still discussed separation of Damasus from his abbey, "It could not have been easy [for him] to carry the additional burden of knowing that in the true sense of a Greek tragedy, he was the protagonist who contributed to his own downfall."[1]

Roarke convincingly demonstrates that the real reason Damasus was sent to the United States sprang from the positions he maintained on monastic issues contrary to those of his abbot, Ildefons Herwegen. Only after they were tragically involved, did the abbot and the community of Maria Laach realize that they had been duped by the National Socialist German Workers' Party and its fanatic leader. Damasus was by no means the only member of the community in this compromised and dangerous situation, yet his involvement did provide an excuse for the abbot to choose him for the mission to North America. Roarke exposes the cover for the real motive, and it may shed light on what Father Leo meant by "deeper reasons and loftier aims which we hoped to accomplish in America." She reports:

> There is a single sentence used by Damasus when it was necessary to explain his presence in the United States. It did not vary and was never further explained. "In 1938 my abbot, fearful that Maria Laach would be suppressed by the Nazis, sent me with two other monks to America to have a place to which the assets of the monastery could be secured." That explanation was taken at face value by those who heard it, and it satisfied the normal interest of those to whom it was addressed.[2]

From all appearances, this was the explanation accepted by Leo. Neither at the time nor later, did he indicate that he had any knowledge of a subtext for the choice of Damasus by his abbot. Roarke quotes Maria Laach's Burkhardt Neunheuser on this question:

> If there were other reasons under the official reason for his being sent to the States, it was because he was more and more disagreeing with the ideas of Abbot Ildefons, especially concerning the role of the abbot in a Benedictine monastery.[3]

In the end Roarke weighs the German situation in light of the mature man:

> An original thinker, always a bit avant-garde, Damasus was also a very persuasive and popular teacher. One can only assume that his ideas soon took root in the young monks and were the topic of lively discussion. Perhaps too lively. His thoughts then were most likely in line with and seminal to his later writings and teachings on monastic renewal. Perhaps the most radical was his call for the abolition of the distinction between choir-monk (priest) and lay-brother.... He also held that the number of priests should be limited to the needs of the community, that communities should be smaller in [size], which called for a rethinking of the role of the abbot. Indeed, Damasus had become, for Abbot Ildefons, rather hard to digest.[4]

War in Europe was immanent, Hitler having announced his plans at the Hossbach Conference on November 5, 1937. Amid fear and confusion the two young monks took ship for America on September 1, 1938. Leo was thirty-six years old when they left the German port of Cuxhaven aboard the SS

Hamburg. Suddenly he was uprooted from the familiar and satisfying life he had led.

> It was doubtlessly a real friendship that motivated Father Damasus and which made me ready to join him. In Rome we had many a time together and were unanimous in many expressions of our taste and our opinions and judgments. We "clicked." But I also think now, that, because I had often expressed open criticism about a certain narrowness at Gerleve, in contrast to Maria Laach, that he thought to help me to get into a freer atmosphere. He was right in some sense there, but I believe he was mistaken in another. Although I was critical about certain aspects of our life in Gerleve, I was nevertheless completely loyal to it. I had never contemplated, or even played with the thought of, leaving Gerleve.

Crossing the Atlantic Ocean in 1938 was, for Leo, a taste of Exodus, an experience that would change his life radically. Preceding them to the United States in 1934 was Albert Hammenstede, the former prior of Maria Laach. Father Albert had been a professor at Bonn University, where he taught philosophy and conducted seminars for students. That his was a dangerous position had become clear when Hitler revealed his plans for freeing youth from the influence of the church.

In the turmoil of the time, no clear plans had been worked out for the venture in North America. The three monks were to establish a Benedictine house, but key questions remained. Was it eventually to be an independent North American monastery, or simply a temporary haven for exiled German monks? Was it to take on the observance of Maria Laach or Gerleve, or something new? Who was responsible among the three monks? Was it Albert because he was the senior member,

above: Damasus, Albert, and Leo at Darlington Seminary in 1938.
below left: Leo at his desk in Gerleve. *below right:* At Darlington
"Some of the happiest years of my life."

or were Damasus and Leo equally responsible? The situation of crisis as the German monks took leave of Europe left such questions unanswered. They would have to be dealt with later. During the ocean crossing, amid all the uncertainties and new experiences, Father Leo had one happy epiphany: "Right then and there I established and confirmed my great love for ships and for the sea."

Exiles in the New World

The boat carrying the two refugees sailed past the Statue of Liberty eight days later. Waiting to greet them in New York were Father Albert, Father Thomas Boland (later Archbishop of Newark), Father Hugh Duffy, a Benedictine monk of Morristown, and Tom Stanley, a layman. The newcomers were quickly settled in New Jersey at Darlington Seminary, conducted by the Archdiocese of Newark. The seminary setting was ideal for beginning the mission of the Germans, whose first task was to learn English. The new arrivals were grateful to have employment as professors, which could generate needed income and provide a home while they searched for a location for their new monastery. They agreed to a three-year contract with the Newark Archdiocese.

With their doctorates in philosophy or theology, they were a welcome addition to the faculty of this North American seminary, and it was not long before they were in the classroom. Albert had already carved out a niche of his own at the seminary and spoke adequate English. Damasus began to lecture in Latin but found that the seminarians hardly understood a word. While he was not fluent in English, he moved on, with much hard work, to writing out his classes beforehand. Leo recorded his own introduction to seminary teaching in America:

> The beginning in Darlington was not easy for me, either socially or academically. My English was embryonic. I had been told that I could teach in Latin. It worked, after a fashion, in theology, but in philosophy the boys just grinned and said, "Father, we don't understand a word. Please speak English." So I launched out in my elementary English. Fortunately, the students were extremely nice and cooperative. They kind of enjoyed their experience with us.

Being more youthful than Albert, Leo and Damasus made friends easily among both the seminary faculty and the students. For the elder monk, the whole process of adaptation was more problematic, and he became increasingly disgruntled. While the two younger men settled in to spend the next years assimilating the North American spirit and learning to feel at home in their new surroundings, Albert traveled about the country. Uncomfortable in North American society and culture, he could at least find an agreeable climate. California was especially attractive to him; Florida, his second choice. He was not keen on establishing a real monastic foundation, thinking more in terms of a temporary haven for exiles.

In a surprisingly short time, Leo and Damasus were conducting lively classes in reasonably good English. The American seminarians responded with enthusiasm to the fresh theological insights of their youthful European professors. New approaches and ideas in theology and liturgical practice had barely reached North American shores in the 1930s. Openness to ecumenical dialogue, emphasis on the role of laity in the church, renewal of the liturgy—all stimulated the interest of the students. They were ideas that would influence a whole generation of future priests. At the same time, the students had effects on their foreign professors. The informal and amicable spirit of the American seminarians, marked by spontaneity, drew the German monks into friendships that would last the rest of their lives.

While Damasus basked in new social and cultural opportunities, Leo enjoyed the New Jersey countryside with its abundant vegetation, flowering shrubs, and pleasing woods. An added treat was the opportunity to go sailing at the summer home of one of the students. Life in America was a satisfying surprise. As Leo recalled, "I still think of our time at Darlington with a certain nostalgia. It was our introduction to American life. Those were some of the happiest years of my life."

The young monk-guests from Europe confided in the American Benedictines of Saint Mary's Abbey in Newark, sharing their hopes for a new monastic foundation that would be more than a haven for monks fleeing Germany. Damasus and Leo also sought to introduce to North America a different approach to monastic life. Up to that time Benedictine monasteries in the United States were devoted to external ministries—teaching, serving in parishes, or providing pastoral assistance to European immigrant groups. The younger German monks were intent on a return to a more contemplative form of Benedictine community life. Several of the Morristown monks offered support and encouragement.

The small band of refugees quickly realized that they had departed their homeland barely in time. Hitler launched his battle for Europe in 1939. Soon England, too, entered the war. Meanwhile, communication with their home abbeys in Germany was cut off. A year after Father Leo's arrival in the United States, the Nazis found a ruse to suppress Saint

Joseph's Abbey in Gerleve. The Gestapo arrived at the door of the monastery, demanding to enter and search the buildings. In the library they discovered the complete works of Vladimir Solov'ev, the important Russian religious philosopher and lay theologian considered a forerunner of the ecumenical movement. They accused the community of spreading Communist propaganda. Some monks fled; others were conscripted. The community dispersed, and the monastery became a hospice for unwed mothers. Maria Laach, the home of Damasus and a far more prominent Benedictine monastery, was spared a similar fate.

St. Paul Priory, Keyport, New Jersey, 1942. "Finally, we bought the Longview Farm from the De Luca brothers and sisters in the township of Holmdel, New Jersey…on the whole the Keyport endeavor was fraught with problems."

3

Experiment in Keyport: On a Confused Mission

The search for a location for the new monastic foundation was not without tensions. Father Albert's distaste for the East Coast and the Northeastern climate in particular was one factor. The arrival of a third monk of Maria Laach, Father Thomas Michels, another monk of Maria Laach who had been teaching theology at St. Michael's College in Winooski, Vermont, further complicated the picture. Thomas had been a professor of church history and liturgy at the Theological State Faculty at Salzburg, Austria, from 1928 to 1938. "Like Albert," Madeleva Roarke reports, "Thomas found the adjustment to life in the New World very difficult. Teaching farmers' sons in rural Vermont was a far cry from teaching at a prestigious institution in Salzburg."[1] She described him as a "shadowy" figure who only came into the foreground when plans had to be made for the group's future.

Insisting that he had been named superior of the new community by the Abbot of Maria Laach, Albert wanted to locate in a warm climate, preferably California, or as a last resort, Florida. In poor health, his heart was not really in the work of establishing a new foundation. Through Thomas came an offer from Francis Kervick, longtime head of the architecture department at Notre Dame, to take over his property in Randolph, Vermont. Favoring location in the Northeast, Damasus and Leo examined sites in Connecticut, Pennsylvania, Vermont, and New Jersey. They finally agreed that they wanted to settle in New Jersey where they had established friendships.

Assuming the role of mediator, Damasus persuaded Albert to accept a New Jersey location with the proviso that he would be the prior. Only Thomas favored the Vermont location. A decision was reached for Keyport, New Jersey, which had a Holmdel post office address. It was not far from friends and the monks of St. Mary's Abbey in Newark and Morristown.

In the absence of contact with the abbots of Maria Laach and Gerleve, Abbot Patrick O'Brien of St. Mary's gave formal approval for the foundation. David O'Leary and Emmet McEvoy, both monks of Newton Abbey, and Hugh Duffy and Stephen Findley, monks of Morristown, became the first trustees of the new Benedictine monastery.

The group of four German monks and an American candidate, Columban McEvoy, moved into their new quarters in the spring of 1942. An article in the *Asbury Park Evening Press* on Wednesday, June 24, 1942, reported the beginning of the new monastic venture called St. Paul's Priory. Photos illustrating the story showed the new monastery building, the Abbey of Maria Laach, and the interior of the Keyport chapel (with a hooded Prior Albert praying in a choir stall). Right beside the priory piece entitled *Three Refugee Monks from Germany Carry on Holy Week at Holmdel Farm,* was an article headlined *Germans Report 11,000 Red Prisoners Taken in Sevastopol Region.*

The newspaper story on St. Paul's put forward the purposes of the new foundation, at least from the perspective of Father Albert, who was quoted extensively.

> On the fertile rolling terrain of rural Holmdel township, along the Centerville road, three refugee monks, whose holy work was disrupted and whose lives were imperiled by Nazi tyranny, are carrying on from where they left off when driven from Germany. These Benedictines have transformed a rugged old farmhouse into Saint Paul's Priory and are fulfilling the ideals of monastic life as they knew it at the venerable Abbey of Maria Laach in the Rhineland which looks back on a history of eight centuries and which had become the center of the liturgical movement in Germany.
>
> Although this renowned lighthouse of Catholic piety and Christian civilization has been extinguished, its glow has been revived in a new land and shines brightly as a beacon of faith and courage....

Albert left no doubt that the monastic lifestyle of the new foundation would mirror the life at Maria Laach:

> One of the chief concerns of the group, according to the Rt. Rev. Prior Albert Hammenstedde, S.T.D., is the building up of an American Catholic culture. Since the hierarchy in this country has succeeded in erecting a highly developed parish organization and the most perfect system of Catholic education to be found, it is not their intention, the prior explains, to take over either parishes or schools, but rather to be primarily a "Holy Choir" in order to celebrate religious services in their sanctuary in accordance with the precepts of the church and in the spirit of sacred liturgy....

> So the monastery will be, according to the idea of Saint Benedict, not only a place of prayer and contemplation, but also a workshop of fruitful toil. Both intellectual and manual labor have their indispensable role in monastic life.

The new foundation would avoid the pitfalls of adopting modern technology prevalent in North American life:

> In working the extensive farm, the machine will be used sparingly and manual labor will prevail. Potatoes, for which this section is famous, will constitute the principal crop. Soil testing and other agrarian advice is being given by the county agricultural agent. Above all, the prior said, "We wish to offer our services to our fellow priests, not only by directing retreats, but also by providing them from time to time with the rare opportunity of a rest for soul and body."

An undertaking blest by the 'highest authority':

> For these aims the group has had words of encouragement from Pope Pius XII, who on Aug. 22, 1938, wrote these words to Father Hammenstedde on his departure for these shores: "Certainly it must be difficult to leave behind so many things that are dear to your hearts, but the ways of Providence are not our ways and perhaps some greater good will result from this sacrifice. I am sure that the fathers of Maria Laach will bring to their new field of effort a zeal and charity that will redound to the glory of God."

This first public description of the goals of the new Benedictine community elucidated hopes shared by the founding monks. Simultaneously, it held the seeds of confusion and division that were to plague their years together.

All four monks were in agreement that they would not assume a pastoral ministry after the fashion of other North American Benedictines of the time. They also looked forward to the celebration of liturgy and the chanting of the monastic office in common. In theory at least, they envisaged manual labor together with intellectual pursuits as integral to their life. Hospitality, especially to the clergy, and the direction of retreats were common interests.

What was not agreed upon was the establishment of monastic life patterned on the monastery of Maria Laach. In the opinion of Albert, that was the only possibility. His reference in the local newspaper story to the "building up of an American Catholic culture" underlined his personal antipathy for the American culture he had encountered.

Father Leo was not looking forward to becoming part of a North American Maria Laach. Neither did he hope to found another Gerleve. He had already become captivated by the youthful spirit of North Americans. Beyond that he was not yet ready to formulate his hopes. Father Damasus again assumed the role of mediator in the group. Though he was always loyal to his home monastery and its abbot, he did not want to create another Maria Laach in America. From Laach he drew his love for Gregorian chant, monastic studies, art, and classical architecture, yet he strongly rejected the prince-prelate version of the abbot. Even at that early date, he embraced a return-to-sources approach to monastic renewal. For him, Keyport represented the opportunity to make a new beginning in America, and he was willing to stake everything on that hope.

Dissension in the Ranks

Community life began at Keyport with unspoken differences in the background. For the financial support of the monastery, Damasus and Thomas began teaching at Manhattanville College, then located in New York City. Albert continued traveling, lecturing, and writing journal articles. Leo preached retreats at several Benedictine monasteries, served as a weekend minister at New Jersey parishes, and gave conferences to the cloistered Maryknoll Sisters. Active in the liturgical movement, he traveled to St. Paul, Minnesota; New Orleans, Louisiana; and Denver, Colorado to deliver lectures under the aegis of the National Liturgical Conference. He also lectured regularly at the motherhouse of the Sisters of Mercy in North Plainfield, New Jersey.

The monastery farm proved to be beyond the capabilities of the priest-monks. In Europe, the lay brothers had done the farm work and menial chores. Just how the question of manual labor was to be worked out in the North American setting remained unclear. A solution came through Vermonters, friends of Thomas. Offering their services to the new monastery, the members of the Norman Langlois family came to Keyport from Winooski. Norman, who had once run the Catholic Worker House of Hospitality in Burlington, Vermont, worked the monastery farm and was a much needed all-around handy man. His mother and his wife, Margaret, cooked meals and did housework for the monks. The six Langlois children brightened the empty spaces in the monastery. Father Leo enjoyed the presence of the Langlois family and the opportunity to work with Norman. As he described the experience, Keyport was the place where he developed his love of manual labor. Recalling one of the several chores he threw himself into, he wrote: "Once I tried to milk the goats. I'll never forget the look of haughty derision, so it seemed, on the face of the goat as she looked back at me as if she were saying: 'First time, buddy?'"

Sundays were the focus of life at St. Paul's. The monks chanted the monastic office and celebrated Mass together as they had done in Europe, where Maria Laach, as the center of liturgical reform in Germany, had revived the artistic and ritual splendors of the Middle Ages. In this vein, at St. Paul's in the early 1940s, the Mass was celebrated facing the congregation—a striking innovation at that time in America. Flowing Gothic vestments replaced the so-called fiddle-back chasubles customary in American parish churches. Incense and Gregorian chant enhanced the solemnity of the celebrations. A homily or reflection on the scripture readings took the place of the customary parish-church sermon.

Word circulated among the professional elite in the area that a rich quality of worship was available at the priory in Keyport; as a result, attendance at Sunday Eucharist increased. Friendships developed between monks and visitors, and a discussion group addressing liturgy, scripture, and spirituality sprouted. Signs of hope for the new community emerged when several young men asked to be admitted to the monastery. Yet there was little sense of how to assimilate new admissions into the community. With the prior frequently away and the other monks engaged in outside activities, there was little true community life.

Unity emerged briefly when representatives of the United States Immigration and Naturalization Services confronted the little community at the Keyport monastery, situated as it was on a bluff overlooking Raritan Bay, a large inlet of the Atlantic Ocean. With German submarines lurking off the eastern seacoast after the U.S. entered the war in 1941, American cities quickly became alert to possible attacks.

Pursuing a tip by a nervous citizen, U.S. authorities wanted to know why a group of German monks would choose such a location for their monastery. With the help of friends and the influence of Abbot Patrick of St. Mary's, the monks were able to persuade the authorities that they were not spies intent on sending signals to preying enemy submarines.

As time passed after that incident, Leo became more and more estranged from his companions. He found friends among people who visited the priory for worship. He was invited to their homes, and such company became preferable to being alone at the monastery when confreres were largely absent. Increasingly, he found himself at the Edgewood Avenue home of Dr. Leon Smith and his wife Dorothea in Clifton, New Jersey. The Smiths, with their two children, became a New World family for him. Dorothea was active in diocesan affairs, especially in promoting liturgical renewal. Leon, a cultured man and a successful surgeon, was a music lover. The couple welcomed Leo into their life as if he were a brother and an uncle to their children.

The Last Straw

By 1944, Leo found the situation within the Keyport community intolerable. For him, the final indignity was the occasion when he, Damasus, and Albert were to become naturalized U.S. citizens. He recalled the breaking point between himself and the other German monks:

> In the beginning I never thought of becoming an American citizen. I was always quite homesick for Gerleve.... To

> change my nationality was at first an abhorrent idea. It was Father Albert and Father Damasus who finally prevailed on me to join them and become a United States citizen.... I fully relied on the fact that Father Damasus and I would be naturalized together in due course....
>
> Finally I received my summons to come to the courthouse in Freehold to be naturalized on a certain day.... I was puzzled because I didn't see Father Damasus receiving his summons, so I asked him about it. Then both he and Father Albert told me quite coolly: "No, we have decided not to go ahead with it." The reason given was America's attitude towards Germany. I was absolutely stunned and completely shaken. I never fully got over that shock, it had hurt me so deeply. My trust was betrayed and I never trusted them fully afterwards.

Leo went alone to the courthouse and received his naturalization papers. Although Albert never renounced his German citizenship, Damasus did swear allegiance to the United States two years later. It is interesting to compare the account by Damasus of the same incident. It illustrates the difficulty of reconstructing personal history from the memory of participants. Despite the vivid details of both accounts, they clearly present different pictures. Madaleva Roarke told Damasus's story:

> The property of Keyport was on a rise of land that overlooked the harbors of the New York region, harbors in which German submarines had been spotted. They [Damasus and Leo] were informed by friends that they were being kept under some sort of surveillance as possible Nazi spies. Both had been in the country long enough to qualify for citizenship, and they were advised to apply

> for this; the process would serve to clear up any suspicions of the authorities. They agreed, with great reluctance, to do so. When Damasus got to the courthouse for his naturalization ceremony, he read the oath he would have to take, renouncing all allegiance to his fatherland in rather stern language. He was also disturbed by the terms of "unconditional surrender" being proposed by the Allies. For him the wording of the oath was tantamount to a betrayal of his family and friends being battered by the war, of his heritage and culture and he could not bring himself to do that, but slipped out of the courtroom. He did so unnoticed by Leo Rudloff, who took the oath, which was just as distasteful to him and, he said, "nearly broke my heart." Leo was unaware for some time that Damasus had not become a citizen and was furious when he learned of it.

As the war drew to a close in 1945, the divisions within the community of St. Paul's became more acute. Leo felt isolated and often despairing. Without going into details, he described the situation:

> On the whole, the Keyport endeavor was fraught with problems.... Our main difficulty was a lack of true unity in our monastic group. Rivalries grew. The question of the source of responsibility for the foundation in the future—Maria Laach alone or together with Gerleve—was unsolved.... The inner problems, however, were too great.

As soon as the opportunity presented itself, Prior Albert returned to Germany. Thomas became the new prior. Together, Thomas and Damasus were making the decisions. Leo was completely disillusioned; he felt only bitterness and confusion.

From the perspective of much elapsed time, he evaluated the New Jersey period, speaking first as an emigrant:

> All the securities you have are falling away. You are like a bird pushed out of the nest so it may learn to fly. But there is also a positive element in emigration. The tearing away from the past is a challenge. You must be on your own. You must find yourself in the new situation, reorient yourself, adapt to new people, new circumstances, surroundings, places, climates, and more. There might be a deeply religious meaning in this wrenching. Looking back to those years, I see they were a time of floundering, groping, searching.
>
> Darlington was our initiation into American life. Those are perhaps the most happy memories and invaluable. After that—in Keyport and elsewhere—it was more of floundering, often erring, insecurity, looking for new security, finding oneself in the new relations. Much of it seems to me unsettled, turbulent, often nervously groping for a hold here and there. Often quite confused. Often petty in the search. Sometimes like a drowning person groping for anything that might look like a support....

After nearly a decade in the United States, Father Leo returned to Gerleve, the community of his monastic beginnings, a changed man. Having set out as a youthful, open but anxious monk on an exciting adventure as an exile in a foreign land, he returned to a devastated Germany and a fragile monastic community beset with feelings of failure, betrayal, darkness, and confusion. His return journey to St. Joseph's Abbey by way of Holland in 1946 was difficult and perilous. Lacking the necessary papers to enter Germany, Leo crossed the border secretly under the protection of the Pontifical

Mission for the Netherlands that was actively repatriating displaced Dutch citizens. Distrust, animosity, despair, and bitterness prevailed throughout Europe as much as in his own spirit.

The aging and ailing Abbot Raphael had managed to reunite some of the members of the Gerleve community and to restore the basic elements of monastic life. The monks were gathered in an old farmhouse because the monastery buildings had not yet been returned to them. The community had changed as well as Leo. While Leo had experienced valuable personal friendships and the sense of equality and mutuality in a democratic country and culture, his brother monks had experienced brutal oppression, anxiety, and violence in war. Though he was warmly welcomed by the Abbot and the community, Leo sensed at a very deep level that he was both an alien in the land he had adopted and an exile in the land of his birth. A sense of disorientation and dislocation marked his reentry to Gerleve.

After a year of calm and having achieved a degree of peace at Gerleve, it was time for Leo to return to New Jersey to settle affairs at Keyport. Once again, in 1948, he crossed the ocean. His friends, the Smiths, received him warmly at their home in Clifton. By this time the decision had been made to sell the Keyport monastery. Father Thomas had vainly tried to find a solution to keep it going. Abbot Ildefons of Maria Laach, seriously ill and burdened with his own battered community, had withdrawn his support for continuing the venture before he died in 1946.

Subsequently, Father Damasus took up residence as chaplain of the newly founded monastery of Benedictine nuns, Regina Laudis, in Bethlehem, Connecticut. It was left to Damasus and Leo to come to terms for the dissolution of St.

above right: Dr. Leon and Dorothea Smith of Clifton, New Jersey, welcomed Leo, *above left,* into their life as if he were "a brother and an uncle to their children." *below:* Damasus and Leo at Regina Laudis closing the project of Keyport.

Paul's Priory. They met at Regina Laudis and, with the help of loyal friends, were able to agree on the dispersal of funds and property. Lambert Dunne, canon lawyer and monk of St. Mary's Abbey in Newark, who would later be secretary to the Abbot Primate, was asked to serve as administrator of the settlement. The breach between Damasus and Leo was not healed on this occasion. The reunion was cool; the discussion objective. Afterward, Leo departed to spend some relaxed days with his friends in Clifton.

Damasus remained at Regina Laudis, continuing to nourish his hopes for a new monastic foundation in North America. When he had left Keyport, the Langlois family accompanied him to Bethlehem where they again absorbed themselves in the needs of the community of Benedictine nuns. Other friends of the Keyport foundation continued to meet regularly with Father Damasus for explorations of liturgy and spirituality. Within a few years, he was able to recruit interested monks from Portsmouth Priory in Rhode Island and a monk from Newton, New Jersey, to venture with him into founding the monastery he dreamed of: Mount Saviour in Elmira, New York.

After a few days at the Smiths' in Clifton, Leo received news of the death of Abbot Raphael at Gerleve. Once more he boarded a ship, destined for a new phase in his life.

above: The Abbey of St. Joseph in Gerleve, Westphalia, Germany. *below:* The Benedictine community at Gerleve with oblate students in 1936. Subprior Leo (circled) at left of Abbot Raphael Mollitor. "I was very happy and settled there; there was a good discipline and also brotherly love." *Archiv der Benediktinerabtei Gerleve*

4

Jerusalem Calls: To a Distant Port

By the time Father Leo reached Gerleve, the community had elected a new abbot, Pius Buddenborg, a contemporary and close friend of Leo's. The monastery was gradually being restored as Leo remembered it. Buildings were under repair and the scattered monks returning. Life was gradually resuming its normal, peaceful rhythm at the abbey.

The abbots of the German Benedictine Congregation of Beuron held a national meeting the year after Leo's return. Abbot Pius was present for the meeting. Discussions focused on the plight of several monasteries of the Beuronese Congregation in the aftermath of the war. A major concern was the Dormition Abbey on Mt. Zion in Jerusalem, Israel.

The German Emperor Wilhelm II had acquired the site on Mt. Zion from the Turkish Sultan Abdul Hamid while he was on a journey through the Middle East in 1898. The land was handed over to the German Association for the Holy Land, and an imposing church and monastery were built "for the benefit of German Catholics." The first Benedictine monks from Germany arrived on Mt. Zion in 1906.

Situated on Mount Zion beyond the wall of the Old City of Jerusalem, the abbey occupies the site of an early Byzantine church commemorating the "falling asleep of Mary," hence the name *Dormitio Mariae*. Adjacent to the monastery are buildings commemorating the place of the Last Supper and the Descent of the Holy Spirit after the Resurrection of Jesus. All three major monotheistic religions, Jewish, Muslim, and Christian, are represented at shrines on Mt. Zion. Near the abbey are a synagogue and a mosque with a minaret.

The Benedictine community on Mount Zion grew to number more than forty members under the first abbot, Maurus Kaufman, originally a monk of Maria Laach. The ordained monks staffed the seminary of the Latin Patriarch at Beit Jalla. Numerous pilgrims visited the towering abbey church with the lovely wooden statue of Mary in repose in the crypt. As in other monasteries of the German Beuronese Congregation, lay brothers performed the menial tasks and did the manual labor at the monastery while the priest-monks chanted the monastic office and liturgy and taught in the seminary.

Immediately following the division of Palestine and the foundation of the State of Israel, war broke out in 1948 between Israel and Jordan. The monks were evacuated from the monastery. Some fled the country, others found asylum with their abbot in the convent of St. Charles Borromeo located in the German Colony in West Jerusalem.

On February 28, 1949, the aged and ailing abbot died.

Jerusalem became a divided city, the Old City behind ancient walls belonging to Jordan, the section outside the walls a part of Israel. The massive stone church of the Dormition Abbey overlooked the walls of the Old City from the Israeli sector. With its heavy walls and high open balcony around the roof of the church, the Abbey was a strategic military site for the Israeli forces. The soldiers continued to occupy the monastery at the close of the war.

The fate of the Dormition Abbey community was in the hands of the Beuronese abbots meeting in Germany in 1949. The abbots agonized over the thought of abandoning the Benedictine presence in the Holy Land. Their German monasteries were still struggling to recover from their own recent experience of World War II. More troubling was the relationship between Israel and German citizens in the aftermath of the Holocaust. What would be the status of German monks in the monastery in Israel? Would the aging and demoralized monks be capable of carrying on a monastic life in the Holy Land? Where would the community turn to find personnel and vocations for the future?

Seeing no options, the abbots were of a mind to suppress the monastery and to recall the monks to Germany. Only Gerleve's Abbot Pius objected.[1] He suggested that a Visitator be appointed to assess the situation with the hope that some solution could be found to maintain the presence of the Benedictine community in the Holy Land. But who among the German Benedictines could be acceptable to both the monks of Dormition Abbey and the Israeli authorities for such a task? The assembly of abbots named Abbot Pius administrator of the abbey in hopes that a solution could be found.

Abbot Pius had a ready answer. A monk of his community had only recently become a citizen of the United States. He would be eminently acceptable to the Israelis. He was a German by birth and was fluent in English and German. He would be equally acceptable to the community. At forty-seven years of age, Leo Rudloff had both the experience and the youth to take on the assignment.

The moment was right for Leo. Since his return to Gerleve after the Keyport experience, he had been restless. Dispirited and with a sense of failure, he was unable to find his place and a sense of purpose in the community. He was easily persuaded to undertake the journey to the Holy Land for the Visitation of Dormition Abbey. This time he sailed east—across the Mediterranean.

A Flock Without a Shepherd

Emerging from the gloom of the Keyport experience and the extended period of disorientation on his return to Gerleve, Father Leo immersed himself in the role of Visitator to the troubled and threatened abbey in the Holy Land. He could identify with the floundering community and nursed a spark of hope that both he and the Dormition Abbey could rise out of the darkness of defeat. As the representative of the Beuronese abbots, he embarked on his first voyage to Israel in 1949 with an open mind and guarded hope.

The Visitation began near the end of June. He went directly to the convent of St. Charles Borromeo, the German hospice on Lloyd George Street in West Jerusalem, where he found twelve elderly monks still grieving the loss of their abbot. Most of them were lay brothers. All but a few of the ordained monks had fled to Europe or America.

Far from their homeland, but within a safe enclosure, the monks had for years lived a protected and quite isolated life at the abbey on Mt. Zion. Now, as a handful of German nationals in a foreign and hostile country, they were filled with anxiety at the prospect of returning to their monastic home. Without leadership and with no sense of direction, the little band huddled in fear.

Leo arrived without agenda. Following his meeting with the community at Saint Charles convent, he proceeded to the abbey. There he found empty, disintegrating monastery buildings. Artillery fire had pockmarked the bell tower, and shells had left gaping holes in the church roof. The exquisite Beuronese mosaics of the apse were riddled with bullet holes. Rubble was everywhere—and trash left by occupying soldiers. Water, electricity, even road access, had been cut off. Together with its absent, beleaguered community, the once proud monastery was in complete disarray.

Despite the ruins surrounding him, Leo was able to glimpse the possibility of new life. The derelict monastery and its helpless community touched his heart in a way that he did not fully understand, but he responded with a mixture of compassion and hope. Before leaving Israel in the first week of August, Leo called at the government's Ministry of Religious Affairs. Dr. Jaacov Herzog, head of the Department for Christian Communities, received him. The Israelis found it a reassuring sign that an English-speaking United States citizen had been chosen to represent the German community in Jerusalem.

Leo returned to Germany to make his report. With his findings he presented a recommendation that the Dormition community be internationalized. The beleaguered abbots did not want to suppress the monastery if there was any real hope for its survival. At the same time, they were powerless to accept responsibility for the presence of the community in Jerusalem. Leo later noted the results of his efforts:

> On my return to Germany I reported not only to my abbot but also to the president of the Beuronese Congregation, Abbot Bernard Durst of Neresheim. We held several meetings. The conclusion reached was that the Congregation would not press for the suppression of the abbey, but they insisted that it be removed from the Congregation of Beuron.

Only Abbot Pius of Gerleve continued to have faith that something could be done to save the distressed community in the Holy Land. He proposed that Abbot Primate Bernard Kaelin, by virtue of a special provision of the *lex propria* of the Benedictine Confederation, take the abbey under his personal supervision. With Leo's agreement, the Abbot Primate named the recent visitator prior-administrator of the Dormition Abbey under its new status. With the support and encouragement of Abbot Pius, Leo assumed his latest responsibilities with enthusiasm.

He took the plunge into the thicket of ecclesial bureaucracy to clear away all canonical obstacles. The Dormition Abbey property was owned by the German Association for the Holy Land *(Deutscher Verein vom Heiligen Lande)* under the Archiepiscopal See of Cologne. All decisions related to the status of the Zion community and the property had to be cleared with that office. Prince Franz Salm-Reifferscheidt was the official in charge of the monastery affairs.

> There was a particularly good understanding between Prince Salm and myself. My agreement with the prince stressed one point: I accepted the priorship on one condition: the community must become international. This was so essential that I stated that I stood or fell on that decision. The prince said, "I am one hundred percent behind you."

Making a trip to Rome, Leo sought support for his enterprise from Cardinal Eugene Tisserant, the powerful Secretary of the Oriental Congregation, the Vatican office that supervised religious congregations in the Middle East. While there, he discussed his strategy with the Abbot Primate and was assured of backing from that quarter as well.

above: Dormition Abbey in Jerusalem with a view to the Judean Desert and the Dead Sea. The roof of the basilica was scarred by mortar shelling in the 1948 Israeli War of Independence and the Six Day war of 1967. *below left:* Maurus Kaufman, first abbot of the Dormition. *below right:* The choir and apse of the monastery church with Beuronese mosaics, altar, and abbatial throne.

When Leo returned to Jerusalem in 1950, the number of monks in residence at the nuns' convent had risen to fifteen, and there was hope that a few more of the dispersed monks would return. Still, the monastery buildings and property remained in the hands of the Israeli military. Armed soldiers patrolled the open balcony encircling the roof of the monastery church. The rest of the monastery, used during the war as military barracks, was vacant. Outlying buildings that formerly served as the seminary were also in government hands.

An early test of Father Leo's diplomacy came in negotiations with the Israelis for the return of the monastery buildings. After the first friendly exchange with the Ministry of Religious Affairs, the two sides moved to substantial issues. Dr. Herzog's first request was that Leo dismiss Father Willibrord, an eccentric monk who had made some imprudent remarks publicly. Stressing the small number of ordained monks in the Dormition community, Leo politely, but firmly, declined to take that action. The second request of the Ministry: that no additional German monks be brought to the community. Leo acquiesced out of his own conviction that for a long time to come no new German monks should be sent to Jerusalem. Reaching this initial understanding, the two men had a promising beginning.

Leo returned to Saint Charles with the news that the monks would soon be able to return to the Abbey. But first there was work to be done. Brother Hilarion, the youngest lay brother, and some of the nuns of the convent volunteered to join Leo in the exhausting work of cleaning up the trashed monastery. Because there was no road leading from the Gehenna Valley floor up the steep slope of Mount Zion to the monastery, all materials for cleaning and repairs had to be carried up the hill on foot in the blazing Jerusalem sun. Inside, there was still no water or electricity. The demanding combination of strenuous menial work, continued negotiations with the government, and supervision of the church restoration drained Leo's energy. As these projects advanced, his health showed signs of deterioration.

After months of backbreaking effort, the monastery was finally habitable. Running water was operative, but not electricity. Father Leo and Brother Hilarion were the first residents to move into the reclaimed abbey. The older German monks feared reprisals because of the Holocaust and were hesitant to leave the relative security of the convent. Leo sought to assure them that it would be safe to return to their former home.

The Benedictines Return to Mount Zion

Abbot Primate Bernard Kaelin had asked Lambert Dunne of St. Mary's Abbey in Newark, a friend of Leo's since his days in Keyport, to be the American Representative of the Dormition in its present sore straits. In a letter dated May 28, 1950, Leo announced joyful news to Lambert.

> What a day! A true resurrection of our sanctuary, and, I must say, one of the happiest days in my life. Today the Church of the Dormitio was returned to us and the first solemn High Mass celebrated, people crowding the beautiful building.... On Friday, May 19, the liaison officer of the Ministry for Religious Affairs turned over to me the keys of our church and monastery. By that act we were reinstated to possession of our sanctuary.... On Tuesday, May 23rd, I moved in and slept in the monastery for the first time. I was all alone the first night. It happened to be rather stormy,

> and all the doors on the floor below were banging all night long. But I was so extremely happy, that it mattered little. To think that probably in this place Our Lady also slept, maybe our Lord (?). At least he was near here.

On August 26, he sent Lambert a glowing account of the situation at the Dormition, for release to the Catholic News Service in the U.S.

> It was a memorable day, when on Friday, May 19, 1950, the liaison officer of the Ministry for Religious Affairs, Dr. Meir Mendes, gave the keys to the Sanctuary and the Abbey of the Dormition on Mount Zion over to the Prior, the Very Rev. Leo A. Rudloff, O.S.B....
>
> It would not have been possible, had not the Israeli Government through its Ministry for Religious Affairs, in cooperation with the Department of Public Works, carried out extensive repair work in the church and monastery, which were severely damaged during the hostilities between Jews and Arabs.... Not all hopes have been fulfilled as yet with regard to the *Dormitio,* but...the actual situation is eased by the truly exemplary behavior of the overwhelming majority of the soldiers on duty at the abbey....

Evidence that all was not quite as smooth and easy as it appeared in the news release came in a September 9th letter to Lambert. Fearing Israeli censorship, Father Leo channeled the letter through the Latin Patriarchate in Jordan.

> Unfortunately, I have to report a thing that is very unpleasant and has aroused me to a very violent protest with the Ministry for Religious Affairs. The contingent of soldiers here on duty on Mount Zion as observers on the

> roof of our church and quartered in our annex building (which is not accessible to us but by a special permit), have twice in the last months committed theft.... It is evident that these things could not have been stolen, other than in an organized way, under the command of the noncom officer in charge of the contingent. That, of course, makes the situation the more serious.... For the rest, we are working to make our monastery more and more able to receive the community. I am living in it alone with two brothers....

Convinced of the rightness of his cause, Leo approached the Ministry of Religious Affairs in Jerusalem again and again. The value of his status as a U.S. citizen became apparent. He was soon treated with respect and as an equal by the Israeli officials. Avoiding accusations and inflammatory language, Leo asserted the rights of the Benedictine community in clear and direct terms. In later meetings with the Israeli Minister of Religion, he successfully pressed for compensation for damages and for the complete repair of the church roof that had been almost wholly destroyed by shelling.

Finally, on Ash Wednesday, 1951, the community as a whole returned to Dormition Abbey, and some elements of monastic life were revived. The lay brothers took up their tasks of caring for the garden and the chickens, housecleaning, preparing meals, and other manual work as they had done in years gone by. They prayed and practiced their devotions. The few ordained monks began praying the monastic office in the church with Father Leo. With the voices of the tiny group swallowed up in the cavernous edifice, Leo appealed to the lay brothers to join the monastic choir for prayer, but the brothers felt that the Latin chant was beyond their capabilities. They cherished the simple prayers and devotions that had marked their lives. Only Brother Hilarion responded to Father Leo's invitation.

The physical occupation of the monastery was a first and difficult step, but for Leo, the presence of a Benedictine community in the Holy Land meant, above all, the establishment of a house of prayer. Praying the monastic office and living according to the Rule of St. Benedict were the essentials of Benedictine presence. It was apparent to him that the small number of priest-monks was insufficient to celebrate the monastic office and liturgy properly in the large monastery church.

The few ordained monks in the community were set in their ways; though they were not happy with their diminished situation, they saw no options for improving it. Leo held regular conferences with his small community. He insisted that vocations would no longer be coming to Israel from Germany; the hope for the survival of the community rested in other lands. He was met with uncomprehending faces and silent resistance. The aging monks were fearful of losing their German national identity as well as the security of the strict and unchanging Beuronese observance of Benedictine life. They did not agree with the idea of trying to attract vocations outside of Germany. They neither accepted nor understood Leo's ideas for a more open and contemporary approach to monastic life. To them, the new administrator of their abbey seemed to have lost something of authentic Benedictine practice during his sojourn in America.

Pressing further, Leo asked that the monks be open to exchanges with Jewish neighbors, the surrounding culture, and the emerging Jewish State of Israel. Even ecumenical exchanges among Christian churches were foreign to the enclosed community. Writing in Vermont in the 1970s, Leo recalled the mindset that he encountered in the late 1940s among the Dormition monks.

> When I arrived, I found the mood of the Dormition community anti-Semitic, almost to the point of virulence. The monks had been living almost exclusively among Arabs and had had little contact with Jews. Thus, they shared in that anti-Jewish attitude of so many of the clergy who had worked among the Arabs earlier. I still remember the terribly anti-Semitic remarks that were almost commonplace among the members of the Dormition community. So one of my first tasks was to change that attitude. It took a long time, but I think I finally succeeded to a great extent. I want to make one thing very clear; in the beginning I also often wished that Dormition Abbey were located in the Arab section of Jerusalem. The upbringing in my home was not particularly friendly to Jews. I even remember a mild, yet quite noticeable anti-Semitic attitude. The Nazi period shook me out of some complacency.

above: Leo, seated at center, at visitation of Dormition community interned at convent of St. Charles Borromeo in 1949. *below:* Leo with elders of the Dormition community at the abbey in 1950. "We were lucky at that time that we still had among our brothers some excellent craftsmen to restore the house."

5

Shepherd's Crook: Gentleness is Power

Breaking the Colonial Pattern

During his two years as Prior-Administrator of Dormition Abbey (1950–1951), Father Leo worked tirelessly to nurse the moribund community back to life: gathering as many of the dispersed members as he could find, negotiating with the Israeli authorities for the restoration of buildings and land, seeking reparations for war damage, obtaining essential financial support from the German Association for the Holy Land, responding to the Abbot Primate on canonical issues. All the challenges of day-to-day survival fell on his shoulders—and filled his days.

Surrounded by aged monks in the grip of fear and insecurity, Leo continued to coax them to join him as he searched for an alternative mode of Benedictine presence in the Holy Land. Later, writing his memoirs in Weston Priory, he felt pangs of regret that, giving attention to so many concerns, he had not been more sensitive to the personal needs of the Dormition Abbey monks:

> Looking back, I put too much emphasis on things over persons. I don't think I neglected the persons, but perhaps my preoccupation with reviving the Abbey, as a building and as—should I say?—an institution, overshadowed and unbalanced the care for the persons who were that abbey. I am afraid some monks felt that. I feel bad about it.

The detailed and sensitive descriptions of the community members of those early days that Leo presented in his "Reminiscences" indicate that he was perhaps judging himself more harshly than he deserved. He spoke with affection and appreciation for them. A few examples illustrate his feelings of respect:

> We were lucky at that time that we still had among our brothers some excellent craftsmen to help restore the house. There was old Brother Columban Nienhaus, a venerable figure, tall and dignified, with a long beard. He was a fine carpenter. First, however, he had to have tools, and all the tools of the monastery had been plundered. Finally, he himself made many of those he needed. He was a genius, in his way.... He restored the choir stalls and many other things. He even made himself a set of wooden dentures! After some years he returned to Maria Laach.... I visited him there a couple of times.... In the very beginning there was Brother Norbert Sauter. He was already old and broken when I came to the abbey, and he could no longer work. He was quite a character, a living chronicle of the early days. His memory was fabulous. He could be very rough and outspoken, but he had a good heart. Father Nicolaus Zieri, a Swiss, was a thoroughly lovable man, but also completely helpless, full of fears and feelings of inferiority. He was funny looking, very

> short of stature, with a forehead constantly furrowed with horizontal wrinkles. But I did love him, and I think he felt comfortable with me. He was like a child in many ways.

On the other hand, Leo's descriptions of some of his priest-monk confreres were not so affirmative:

> Father Prior...no doubt an honorable and very pious man. There was some personal contact and relationship between us...he was the source of unspeakable trouble for me. Unfortunately, he has a bias for extraordinary "supernatural" phenomena. Holy nuns, visions, and revelations take his whole interest. He could talk about almost nothing else.... Father Willibrord...was truly a mental case.... He had spells when he was just lying in bed, sleeping to all appearance, covered completely by his sheets, and unapproachable for days.... Father Paul...has good lovable qualities. I think he has a yearning for love, and I am not sure if I showed him enough of that. On the other hand, he is terribly narrow, set in his ways, conservative to the extreme, frankly quite neurotic, if not psychopathic.

While much of his attention was directed to internal matters of the community and the repairs to the monastic buildings, Leo did not confine himself to the enclosure of the monastery. With his Vatican credentials for travel, he passed easily from the Israeli sector of Jerusalem to the Old City in Jordan, where most of the Catholic religious communities, caring for the holy places and shrines, were located. A variety of Christian denominations and communities were also present in that part of the Holy City.

The divisions, competition, and hostility among the churches and the individualism prevalent in the "shrine spirituality" stood in stark contrast to Leo's understanding of the Benedictine monastic spirit of hospitality and reconciliation. Gradually he was clarifying his long-range objectives for the Benedictine abbey:

> The administration of the Church in the Holy Land—and that means the running of the dioceses, of the hierarchy (oriental as well as occidental), and of the monasteries—reflects very strongly the colonial attitude prevailing there before the establishment of the State of Israel. In that, incidentally, I also see to a great extent the cause of the enmity to Israel of so many clergymen in the Holy Land who cannot get used to the new situation. They are nostalgic for the time when they were treated like overlords by the simple Arab people of the land. The Latin Patriarchate is Italian to a great extent.... The Greek Orthodox are very much *Greek* Orthodox. There are all the other national churches.... In the sanctuaries and monasteries the situation is even worse.... The Custos ("Guardian" of Franciscan communities) must always be Italian, the vicar French, the treasurer Spanish. Similarly, the Holy Places are in the hands of specific European nations. Thus, the Dormition had been considered the German monastery.

At this very early date, 1950, Leo, while not clearly articulating it, was grappling with the issue of the inculturation of his monastic community—an insight that would not gain widespread acceptance in the Church until many years later:

> From the outset I wanted to break radically with the principle of the colonial church. The moment of the revival of the Dormition in the newly established State of Israel seemed to me the *kairos,* i.e., the Providence-appointed time, pregnant

with meaning and momentum for the future. Once it had passed, I thought (and still think), it would be much more difficult to change the character of the monastery from German to anything else. Eventually, the language had to be Hebrew, or Ivrit, as the modern Hebrew is called in its own tongue, but that would take time.

An Extraordinary Visitor

Leo arrived in Israel with no detailed plan. He learned from observation and reflection on his experiences. An early incident provided a crucial point in his emerging vision for Benedictine presence there.

He was surprised one day when the brother porter, who had the task of receiving visitors, informed him that a uniformed officer of the Israeli military was at the monastery entrance asking to speak with him. The visitor was a tall, burly man, completely bald, with a brusque manner. Leo later recalled that first meeting:

> One of the visitors in those early days was Joshua Blum. We clicked almost immediately. He was shocked to see the bullet holes in the mosaics of the apse. He asked whether he could come back some day, maybe with his wife. This, of course, was gladly agreed upon. He returned often, and I visited him.

The friendship and frequent visits exchanged by the Benedictine prior and the Israeli military man resulted in an unexpected request. The major asked to be instructed in the Catholic faith. Leo was both surprised and pleased. After the period of instructions, Joshua was baptized. As a consequence of his baptism, he suffered ostracism in Israel. Stripped of his rank in the military and cashiered, unable to find employment, his marriage collapsed. His request to rent a place to live was denied. Prior Leo received him as an "enclosed oblate" in the monastery. Living at the abbey, Joshua wore the monastic habit and joined in the prayer and work of the community, though he was not included in the monastic chapter.

Up until that time, Leo had held the prevailing Catholic position regarding the relationship between Christians and Jews. While he did not accept that active proselytizing was appropriate in the Jewish country, he considered conversion to Catholicism to be the road to salvation for all. That outlook also colored his understanding of the monastic presence in Israel.

The conversion of Joshua Blum and its aftermath gave Leo an unexpected opportunity to re-examine his approach to Jewish-Christian relations and what that might mean for Benedictines in the Holy Land. He was confronted with a challenge to preconceived ideas about Judaism, and the role of the monk in Israel. Joshua's new situation was disturbing, but Leo refrained from reacting defensively. Instead, he began to listen and observe more thoughtfully. Before he articulated the theme that was to become the fundamental guide to his life—"Stay open to the Holy Spirit"—he began to practice it.

When Leo accepted the role of prior-administrator of Dormition Abbey, he knew that the community must free itself from its image as a German monastery. He had no preconceived idea of how that could be accomplished. A degree of economic independence presented itself as one related issue.

He consulted his North American representative in the United States, Lambert Dunne, of St. Mary's Abbey in New Jersey. They investigated schemes for raising funds for the Dormition—including shipping bottles of Jordan River water for sale in the United States! An Israeli businessman named Katz proposed the peculiar venture. Leo reported to Lambert in a letter in July:

> I am rather favorably impressed by the possibilities offered by this corporation. They want to fill little flasks, which we would design, with Jordan water, but they would make them here. They would take over the supply of all the apparatus necessary (such as a distilling machine), and they would take care of the shipping to all sections of the world, particularly the USA.

Other possibilities—like seeking donations—proved more realistic and successful. A first step was to have a center in the United States to receive funds. Initially, the idea was to establish a "procure" (a type of temporary monastic outpost primarily intended to raise funds) in a diocese in the Northeast. Such a canonical establishment required permission of the local bishop. Several sites were investigated. When contacted, the various bishops required further details on the purpose of the proposed procure.

By the time Christopher Lind, another monk of St. Mary's, replaced Lambert as representative of the Dormition in the United States, the idea of a procure had begun to develop further. First it had been suggested as a house to receive funds, staffed by a layperson. In 1951, a memorandum from Leo indicated that eventually a novice master would be on staff at the procure to train one or two postulants and prepare them to go to the Holy Land.

Faced with reluctance from North American bishops to authorize a somewhat vague religious entity in their dioceses, Leo asked Cardinal Eugene Tisserant, head of the Oriental Congregation, to intervene on his behalf. The Cardinal wrote to the Archbishop of Philadelphia endorsing Leo's request. In spite of the support of an influential cardinal of the Curia, Leo's appeals were denied.

At length he turned to his friends Dorothea and Leon Smith in Clifton, New Jersey. When he wrote them that he hoped to establish a monastic house in North America, they were enthusiastic. Memories of Keyport and their friendship with Leo resurfaced readily. The Smiths began making inquiries for possible venues.

Other friends from his time in the United States became involved. The Smiths visited Norman and Margaret Langlois, now established at Regina Laudis monastery in Bethlehem, Connecticut. Dorothea and Leon shared Leo's latest news. Suggestions were generated. Norman remembered Professor Francis Kervick of Notre Dame, who previously had offered to donate his property in Randolph, Vermont, to the German monks before they settled in Keyport, New Jersey. It was one of several possibilities to be investigated. Leo was alerted that he should come and pursue these prospects.

Exploring the Green Mountain State

Soon a letter dispatched by Christopher Lind to Bishop Edward Ryan of Burlington, Vermont, was persuasive in obtaining the welcome from at least one member of the hierarchy:

> Father Leo Rudloff, O.S.B. Prior and Apostolic Administrator of Dormition Abbey, Jerusalem, is expected to arrive in this country at the end of the month. He has been instructed by the Oriental Congregation to establish a foundation within the United States. Such a foundation would be dependent upon and serving Dormition Abbey

> for some time. If God should favor its growth, it would eventually be developed into a permanent foundation and monastic center....
>
> Actually this instruction of Father Leo's was made about a month ago, but heavy duties for my own abbey caused me to delay in fulfilling it. A letter that I received this morning from His Eminence, Cardinal Tisserant, urged me to proceed without further delay.

The references to the Oriental Congregation and Cardinal Tisserant mark a dramatic shift in Leo's vision of his projected foundation in the United States. What he referred to previously as a procure for raising funds with the possibility of a few candidates to be prepared for the Dormition Abbey, was now expanded to a genuine monastic foundation. He alluded to this new understanding in a letter to Christopher Lind on July 17, 1952:

> Yes, I intend to make a permanent foundation. Things were talked over with the Oriental Congregation in Rome. Only thus can we realize our plans for the future. My idea is to make the place in the United States more and more the center of our activities that, according to our plans, will outgrow support for Dormition Abbey into further fields of action—more by word of mouth. Whether I personally shall eventually be more there than here, that I leave entirely to God, in Whose Providence I put my trust.

Christopher wondered who would staff the new monastery and asked Leo in a letter where the monks for the new foundation would come from. Leo replied with perhaps a little more bravado than he actually felt:

> To begin with, I shall order our Father Luke Joerg, now in St. Joseph's Abbey, Louisiana, to the new place. I have

> mentioned it to him. Then, I shall as soon as possible try to get our Father Matthias there, who is in Beirut, and our Father Cyril, who is in Westphalia. Our Father Placid is at present in New Subiaco, Arkansas. He also can join the community in the new foundation. So you see, I also want to collect all the stray members of our Abbey in one place, so as to reunite them all in the common effort for our community. Father Andreas in North Italy could perhaps also join.
>
> So you see, I hate to call the place a procure. Yet, at least for some time, it will be dependent on us and serving us. How things will then develop is in the hands of God. I visualize the place as a real foundation in the future, and a monastic center....

Although the location in Randolph proved to be inadequate for the projected foundation, Bishop Ryan was open to Leo's plans and suggested that he look for another location in his diocese.

Leo continued to prod Christopher Lind by mail not to give up on the search for a suitable property in the U.S., "The other day, there visited here a certain Paul Freytag of Bernardsville, New Jersey.... In the time of Keyport he had contact with Father Albert Hammenstede.... He is now very interested in the abbey and our need for a location in the States."

Paul Freytag informed Leo that he spent his summers in Newfane, Vermont. He also indicated that he dealt in real estate and knew many suitable places for a monastery. When he returned to the United States, Mr. Freytag joined Leon and Dorothea Smith in their search, driving to Vermont together.

They viewed several beautiful remote estates in the Green Mountains, all priced in the $70,000 range, a far cry from Father Leo's limited budget of $2,400. As the Smiths prepared to leave for home, checking out in the lobby of the Newfane Inn, they overheard a woman ask for Paul Freytag's room.

Introducing themselves, they offered to show her the way. She was Mary Mitchell Miller, who also dealt in real estate in Vermont. When the Smiths shared the failure of their mission, Mary Miller told them that she had the answer to their prayer. She drove them to the little town of Weston.

Located in south central Vermont, Weston was approached in those days only by unpaved dirt roads. The quiet village was known for its crafts, summer theatre, and country store as well as the beauty of its natural setting. The peaceful West River coursed through the center of town past the village green with its pre-Civil War-period bandstand. Forested mountains framed the picturesque scene. Four miles north of the village the visitors drove up a winding road to an abandoned farmhouse. The barn attached to the house had been partially burned to the ground. The house was decrepit, but standing upright in comparison to the sagging chicken coop in the backyard. The open fields had not been tended for years; scrub was taking over. Yet there was a wonderful air of peace and quiet. The view to the surrounding mountains and Green Mountain National Forest was striking. The land seemed to invite someone to care for it. The Smiths agreed that it was just the answer to Father Leo's hopes and needs. It had potential and the price was right. Dorothea Smith described their arrival in Weston in detail:

> After lunch we all got into a Jeep and went to look at the site. It was rough going, for the road up the hill was in very bad shape. Priory Lane was not a useable road then. When we reached the top, what did we see? Fields of overgrown grass and weeds waist high, a tumbledown house with a large chicken house attached. It was nearly impossible to walk through the weeds and shrub.... The house was an old New England type of simple lines. When we entered, we found the inside far worse than the

> outside. Nevertheless, we were later told that it was structurally sound and could be put into good shape. There was a small opening near the ground into the chicken house. I crawled in on my hands and knees to find that it was just one big space. One of the rafters had fallen down and was lying across the floor....
>
> In the house we found an old piano in the front room. And in the entrance hall a large picture of the Sacred Heart. Who would ever have expected this in a deep-seated stronghold of Anglo-Saxon Protestantism? It certainly took us by surprise. I'm afraid that we took it as an omen! Some two hundred acres went with the buildings and the price was such that Father Leo could make an initial payment.[1]

Mary Miller introduced the Smiths to Jean Wilcox, her real estate partner. Jean, only recently baptized a Catholic, represented half the Catholic population of Weston. George Conley, a retired businessman was the other half. Jean's husband Al was a partner with Raymond Austin in the firm Architects and Builders of Weston. Al assured the Smiths that, in spite of its appearance, the building was sound enough to be rejuvenated. In high spirits, Dorothea and Leon returned to their home in New Jersey.

Jean Wilcox sent this appraisal of the property to Father Leo:

3 acres (Shattuck Place)	$ 800
50 acres (Hodges Place)	1,000
20 acres (Dave Wilder Place)	150
100 acres (Eastman Place)	500
85 acres (Glebeland)	1,000
258 acres appraised value	$3,450

above: Weston Priory at time of purchase in 1952. *below left:* Mary Mitchell Miller, a Vermont Real Estate dealer 'discovered' the Weston property. *below right:* Jean Wilcox, Mary's Real Estate partner with husband Al who negotiated the purchase and with his partner, Ray Austin, renovated the original farm house.

The Smiths hastily informed Leo of their find in Vermont. Sensing that this was the best opportunity, he hastened back to the United States. On his arrival, Dorothea and Leon filled him in on their findings in Vermont, "We told him in detail of the condition of the Peabody property in Weston, for we did not want him to be shocked by the first appearance."

Leo drove to Weston to inspect the Peabody property that the Smiths had unearthed, accompanied by Hugh Duffy, a monk of Morristown, New Jersey, who had agreed to serve as first prior of the envisaged foundation.

Traveling up the winding lane north of the village, Leo's hopes were high. At the crest of the hill, he was not disappointed. Wilderness framed the scene. He thrilled to the beauty around him. He loved the remoteness and the quiet. The woods brought back his silent walks with his father in the Sauerland forests of Germany. He was not taken aback by the run-down appearance of the buildings. The deserted house did not daunt him. This forsaken place, at the edge of wilderness and civilization, called out for a new beginning.

As Leo surveyed this landscape for the first time in the fall of 1952, all that remained of the thriving community of fifty years earlier were the cellar holes and remnants of foundations, the stone walls and hints of fields, the memories and hidden signs of a life once lived—a culture rooted in the rocky soil worked by early Vermont settlers.

The Old County Road, rising from the flood plain just north of Weston Village, had once been the stage road linking two southern Vermont counties. It followed a mountain ridge from Weston over Mount Holly to the town of Rutland. Along the way, in the nineteenth century, it was lined with the homesteads of Yankee families. The Hodge, Stevens, Peabody, Eastman, Wilder, and Shattuck families sent their children to the one-room schoolhouses scattered through the now dense woodland.

With their raw strength and the aid of oxen, the Yankee farmers had built rock fences to mark their property and create enclosures for livestock. Flocks of sheep and turkeys grazed the open pastures. Lumber mills and charcoal kilns provided work, income, and fuel for families with numerous offspring. Each farmhouse had its own apple orchard, sugar bush, and sugar house for the seasonal occupations of autumn and spring. Hard and sweet cider and maple syrup were processed, consumed, and marketed by frugal people, who lived simply and sustained their families by dint of hard work.

For Leo, abandonment, neglect, and failure had already become the occasion for hope and new life. As he gazed for the first time at the old Peabody Place, forlorn and neglected, he experienced the feelings of love and promise similar to those he felt when he first set foot on the soil of Israel.

The Weston property met his desires and nourished his dream. Here, even before he had been named Abbot of Dormition Abbey, the promise of new life was born. Later, he would call this place his child; the monastery of Weston Priory. Dorothea succinctly portrayed his reaction on his return from Weston to New Jersey; "When Father Leo returned from his visit, he was full of anticipation and excitement at the possibilities of the house and acreage—all for a price less than $2400.00!"

The purchase of the Weston property was complicated. The previous owner had declared bankruptcy. The government had appropriated forested parcels of the land in lieu of taxes. Claims had to be cleared. Leo had neither the time nor the expertise to deal with such problems. More than that, Abbot

Primate Bernard Kaelin informed him from Rome that he was to become the second abbot of Dormition Abbey. Abbot Bernard was to conduct a Visitation of the Abbey and confirm his selection as abbot in the fall. It was necessary for Leo to set out at once for Rome and Israel.

He entrusted the negotiations for the Weston transaction into the hands of Hugh Duffy and Christopher Lind, monks of Morristown, New Jersey, and his newfound Vermont friends, Al and Jean Wilcox and Mary Miller. The formation of the Board of Directors of the Benedictine Foundation of the State of Vermont, Inc., the drawing up of the By-laws and Articles of Association for the legal corporation, and the transfer of property had to be accomplished in the absence of Father Leo, the Chairman of the Board. He could only be present in faith and trust.

MANSUETUDO—POTENTIA

above: 1953. Abbatial blessing at Sant'Anselmo in Rome. Abbot Pius of Gerleve on Leo's left, Abbot Albert of Neuberg on his right, Bishop Johannes von Rudloff in background. *center left:* Cardinal Eugene Tisserant officiated at the blessing. *center right:* Abbot Primate Bernard Kaelin, Cardinal Tisserant, Abbot Leo after the blessing. *below left:* Installation at Dormition Abbey with Latin Patriarch Albert Gori, Fathers Willibrord and Joseph. *below right:* Recession following installation. "It was a big affair."

6

From Mount Zion to the Green Mountains

Time passed quickly as the Dormition Abbey community prepared for the Visitation by the Abbot Primate. Father Leo assembled as many of the dispersed members of the community as he was able to persuade to be present for the occasion. He informed them that progress was being made toward a foundation in the United States. Relations with the Israeli authorities were vastly improved, and there were promises of cooperation in restoring all the monastic properties. There were at least faint signs of hope that support and recruits for the beleaguered community were in the not too distant future.

The Abbot Primate arrived in Jerusalem near the end of November of 1952. During the week long Visitation, he interviewed the monks and determined that the community supported Leo's leadership. While he did not detect enthusiasm for Leo's vision of a renewed monastic life, all members of the community agreed that only he could assume the responsibilities of abbot. On December 8, Abbot Primate Bernard Kaelin confirmed Leo's election as second abbot of Dormition Abbey.

The abbey in Jerusalem and its meager community were not prepared to host such a celebrative event as the blessing of an abbot. Guest facilities were not available to house the dignitaries who were to be invited. The kitchen and refectory were not adequately equipped for such an occasion. The monastic community itself was not yet sufficiently united or ready to offer the hospitality or to conduct the solemn service.

In consultation with the Abbot Primate, Leo decided to have the blessing take place at the Benedictine College of Sant'Anselmo in Rome, the resident monastery of the Abbot Primate and Leo's alma mater. The student community of Sant'Anselmo would offer the music and trained ministers for the service. There would be appropriate hospitality for bishops, abbots, and other dignitaries. A few of the ordained monks of the Dormition community would accompany Leo to Rome.

In the midst of the flurry of these preparations, Leo received a disturbing telegram from the United States. In December, Hugh Duffy, who had consented to serve as prior of the new foundation in Vermont, had set out for Weston from New Jersey with his nephew. On the way he stopped to visit his sister in Boston. While there, he suffered a disabling heart attack; he was unable to continue his journey. It was unclear when he would be active again, and he was unable to continue as prior.

The news spread quickly. Michael Ducey, a monk of St. Anselm Abbey in Washington, D.C., had been with Hugh at the experimental monastery of Christ the King in Fifield, Wisconsin, the previous year. They shared the hope for a simpler Benedictine monastic lifestyle than was currently available. When he heard of Hugh's heart attack, Michael hurried to Boston to the side of his friend. He offered to fill in for Hugh as prior of the Weston monastery.

With relief and gratitude, Leo accepted Michael's offer. There was little opportunity to communicate with his new Prior, who was almost a stranger to him. Prior Alban Boultwood of St. Anselm's Priory in Washington, D.C., graciously released Michael from his jurisdiction. With lessened anxiety, Leo set out from Israel to Rome for his abbatial blessing.

The spacious chapel of Sant'Anselmo in Rome was the scene of Father Leo's abbatial blessing on January 6, 1953. The handsome abbey chapel was still decked with greens and decorations from the Christmas season. Numerous invited guests and members of religious orders filled the pews. The student body and faculty of Benedictine monks with monastic tonsure attended in their choir stalls or as ministers around the altar. Cistercian and Benedictine abbots joined with Leo's brother Johannes, the Bishop in Hamburg, Germany, in the procession down the center aisle.

Cardinal Eugene Tisserant, camerlengo to Pope Pius XII and head of the Oriental Congregation, presided at the blessing.[1] With his flowing beard and severe countenance he lent an air of gravity to the occasion. Leo's friends, Abbot Pius Buddenborg of Gerleve and Abbot Albert Ohlmeyer of Neuberg, functioned in assisting roles in traditional vestments.

Following the ceremony Leo remarked to his brother Johannes, "This is my Palm Sunday before my Good Friday." He later pictured the event in a lighter vein, "It was a big affair. Today I would call it almost pompous.... It had all the trappings of a big Roman Pontifical celebration: the Cardinal...then Monsignor Terzariol as Master of Ceremonies, a kind of glorified valet and all the rest."

Photos taken during the ceremony confirm the solemnity of the celebration. They also depict a somber mood. Abbot Leo's face betrays signs of strain and gravity. Absent are indications of joyful celebration. In the atrium of the chapel, three monks of Dormition Abbey, stern and grim-faced, pose formally with Leo for a photo following the celebration.

Nearly a month later, on February 2, 1953, Leo was officially installed as the second abbot of Dormition Abbey in Jerusalem. It was another solemn occasion. Archbishop Alberto Gori, the Latin Patriarch of Jerusalem, presided at the ceremony in the beautiful monastery church. Leo was led to the abbatial throne in the apse of the church. Above the canopied throne hung the shield and motto of the new abbot. For his motto, Leo chose the Latin words, *Mansuetudo Potentia.*

In his "Reminiscences" he wrote a short paragraph explaining the origin of that phrase without indicating its meaning or import for him:

> As my motto, as Abbot, I chose the words: *Mansuetudo-Potentia,* Gentleness is Power. This was taken from a letter of the martyr St. Ignatius to the Trallians (3,2). In that chapter, St. Ignatius gives his impression of the bishop of Tralles, who came to the port when the holy martyr was, as a prisoner condemned to die, conveyed by ship to Rome. The whole sentence reads like this: "I have received the example of your love, and I have it with me in the person of your bishop whose very demeanor is a great sermon, and whose gentleness is power." It is customary to have the motto in Latin. I should have liked to have it in Greek...

In the context of Leo's forebodings and many trials, it may well be that he identified with the bishop of Tralles, "the holy martyr...as a prisoner condemned to die." Leo made no effort to explain why he would have preferred to have the motto in

Greek. His aversion to the Latin word *mansuetudo* may stem from its usual English translation as meekness that evokes the image of servitude or one who quietly submits to authority! By temperament Leo was more inclined toward diplomacy and propriety than to passive submission. As his personality tempered with the passing of years, gentleness became a more suitable attribution of his character.

Father Willibrord, a gaunt and lanky senior monk of the Dormition community, placed the abbatial miter on Abbot Leo's bowed head. Each member of the community then knelt singly before the new abbot, promised obedience, and received the kiss of peace.

At the close of the ceremony, Leo addressed the assembly that included the American Consul General, representatives of the Israeli Government and religious dignitaries. The *Jerusalem Post* praised the speech on behalf of the people of Israel, commenting that "it was one of the most friendly utterances to date by any representative of the Vatican."

With the ecclesial festivities behind him and the departure of dignitaries and friends, Leo turned again to the pressing issue of his new North American monastic foundation. He was pleased with the architect's drawing of the monastery. The simple New England style of the renovated farm house and attached barn chapel blended into the rural surroundings. In a remarkably short time, a loan for funds was secured and the renovations were underway.

As abbot, he appealed to the still absent members of his community. In his earlier letter to Christopher Lind, he had expressed confidence that they would hasten to staff the new foundation in Weston. The "scattered flock" of Dormition monks offered the same resistance to Leo's plea as had the resident monks in Jerusalem. They were not in full agreement with the idea of Dormition Abbey as an international community. They were hesitant about the United States as a source of vocations. They clung to their Beuronese identity and observance. They were not ready to move to the unknown state of Vermont and to cast their lot into a venture that they neither approved nor understood. Only Cyril Berndt, the lone monk who had remained at St. Joseph's Abbey in Gerleve, Germany, during the war, responded to that appeal. Cyril spent several months assisting Michael Ducey, but he found the Vermont climate and manual labor too strenuous and moved on to New Jersey.

A Novel Foundation in the Green Mountain State

So it was Michael Ducey, not the initially appointed Hugh Duffy, who arrived to take up duties as the first resident prior of Weston on a blustery day in January, 1953. A scholarly, unassuming man, Michael was more at home in the classroom than in the rugged outdoors. A past secretary of the National Liturgical Conference, he was author of numerous articles on the liturgy.

In the company of Bert Quaadman, a young layman from Morristown, New Jersey, who was a candidate for the Dormition community, Michael waited through the Vermont winter for the arrival of Abbot Leo in the late spring. While renovations to the monastery building were being completed, the two early arrivals stayed in the rented Plesset house—later the Priory's Bethany Guest House—near the monastery property. There was little to be done until Michael learned in more detail of Leo's plans for the monastic community at Weston.

Leo joined Michael in Weston at the beginning of the Vermont summer in the month of June. Both men were in their early fifties and shared common interests, though their monastic backgrounds differed. Michael's early monastic training took place at Fort Augustus Abbey in Scotland, a monastery belonging to the English Benedictine Congregation that was largely dedicated to service in educational institutions. St. Joseph's Abbey in Gerleve, the home of Leo's formative monastic years, was a member of the German Beuronese Congregation that fostered a strict disciplinary observance of the Rule of St. Benedict and engaged in pastoral ministry and retreat work.

Entering the renovated farmhouse on Old County Road together, the two men were virtual strangers to one another. Yet they shared a commitment to Benedictine monastic life as well as a love of the liturgy, the public prayer of the church. A basic hope also united them in bringing the Weston Priory community to birth: both ardently desired a new expression of Benedictine monastic life, one that would be centered in prayer and faithfulness to the Rule of Benedict.

There was little time in their first encounter that summer at Weston Priory for the two men to explore the views they held, which would prove to be quite divergent. Abbot Leo urged the immediate purpose of the Priory was to provide personnel and support for the Dormition Abbey in Jerusalem. Michael placed priority on the monastery as a center for liturgical prayer and simple monastic living. In light of the present need to form a community and to establish it on a firm footing, their differences did not appear to be irreconcilable, since Leo's hope for the Dormition Abbey also foresaw a new kind of Benedictine presence and monastic life in the Holy Land. Some ambiguity seemed tolerable under the circumstances.

Leo set one goal for the inaugural year: to make it known that a Benedictine monastery was now present in the Green Mountains of Vermont. The two monastic pioneers set about this task without delay. Both traveled around the country speaking in parishes, visiting other monasteries and religious communities, and contacting newspapers and journals.

It was a fortuitous time to launch a new monastic community. In the years after World War II, interest in religious vocations was at a high point. Monastic writers like Thomas Merton, Bede Griffiths, Jean Leclerc, and Louis Bouyer endorsed a simplification and renewal of monastic life. They emphasized the uniqueness of the monastic vocation as different from that of priesthood or religious orders. Experiments in small monastic communities sprang up around the country and beyond—at Christ the King in Wisconsin, Mount Saviour in New York State, Glastonbury in Massachusetts, Pius X and St. Louis priories in Missouri, Our Lady of the Resurrection Monastery in Cuernavaca, Mexico, as well as in Weston, Vermont.

In an early summer interview published by the *Boston Globe,* Leo spoke of the chapel at Weston Priory. In contrast with traditional monastic structures, the architecture of the new foundation would harmonize with its environment:

> When it is finished...it will be strikingly different from its parent, the Dormition Abbey. There will be neither stained glass windows nor elaborate carvings. Instead, the chapel will be made to fit the landscape of encroaching forests, and the song of birds will accompany the Gregorian chants of the monks. The outside of the chapel will keep its simple, barn like shape, with small windows high up in the walls; the interior will be paneled in the pine that grows in the surrounding forests.

In July, when Bishop Edward F. Ryan made his first visit to the Priory, he expressed his pleasure at welcoming the Benedictine community to a section of the Burlington diocese that had a very sparse Catholic population. Confirming that the monastic community would not assume parochial responsibilities, he said his hope was that by prayer and monastic presence the priory would radiate the Christian spirit in its environs.

The formal welcome of the Weston Priory community to the diocese took place at an open-air Mass in South Park in Burlington on a sunny August day. A thousand people filled the bleachers and concrete grandstand. Clergy and religious of the diocese followed an honor guard of Knights of Columbus with plumed hats, capes, and swords in a procession across the field to an altar and abbatial throne arranged on the baseball diamond. The celebrated von Trapp family of Stowe, European refugees like Abbot Leo during World War II, sang German processionals and Gregorian chant during the Mass. They concluded the celebration with a moving rendition of the classic German pilgrimage hymn, "O Maria Hilf," praying for Mary's help.

Abbot Leo celebrated the Pontifical Mass in full episcopal regalia that he borrowed from Bishop Ryan, who chose to be represented by his vicar general. By absenting himself, the Bishop made room for Abbot Leo to vest fully with miter, crozier, and other signs of ecclesial office. In accord with church protocol, two members of the hierarchy garbed in episcopal robes would have given an air of competition. Leo presided with an air of dignity, and in his homily portrayed his dream for the priory in Weston and the abbey in Jerusalem.

A photo taken late in that summer of 1953 shows Leo with architect Ray Austin and builder Al Wilcox playfully at work on the steps of the partially completed chapel at the Priory. The mood is optimistic, even joyful, Leo attired in informal clothes wielding a hammer over his shoulder, his head thrown back in laughter. His two non-Catholic friends seem to be enjoying the fun. There is a spirit of hope and even playfulness that would be absent in the months to follow.

Encouraged by his first summer at Weston, Leo returned to Israel in the fall of 1953. On his way, he stopped in Rome to participate for the first time in one of the regular congresses of Benedictine abbots and priors.[2] At that meeting, Abbot Leo presented a brief report in Latin on Dormition Abbey and Weston Priory. He laid out his hopes of internationalizing the Dormition community and obtaining vocations from the new foundation in North America.

Choir Monks and Communication Problems

While in Rome, Abbot Leo took advantage of the opportunity to broach the subject of non-ordained choir-monks with the Abbot Primate, Bernard Kaelin. The Primate gave little encouragement, saying that men who had previously requested the status of non-ordained monks did not persevere. Leo pursued the question no further at that time, writing to Michael Ducey that he accepted the Primate's advice though he "was not 100% satisfied by it."

Leo conveyed his own hesitation to implement the choir-monk program at this early juncture in a letter to Prior Michael Ducey dated April 22, 1954:

> Now the important question of "lay monk." In principle, I am all for it, but the situation is this. It was mentioned, alas too briefly, at the Abbots' Congress.... It seems that

above: August 6, 1953. Von Trapp family singers at field mass in Burlington. *center left:* Abbot Leo on throne. Father Charles Towne offered welcome on behalf of the Burlington Diocese. *below left:* Among diocesan clergy, Robert Hammond, the future brother John. *below right:* Abbot Leo opened the door to Weston Priory.

> up to the present, it has really been done nowhere successfully. Mount Saviour has it on their program, but so far they have not a single one, as far as I know. Prinknash has it. But do they have recent professions of that kind? I don't think so. The Abbot Primate says the experience is that those choir monks, not in [holy] orders, become malcontent later on, and unhappy.

Following the lead of the Abbot Primate, a compromise should suffice for the time being:

> He suggests, instead, the following procedure. We should lift the brothers up more and more, let them take part in the holy office (at least part of it), treat them as real members of the family, although they might not have a vote in the chapter. As a general rule, I think for the time being there is nothing to be done, other than to make them [lay] brothers and to assimilate those brothers more and more into the choir.... This way, in time, by way of evolution, the thing may eventually come to pass that we have real choir-monks, not in the priesthood.

When Abbot Leo arrived in Jerusalem, a copy of a news release out of Weston, carried by the National Catholic News Service in the U.S., awaited him. Announcing "Prior Named for Benedictine Foundation Which Will Stress Contemplative Life," it read:

> Weston, Vt., Oct. 1 (NC)—Father Michael Ducey, O.S.B., until recently prior of St. Anselm's Priory in Washington, D.C., and one of the founders of the National Liturgical Conference, has been appointed Prior of the new Benedictine foundation here. Abbot Leo Rudloff, O.S.B., of the Dormition Abbey in Jerusalem, made the

> announcement as he left the United States to return to the Holy Land.
>
> Weston Priory, situated on a mountainside overlooking scenic West River Valley in the Green Mountains, has been established as a branch of the famed Jerusalem shrine of Our Lady. Present plans call for a community of 12 monks.
>
> While some 20 or so of the Benedictine monasteries in America are engaged in teaching or missionary work, five others, including Weston Priory, represent a return to the more ancient traditions which stress contemplation rather than action.
>
> Much of the monks' time at first will be spent in farming in an attempt to return the abandoned land to a state of cultivation. It is from farm activities and their crafts that the monks will obtain their sustenance and pay for the operation of the priory. As farm activities become organized and the monks have more leisure time, they will devote it to developing their talents in the arts.
>
> It is expected it will take ten years to fully organize the monastery, and by then the monks might number as many as 50. Eventually the priory will sever its link with the Jerusalem abbey and maintain its own community and personnel.

From his discussions in Rome, Leo realized that some abbots were turning a critical eye on his new venture in the United States. At the same time, within the Dormition community, he had to deal with an entrenched conservatism that feared any change. Betraying his anxiety that the fledgling Weston monastery elude criticism and authoritarian hindrance, Leo responded with guarded praise and a caution to Michael concerning the news release just received:

> About the enclosures: Generally speaking they are quite all right. Two exceptions:
>
> Be careful in emphasizing the difference between the contemplative and the active Order of Saint Benedict. Some people are very sensitive, and it did a lot of harm to Elmira [Mount Saviour monastery in New York State].
>
> I am somewhat upset about the concluding paragraph:
>
> "Eventually the priory will sever its link with the Jerusalem abbey and maintain its own community and personnel." You know, Father, that I consider the connection between Dormition Abbey and Weston Priory essential. True, I have occasionally said the place might develop into an abbey. By that time, many problems will be solved. But it gives an entirely wrong impression if you write it as you did in those articles. Please, do handle this according to my intentions. It is a fact that the connection is the raison d'etre for the foundation. So I should appreciate it, if this were made clear—as I explained it to you and Father Hugh—especially to postulants.

Michael was stung by the implication that his remarks were contrary to Leo's wishes. By return mail he pointed out that the reference "Eventually...sever its link with the Jerusalem abbey..." was actually taken from an interview given by Abbot Leo himself earlier in the summer. With shock, Leo offered apologies to Michael:

> My sincere apologies for imputing to you that article with the statement about "severing relations." Do you mean it was the lady reporter who interviewed me who is responsible for it? That would go to show once more how careful one has to be with reporters, and that one should always request proofreading before publication. Well, the thing is

> not toooo serious, although it really had some nefarious results. I hope that some venomous criticism that reached me on account of the article remains an isolated case.

The mention of venomous criticism arose no doubt from some exchanges he had with other abbots at the Congress before his departure from Rome or from repercussions within the Dormition community. This initial misunderstanding between Michael and Leo was a foretaste of the problems of communication that beset Abbot Leo and the men he chose to serve as priors of Weston Priory in its foundational years. It was clear from the outset that he wanted Weston to be a source of vocations and support for the community in Israel. It was not clear how the Priory would achieve its own identity. As the *Boston Globe* article foretold, it would indeed take "ten years for the monastery to be organized."

For Leo and the first three priors at Weston it was a time of strenuous efforts toward survival and clarification. The inconsistency of creating a stable community at Weston while sending monks from the young foundation to create a new Benedictine monastic presence in the Holy Land was fraught with difficulties.

The Vermont community began without the presence of committed, experienced monks. The first two priors were on loan from other monasteries. None of the first priors had any experience of life in the Holy Land or in the founding Beuronese community of Dormition Abbey. Furthermore, they had little understanding of the issues bound up in Jewish-Christian relations.

Abbot Leo's vision was evolving with his experience and studies in Israel. His understanding of the terms "a monastic mission to the Jews" and "a Benedictine presence in the Holy Land" was in flux. His concept of a renewed form of monastic life was likewise tentative and still in process.

A Lonely Undertaking in Israel

When in Jerusalem, Abbot Leo responded to invitations for civic, social, and ecclesial events. Unable to convince his fellow monks of the value of reaching out to the world around them, he usually went alone. He attended receptions for the presidents and other officials of the Israeli government, mixing easily with distinguished guests. He played a leading role in ecumenical organizations. Ever a gracious participant, he was an agent for harmony among competing religious groups.

Life inside the abbey itself was harsh partly because the monastery buildings were poorly adapted to the climate. The large structure with its thick stone walls towered like a mighty European fortress on Mount Zion. In the winter months, temperatures dropped into the thirties Fahrenheit. Once cold penetrated the walls, it remained for the duration of the season. The cavernous church with its high cupola was equally uncomfortable.

The church and monastery lacked central heating and, for the first ten years after the war of independence, was without electricity. Meals were prepared on a tiny single-burner gas stove. By the time the food reached the dining room, it was tepid. In the kitchen, the brothers did their best with limited supplies that had to be purchased each day because there was no refrigeration. It pained Leo that he could not offer hospitality to guests since there were no guest facilities for lodging or meals.

The lengthy and ponderous rendition of the monastic offices in Latin was far from the desire that Leo harbored for uplifting community prayer. The two-class system of lay brothers and solemnly professed priest-monks remained entrenched; the two groups took work, prayer, and recreation separately. Hierarchic order was maintained; brothers were subservient to priests. In the midst of this bleak picture, Leo noted at least one hopeful sign emerging from his early labors in the Dormition Abbey community:

> Besides working on the external restoration of Dormition Abbey, I found much to do in giving direction in some internal matters. The building up of a real monastic community would have taken much more time than was allotted to me. My plans in that direction did not fully materialize.
>
> But there was one thing that I attacked with great energy, and I think, not without success. When I arrived, I found the mood of the Dormition community anti-Semitic, almost to the point where it might be called virulent.... I still remember the terribly anti-Semitic remarks which were almost commonplace among the members of the Dormition community.... So one of my first tasks was to change that attitude. It took a long time, but I think I finally succeeded to a great extent. It was a hard task, indeed....
>
> In the beginning, I also often wished that Dormition Abbey had been located in the Arab section of Jerusalem.... I also felt greater sympathy for the Arabs. My upbringing was not particularly friendly to Jews.

Tabgha: A Favored Place of Hope

An adventurous and enquiring spirit prevented Leo from falling into discouragement or negativity. He was inspired by the Jewish "love for the land." The Hebrew relationship to the land that plays a central part in Jewish spirituality held special appeal for Leo. The link between people and place had a parallel in the Benedictine value of stability that binds a monk to a monastery, its place, and its members. In view of this value common to both Jews and Benedictines, a place in Israel named Tabgha played a key role in Leo's vision of monastic life in the Holy Land.

A 1955 booklet on the Dormition Abbey pictures the daughter sanctuary located at the site, beside the Sea of Galilee, traditionally linked to Christ's miracle of multiplying the loaves and fishes. The name Tabgha, it explains, is a corruption of a Greek word meaning "seven wells." Indeed, Tabgha and its surroundings are exceptionally rich in fresh water springs. At the site when Leo first arrived, there were the remains of two ancient churches, one built atop the other. In the later ruins, fourth-century floor mosaics are preserved. Of these, one near the altar, showing a basket with loaves and two fishes, clearly represents the miracle. Leo later expressed his feelings for the place:

> From the very beginning I had great love for Tabgha. It had been my idea to develop Tabgha as a real monastery.... It is in the country, in beautiful scenery, and already for that reason very dear to me, who loves the country much more than the city. It became a favored place for me, where I liked to spend a few days off and on whenever possible. I am still somewhat homesick for it.

Tabgha became central to Leo's vision for a Benedictine community in Israel:

> In 1954, I laid the cornerstone to the new building, which was dedicated a year later. It is a handsome structure, which fits into the landscape, gently hugging it; adjoining the church on both sides are wings. There are also some

> ruins of an ancient Greek monastery, an oil press and a wine press.... An Arab architect from Nazareth built the monastery. I had hoped that we could build up a good monastic life there, make it even the headquarters of the community as such, from where the Dormition, a Sanctuary and pilgrims' center, was to be serviced.

The area was sparsely populated and undeveloped; the nearest town was Tiberias at the far southern end of the Lake. On the crest of the Mount of Beatitudes, overlooking the Tabgha monastery, a congregation of German sisters maintained a church and retreat house. A brief twenty-minute walk north along the shore of the lake led to the ruins of the fourth-century synagogue at Capernaum, the place the Gospels indicate as a sort of center of operations for Jesus's ministry.

Beyond the natural beauty of the scene, Leo was engrossed by its spiritual significance. He felt within himself that this extraordinary spot could somehow fit into his emerging vision of a Benedictine monastic presence in the Holy Land.

He set to work on this new project, giving priority to preservation of the precious floor mosaics. A temporary church shelter was constructed over the mosaics on the foundations of the original building. A two-story building, consisting of monastic cells made of stone and concrete, rested unobtrusively on the land. The architecture reflected Leo's taste for simplicity and his desire to avoid imposing alien structures on the natural landscape.

Abbot Leo assigned Father Jerome, an energetic Czech monk, and two elderly German lay brothers, Engelbert and Cletus, to the Tabgha mission. A few farm buildings were added, and with the labor of neighboring Palestinian Arabs, the fertile plain was converted into a banana plantation. When he needed respite from his responsibilities in Jerusalem, the peaceful setting of Tabgha provided Leo with a place for reflection, renewal, and prayer. Although the climate was extremely hot year-round, the water of the lake remained refreshingly cool. He frequently began his day with a swim at Tabgha, then a brisk walk to the ruins of Capernaum and back. Only the hostile presence of the Syrian military on the Golan Heights across the Lake marred the tranquility of the surroundings. Still, the setting of Tabgha enhanced his dream for monastic life in Israel.

The Hanseatic, Abbot Leo's favored ocean liner. "In these years I began my truly nomadic existence.... I must have crossed the Atlantic about fifty times."

7

A Nomadic Existence

The responsibility of directing two monastic communities separated by oceans and cultures was a formidable undertaking. Abbot Leo described his years of heading the venerable abbey in Jerusalem and the fledgling priory in Vermont as "a nomadic existence." Each year for twenty years, he shuttled back and forth between Israel and the United States, usually stopping off on the way for consultation in Rome and occasional visits with the monks at Gerleve and friends in Germany. As he said, "I must have crossed the Atlantic at least fifty times." Fortunately, he loved the ocean. With fondness, he described his shipboard experience:

> I never tired watching the sea and its changing hues and shades from morning to night, from sunshine to cloudy sky, or rain. Sometimes, when the sun was shining on our ship, you saw in the distance clouds pouring down rain in visible streams upon the darkened sea. Where the boat churned up the waves, they appeared to me as precious marble.

The ocean fascinated him and in it he found a striking metaphor for his own approach to the challenges that life offered him:

> I find sailing utterly thrilling. Of course, there is my love of ships and the water in general. But then the play of the elements, water and wind, is such a fascinating thing. To trim the sail to meet wind and water, to feel the pressure of water and wind, to play the tiller against the sail or in harmony with it and thus make the boat move to your goal, that is a real thrill. Often you have to compromise, to deal as it were, with the elements. You may have to tack quite a bit, come about many times, before you reach your destination. You may experiment with a normal come-about wind with a jib. Mainsail and jib become your tools together with the tiller.

The elements of nature conspiring against the man in the watercraft and his attempts to control them with the nautical devices at his command, all combine into the perfect image of the abbot coping with his shifting challenges across the globe. The maneuvers he had to make are just the ones he used to handle a small boat.

Happily, it was crossing the ocean dividing very different worlds—Israel, Rome, and Weston—that provided a spate of relaxation for Leo. He needed time and space to adjust his perspectives. Moreover, the shipboard ambiance, both the vastness of the horizon and the conviviality of fellow passengers, put him at ease. By the time he landed on another shore, he was prepared for the next encounter.

In the first decade of Weston Priory's existence, Leo tarried at least three months of every year in the United States. Each of those visits began with an extended ritual. First, he had a few days of rest with his friends, the Smiths, in New Jersey. Next, he drove—in the aged car he'd been given that he called Suzy—to the home of Jean and Al Wilcox at the south end of Weston, pausing for a little refreshment. From there, a phone call to the Priory announced that Abbot Leo was on his way. The community welcomed him like a father returning after a long absence. To the ringing of the monastery bells, he walked up the stone path to the chapel. Inside, the community was assembled, awaiting his blessing. After this rather formal reception, he settled into the upstairs room reserved for him in Saint Gabriel's, the remodeled farmhouse and main monastery building.

Laying the Foundations

At the Priory he applied himself to community life, joining in the monastic choir, presiding at the Eucharist and meals, leading conversations at evening recreation, and assuming his role as teacher. Each morning at Prime—the common prayer that preceded the period of work—he spoke at length to the whole community. It was an opportunity to share his growing love for Judaism and his hopes for a Benedictine presence at the Dormition Abbey in Jerusalem. In the course of his days at Weston, all of the brothers were eager to meet with him personally. He welcomed them to his room. Joys and hardships poured out freely. He was a good listener and readily offered reassurance and advice.

The brothers looked forward to his classes on the Rule, monastic history, and the Psalms. The group of young men—at times as many as a dozen aspirants—clothed in their black monastic habits sat at desk chairs, filling the makeshift classroom on the ground floor of the refurbished chicken coop. The setting contrasted starkly with the formal lecture halls and polished academic facilities more familiar to Abbot Leo. The loose-fitting windows rattled in the wind. The floors were rough boards hewn at the local lumber mill. The hand-me-down desks were discards from the College of Saint Rose in Albany after renovations there. The room was heated with a small pot-bellied stove. In this primitive setting, Abbot Leo held everyone's attention.

His teaching on spirituality and Benedictine life was a departure from conventional thinking in Catholic circles at the time. Pious books and devotions far removed from Scripture, the Rule, and authentic Tradition, were the common fare for spirituality, even in many monasteries. Liturgy was a rarely used word and usually relegated to regulations addressed to priests for administration of the sacraments.

Generally, monastic communities relied on their religious constitutions, local customaries, and novice masters for the formation of their members. For Abbot Leo, the Rule was the monastery's "Constitution," its primary document. He portrayed the Rule of St. Benedict as a spiritual guide and foundation rather than a set of rules and regulations. At a time when the Rule was often seen in legalistic terms, Leo's perspective was ahead of his times.

He instructed the young community in *Lectio Divina,* the meditative reading of the scriptures for personal prayer. Chanting the monastic office and the community celebration of Eucharist displaced the many pious devotions and individualistic prayers that were current in the 1950s. Further, true to the spirit of Benedict, the monks were "to live by the work of their hands." He demanded that ordained and non-ordained monks participate equally in manual labor, study, and praying the monastic office.

Chapter seven of the Rule of St. Benedict was for Abbot Leo the center of Benedictine spirituality. He underlined humility in radical and inspiring terms—as "the reverse side and underpinning of charity"—calling attention to the derivation of the word from the Latin *humus* meaning earth or rich soil. Growth in humility meant to become more and more down-to-earth, to become real, open, and honest in relating to God and to one another. He taught that humility and magnanimity, far from contradicting one another, go hand-in-hand. It is narrowness and meanness that oppose humility; an open spirit and a large heart are the signs of humility.

In his teaching as well as in his frequently poetic style of writing and speaking, Abbot Leo often made use of images. Out of his experience of life in foreign countries, he spoke of the monastery as an "embassy of the kingdom of God." The monastic 'embassy' was to be a place of openness and friendship, a place of peace and reconciliation.

During Leo's brief visits to the United States, he was intensely active and traveled well beyond the Weston community. His initial charge to Michael Ducey as prior had been to inform the public of the existence of the new Benedictine monastery in Vermont. He encouraged Michael to use all means at his disposal to attract attention to the new foundation, and Leo joined in the public relations effort. He welcomed guests and went out to neighbors. Though Catholics were a rarity in Weston at the time, he didn't hesitate to accept a dinner invitation from any of the priory's neighbors. He also traveled about the country preaching retreats at different monasteries and addressing groups wherever he was welcomed.

The combined efforts of Michael and Leo to publicize the priory and to attract interested candidates produced results. Illustrated articles on Weston Priory appeared in the *New York*

Daily News and the *Boston Globe* as well as in several Vermont newspapers. *Jubilee* magazine, a prominent Catholic periodical of the '50s and '60s edited by friends of Thomas Merton, featured the priory prominently in an early issue. In *The Silent Life,* a book exploring contemporary monastic life, Merton himself singled out Weston Priory and Mount Saviour as monasteries "of the primitive observance." The small remote priory at the edge of the Green Mountain Forest gradually gained visibility within the North American Catholic community.

With the arrival in 1954 of Father Bede Scholz, prior and founder of Pius X monastery in Missouri, Michael found more freedom to travel. He organized a pilgrimage to the Holy Land, and on his return, increased his schedule of lectures for recruitment. Meanwhile, Bede assumed many of the duties of the prior, organizing work, giving classes to the novices and postulants, and receiving new candidates.

Directing from a Distant Shore

Leo was hardly able to control happenings at Weston while he sojourned in the Holy Land, though the exchange of letters makes it obvious that even when in Jerusalem he was the superior of both houses. Correspondence between Michael and Leo addresses largely mundane matters. Financial problems were high on the list. Details of observance and questions of policy were discussed. Acceptance of candidates and problems among the members had to be addressed from afar. Even the most basic household items received mention.

A letter from Michael to Leo, written in the fall of 1953 after Abbot Leo's first visit to the newly established priory, samples concerns at Weston:

above: 1955. Early Weston monks: John Schanhaar, Bede Scholz, Stephen Fronckewicz, William Seegmüller and Cyril Berndt. *below left:* Neighbor Frank Stevens taught Father Bede the art of making maple syrup. *below right:* First resident claustral prior of Weston, Michael Ducey.

> Well, we seem to be making a little progress towards the desired monastic goal. Abbot Patrick recalled Brother Paul but sent us a good man in return, Father Malachy McPadden who seems about the best prospect we have had yet. Father Michael Fronckewicz was advised to wait till June and finish his year of theology at Conception Abbey. Father Bede et al. say they may come at Christmas time....
>
> Dave will bring a Jeep, too, he says, which should help with our car problem for the winter. The Ford is running fine, tho' we've had to put in about $50. worth of new parts.... Building program now at a standstill, no more money. We are getting a good used wood stove for heating the oratory. Al will put in a temporary vent thru the roof. No more word from the Bishop. The South Orange card party was grand, netting $500....

Each paragraph contains a raft of items:

> Some people still trickle in to see the place, a good crowd still on Sundays, this now being Foliage Season, and truly gorgeous.... We can put in the wall insulation ourselves when needed.... Also, Andy Shannon is giving us some pointers on caring for the horse, fixing up some kind of barn by using the wood, etc., from the two red outhouses, but putting it out of sight from the road...also will try to fix up the "garage" better for winter. May be able, too, to get a field plowed under before winter, so as to permit harrowing and planting in the spring....

The vacuum cleaner and the mortgage get equal time:

> Do you know what happened to our vacuum cleaner, which seems to have disappeared? We will sure need some more, soon. That first payment on the mortgage is

> due in about a week. Will need a boost from somewhere to meet it, but I'm not worrying....

Michael was a kindly, generous man, but from all indications somewhat disorganized and quite lacking in diplomacy. His letters often consisted of one paragraph—a full page long, rambling through a tangled stream of consciousness! He was also notorious for unwittingly alienating friends of the fledgling community. His written communications failed to inspire Leo's confidence.

The abbot's responses came with numbered paragraphs, an attempt to sort out the issues and questions and to give clear directions. At one point, no little frustration was expressed, "It is so difficult to answer at this distance. We will have to get our heads together when I come to Weston."

With the growing popularity of worship at Weston Priory, complaints were heard from a local pastor, Father Edwin Buckley, and from other neighboring priests. Priory liturgies were drawing away their parishioners. The use of unusual and aesthetic Gothic-style vestments by the priest-celebrant; the singing of Gregorian Chant, participation by lay people in the responses at Mass; processions for the blessings of fields, animals, and gardens; the replacement of typical devotions like novenas and rosaries, making way for the chanted monastic prayer—all began to contribute to a reputation that coupled the Benedictines with the "dangerous innovations" of the "Liturgical movement." Even some of the young monk-candidates complained of what was seen to be innovation.

Michael aroused the ire of an assembly of the Vermont diocesan clergy at a day of recollection that he conducted in the fall of 1955 in Shelburne, Vermont. At the invitation of Father Francis MacDonough, the pastor of St. Catherine's Parish in Shelburne and chairman of the diocesan liturgical commission, Michael was enlisted to give several lectures on the Eucharist.

A large representation of priests was in attendance in St. Catherine's Parish hall. Michael opened the day with a discourse on the homily of the Mass. He insisted that it should be a reflection on the scripture readings of the day rather than a catechetical sermon. Pandemonium erupted.

The priests' commission of the local diocesan Confraternity of Christian Doctrine had only recently mandated a three-year series of Sunday sermon topics for every parish of the diocese. To be successively treated were the commandments, the creed, and the sacraments. Members of the commission were present at the conference in full force. All their work stood to be destroyed by the initiative that Michael advanced. The CCD priests accused him of conceiving a program that would undermine the faith of the people. The lecturer tried meekly to defend himself. At length, Auxiliary Bishop Robert Joyce intervened, declaring that Michael must desist from promoting his agenda. Needless to say, the day of recollection as well as the standing of both Michael and Weston Priory in the Vermont diocese went downhill from there.

Eventually, Bishop Ryan felt it necessary to clarify relations between the Priory and the Diocese. On Dec. 29, 1955, he wrote Father Michael:

> I am sending you the regulations that I deem proper for you and your Foundation in Weston to follow regarding the use of your chapel as a public oratory.
>
> First of all, it is to be understood that this chapel is in no sense a parochial or even a quasi-parochial church. However, people in the vicinity will be allowed to assist at Mass in your chapel on Sundays and holy days of obligation and at all devotions at any time.

The Bishop continued, indicating that sacramental ministry such as weddings, funerals, and baptism, was the responsibility of the pastor of the church in Chester and was subject to his authority. He concluded with an ominous caveat:

> You will understand that these arrangements are made at the pleasure of the Bishop and may be changed or withdrawn at any time that he may see fit, for good and sufficient reasons, to do so.

It remained for Abbot Leo to employ his gifts of quiet diplomacy with diocesan authorities on his annual visits to the diocese for the restoration of a spirit of calm.

By 1956, just three years after it was founded, Weston Priory numbered seventeen residents—none of them yet in solemn, i.e., final vows. Even Father Michael, the prior, was on loan from another monastery. The prospective members hailed from New England (Connecticut, Massachusetts, New Hampshire, Vermont), the Mid-Atlantic (New York, New Jersey, Pennsylvania), westward (Ohio, Missouri, Utah), and even from outside the country (Canada, Colombia).

The candidates, a disparate group and mostly in their early twenties, were filled with idealism, but had little understanding of monastic life. The two priest-monks, Michael Ducey and Bede Scholz, were on temporary assignment from their respective communities. The stability and identity of the Weston community, at this juncture, was but a hope for the future.

In the 1950s, the idea of a simple form of Benedictine monastic life appealed to many young men who were attracted to Weston Priory in the aftermath of World War II. In the primitive setting of meager rustic accommodations and the stringent manual work of a New England farm, it was no simple task for Leo to articulate how this simple monastic life related to his vision for service at the Dormition Abbey in the far away Holy Land.

His own interest in Judaism and the land of Israel was growing rapidly. Issues within Jewish-Christian relations were in the foreground of his concerns. Three months was a short time out of each year to expose his vision to a community of men who were not yet rooted in the tradition of Benedictine stability or yet introduced to a basic understanding of monastic life. Besides, there was the large turnover of candidates each year. Abbot Leo's task of bringing a simple monastic community into existence out of the raw material of young, inexperienced men from highly diverse backgrounds carried the added burden of the pressure from Israel where the skeptical Dormition monks were impatient for results from his plans.

Three Paths in the Woods

It was not only the instability and inexperience of young candidates that made Leo's task in Weston difficult. There were also the divergent views of the few older monks who came from monasteries with their own distinctive traditions and practices.

Michael and Bede shared Leo's desire for a renewed contemporary monastic life. Yet all three men had differing views on how that would take shape in the monastic community in Vermont. Both Michael and Bede were in their mid-fifties, about the same age as Abbot Leo. They had years of monastic experience behind them, although the forms of Benedictine observance and the particular monastic traditions they had been schooled in were not wholly of the same bolt. Neither man had extensive exposure to or profound interest in Jewish-Christian relations. Beyond that, they had no firsthand knowledge of Israel or the situation of the Dormition Abbey in the Holy Land.

While both priest-monks shared an interest in liturgy, Michael was perhaps a more prominent figure on that stage. In contrast to the academic background he brought to the new priory, Bede sprang from a wholly different world. He had been a monk of Conception Abbey in Missouri. While active in the liturgical movement, he was at the same time a leading figure in the Christian Family Movement and the Rural Life Conference in the Midwest. To this son of Midwestern farm stock, the discipline and hard work of life on the land in Vermont were second nature. By contrast, Michael, a former professor and prominent liturgist, was not at all proficient at manual labor and possessed few other practical skills.

Bede's vision of the monastery harkened back to the Middle Ages, when such institutions were centers of religious, civic, and cultural life where neighbors learned from the monks and often worked for them. Michael saw Weston Priory as a center of liturgical renewal, offering an environment conducive to studies and conferences devoted to the liturgy. He made no effort to hide his opinion that Weston was not a favorable location for such a monastery. The new foundation should be near a city, he believed, to be accessible to large numbers of people who would come for liturgical prayer, retreats, conferences, and workshops. At one point, according to Bede, Michael declared that to remain in Weston was "to commit monastic suicide."

To Bede, Weston was the ideal site for his monastery. He reveled in the remoteness of the location. He related easily to the rural Yankee people of the neighboring farms. For him, manual labor held top priority for the formation of monks. In this largely non-Catholic region, he believed, the monastery would attract converts to Catholicism and would Christianize the culture. At first, Michael and Bede handled their differences with light banter. Inevitably, tensions surfaced.

Weston Priory, monastery and attached chapel, 1953. "When it is finished, [Weston Priory] will be strikingly different from its parent, the Dormition Abbey."

8

Turbulence on All Sides

Early 1956 found Abbot Leo in Jerusalem, still uneasy thanks to rumors confided by friends before he left Weston the previous fall to attend the Abbots' Congress. He had learned then that word was circulating in church circles that Weston Priory would be moved to another location. In March, a disquieting letter came from Father Bede. It described, first, discontent among the novices at Weston due to Father Michael's "tactlessness." Next, it reported that people were hearing that Michael had plans to move the monastery from Weston. Bede declared that, no matter what the outcome, he would always remain faithful to Weston and to Leo's wishes.

Uncertain and anxious, Abbot Leo took action on March 20. He sent word to Weston naming Father Bede prior, replacing Father Michael. When Michael, away at the time, received news of the change, he wrote Abbot Leo in shock:

> I remain at a loss to account for the sudden change, news of which reached me without warning, and it will take me a little time to adjust, as I know you will understand.

> Especially since the only specific charge against me is that I am "still working for a change of place," which is simply untrue.

The letter concludes with a request for permission to create a monastic foundation in Michigan similar to Weston Priory, but independent of Weston or the Dormition Abbey. Plaintive lines from Christina Rossetti that conjure up his disappointment at Weston preface the request:

> *"The hope I dreamed of was a dream,*
> *Was but a dream, and now I wake*
> *Exceeding comfortless, and worn, and old,*
> *For a dream's sake."*
>
> Yet I am confident, on the basis of our friendship over the years and happy association up to now in working for the liturgical and monastic revival in this great land of ours, with fruitful results under God, that you will find it possible to somehow encourage another center similar to Weston, from the vantage point of your eminent canonical position, in a region that literally cries for it.

In reply, Leo affirmed his friendship with Michael, but expressed regret that he could not assume responsibility for another monastic foundation, and he wished the departing ex-prior well.

Bede, who was already fulfilling many of the prior's duties during the frequent absences of Michael, readily assumed his new role. John Wynhoven, a young Dormition monk, pursuing studies at St. Benoit-du-lac monastery in Quebec and helping out at Weston at the time, was commissioned by Abbot Leo to make the public announcement of the change. He then reported current news in a letter to Abbot Leo:

> Father Bede is gone for some days now. First of all, Harold quit his job during Father Bede's absence. He had too much (and difficult) work here. So we sit with the barn.
>
> Nobody understood milking, and the first days Brothers Mathew and James needed hours to get the cows milked. Frank taught them, and now the mother cow is sick. She takes an hour to be milked, as you have to tie her up. The pigs broke out because Harold neglected to feed them for a couple of days. I think, on the whole, that Harold had not the necessary capacities. Farming is too complicated for him. He wastes things, and piles of dirt and dung are heaped around the barn.
>
> We made 350 gallons of syrup this year—the result of "blood, sweat and tears!" We could have made much more if we had not the transport problem. The sugar lots are too widespread, and this year we had to shovel first all the roads for the sledges on account of the extraordinary amount of snow. So you understand that we need every minute to keep things going. The buckets are down from the trees but have to be gathered and washed.
>
> Ettinger's barn, which he gave us, has to be picked up before his return—end of May. And we are only six at the moment. Prior Michael was in the hospital when he last wrote. He had pneumonia. For the rest, all are in good health.

This first account of the conditions at Weston, as Father Bede began what would be his brief tenure as prior, was hardly reassuring to Abbot Leo. Nonetheless, by autumn Bede was able to announce that, with a dozen novices and postulants on hand, the monastery was again filled to overflowing.

Abbot Leo did his best to direct the life of the two far-flung communities. Responding to the questions and problems arising in daily life in two places taxed his energies and resources. He did not always have a clear answer at a time when his own vision was still in the process of formation.

An urgent question came from Weston. Young men arriving at the monastery were seeking a monastic life but not ordination to the priesthood. This was not a new question, but continued to be a nagging one. How was Bede to handle the matter? His own inclination, stemming from the medieval view of monastic life, was that priesthood enhanced the monastic state and would enable the monks to offer services such as celebrating the sacraments, offering spiritual direction and retreats, and performing other priestly tasks. Ordained monks fit more neatly into his understanding of monastic life as he visualized it for Weston.

Leo replied cautiously in April, 1956, and with some ambivalence:

> I am afraid too many want to be non-priests. It is not they who should decide, but the superiors! They should accept the decision in obedience, and if a postulant shows ability etc. for priesthood, he should go on for it.

Embattled on All Fronts

Meanwhile, apart from the internal problems of both Weston and the Dormition, major geopolitical events were occurring right next door to Jerusalem. In July 1956, Egyptian President Gamal Nasser had nationalized the Suez Canal, barely two hundred miles from the abbey. In response, Israeli forces moved to seize the whole of the surrounding Sinai Peninsula. The following year Abbot Leo described life inside the Dormition during the brief war that ensued.

above left: 1948. Roof of Dormition Abbey church, ravaged by two wars. *above right:* 1967. *center left:* Abbot Leo with president of Israel, Zalman Shazar. *center right:* With mayor of Jerusalem, Teddy Kolleck and his wife, and Prior Benedict. *below:* Greeting King Baudouin of Belgium. "Exercised in diplomacy."

> Last October, I arrived only a few days before the outbreak of the war. No doubt, the situation in the whole of the land was tense and dangerous, but with the grace of God we remained unmolested. We had to comply with blackout and other security regulations, and we did hear the thunder of guns and an occasional outburst of machine-gun fire. We were surrounded by soldiers, but we were able to carry on our normal monastic and liturgical life with only slight alterations in the schedule and by saying the night offices in the crypt instead of the church. As time passed, little by little everything returned to normal and, after a while, pilgrims started to come as before, first in a trickle, then more and more.[1]

In the same period, growing tensions within the Dormition Abbey community took a toll on Leo's health and spirit. The monks in Israel were impatient for results from the foundation in the United States. Aging lay brothers wanted to return to their German homeland to die. There was general concern that the monks from North America would not accept the discipline and observance required at Dormition Abbey. Apparently in response to such contentions, in March 1957, Leo wrote Bede, giving guidelines marked by uncharacteristic severity:

> The recreation [at Weston] is to be held absolutely in common.... Persistent private conversation by two or so is a grave offense against the monastic discipline.... Also, the walk on Sunday afternoons is to be held in common, certainly not in pairs.... Outside of the cases mentioned above, no conversation whatsoever, under whatsoever pretext, is permitted, and the rule of silence is to be enforced in the strictest manner. Any transgression is a serious offense, especially if repeated.

As pressure mounted in Jerusalem for bringing monks from Weston to the Holy Land, Abbot Leo broached the subject during his annual Vermont visit in 1957. For Father Bede, who was convinced that all hands were needed to build up the farm, it was not an easy request to hear.

At that point, only one member of the Weston community, Stephen Fronckewicz, had made his final monastic profession. He was completing studies for priesthood at Saint Bede's Abbey in Peru, Illinois. The other brothers were either in temporary vows, or novices, or postulants. Father Bede had encouraged members in temporary vows to study for priesthood, and they were sent off for seminary training immediately after their first profession or commitment for three years.[2]

Because the lay-brother who was the Dormition Abbey's cook was soon to leave for Germany, Leo insisted that a Weston brother was needed to work in the kitchen there. Reluctantly, Bede acceded to Leo's wishes, promising that brother Bernard, who served as the cook in Weston, would be released to go to Jerusalem the following year.

Before returning to Israel at the close of the 1957 summer, Leo observed that the Weston community was overburdened: farm work was encroaching on times of prayer and study. He had special concern for the novices and postulants. Because of Bede's resistance to lighten the burdens of work, communication between Leo and Bede became increasingly a stumbling block.

In May of that year, Damasus Winzen, once Leo's closest friend, had suffered a near fatal heart attack. While he was recovering at Mount Saviour, Leo went to Elmira to visit him. That meeting was the occasion for mending broken fences and healing the personal wounds of their past relationship. During their visit, the two monks became fully reconciled. After the years of separation that succeeded their days at Keyport, they re-explored their common purpose of creating a renewed form of monasticism in the United States. Pledging to join forces in their shared vision, they would once more walk that path together.

By 1957, Mount Saviour showed all the signs of flourishing monastic life. The community numbered more than thirty members. Seasoned monks were in positions of leadership. Gregory Borgstedt, former prior of Portsmouth Priory was subprior, and Peter Minard, a revered monk of the French abbey at Ligugé, served as novice master. The monastic community was fast gaining recognition as a center of spirituality, noted for its exemplary monastic observance and its celebration of the liturgy.

Leo laid out before Damasus the situation in Weston. Bede was overburdened with the tasks of prior, novice master, director of work, and finances; he bore total responsibility for the community. The young monks were not receiving adequate training and were showing signs of discontent and overwork. In response to the immediate problem of training, Damasus offered to receive Weston novices at Mount Saviour, where they would come under the guidance of the redoubtable Peter Minard.

Leo's visit to Mount Saviour relieved him of the sense of isolation he had felt in his efforts toward a renewal of monastic life in both Israel and the New World. For the next several years, the more established community of Mount Saviour would accompany the budding community of Weston Priory as an elder monastic brother, receiving Weston's novices for a few months of training and sending mature monks to help at Weston with classes and spiritual support.[3]

Back in Weston, Bede did not share Leo's enthusiasm for Damasus's offer to assist the Weston community. Faithfulness to chanting the monastic office and the development of the dairy farm were at the heart of Bede's design for the Vermont community. He had invested time and energy in both endeavors, and he had his own vision of how all this would be done. With some brothers away for studies for the priesthood, another going to Israel, and now the thought of still others going to Mount Saviour for novitiate, he felt that the community was shrinking rather than growing.

As the burden of work increased among the brothers remaining in Weston, so did discontent. Chanting the lengthy monastic office and liturgy became a chore rather than a joyful celebration. Unable to articulate his dissatisfaction with the latest developments, Bede allowed Leo to return to Israel under the impression that the situation in Vermont was showing improvement.

A Tough Decision at Weston

Abbot Leo's optimism was of short duration, as complaints from Weston reached him in Jerusalem. Disgruntled brothers resented their burdens, and friction was increasing between monks and hired men. The brothers felt that Father Bede showed more consideration for employees than he did for members of the community. Equally disconcerting to Leo was the news that Bede was not in accord with the idea that Weston brothers should volunteer to go to Israel. Leo was reluctant to believe all that he was told, especially when it came from young brothers departing the community in anger and confusion. He wrote of his misgivings in a letter to Bede:

> Sometimes I worry myself almost sick. Do the boys get spiritually what they need? I think we do need an additional man, because both temporal and spiritual responsibilities are too much for one man.

> Then, please, be loyal to me in every respect (not that I have reason to doubt it, but I have gotten, I believe, enough stabs in the back from others), e.g., with regard to Weston's responsibility to the Dormition. We must get vocations from Weston, and later, all kinds of help so that it is really—besides being a full-fledged Benedictine monastery (which I emphasize very much)—a kind of commissariat for us (as the Franciscans have their commissariats everywhere) for the Holy Land.
>
> Please, let me rely on you in every respect. Otherwise I will go crazy one of these days. It is too much for me. Well, maybe I have not been feeling well recently and look at things gloomily....

Bede responded sympathetically to Leo, assuring him of his loyalty and of the good progress of the community in Weston. They both agreed that Abbot Leo needed a period of rest and relaxation on his next visit to the United States.

In 1958 Leo stayed in Jerusalem until September. Besides receiving brother Bernard, who arrived in the spring, he wanted to promote the Weston monk's integration into the Dormition community. Brother Anselm, another monk of Weston in temporary profession who was studying at Sant'Anselmo in Rome, arrived to spend his August break from academic work in Jerusalem. He let it be known that he was on vacation. His lax attitude toward the monastic observance at the Dormition gave an unfortunate impression that would influence the reception of all the North Americans who followed him. Anselm's behavior re-enforced the Germans' fear that the Weston monks would not enhance the abbey community.

The threat of war against Israel was pervasive during those years, as Arab nations on all sides maneuvered for advantage.

In full view of the little Benedictine community at Tabgha, armed Syrian encampments on the Golan Heights monitored the Sea of Galilee. Thus, weighed down by war worries as well as unresolved problems at the Dormition and in the Weston community, Abbot Leo set out once again for the United States, making his accustomed stop in Rome. There he pleaded with members of the Curia to take a more conciliatory attitude toward Israel. In those final months of the reign of Pius XII, he found little support at the Vatican for his initiatives.

His visit to Weston that year didn't provide the hoped for rest and relaxation. Morale among the monks was low. He asked each brother for a frank evaluation of life in the community. Conflicts between the monks and the several hired men had only increased. The monks still felt overly burdened with work. Some confided to Abbot Leo that Father Bede dissuaded them from volunteering to go to the Holy Land. The list of complaints lengthened.

Shaken and anxious, Leo presented the complaints to Bede. As a first step in restoring the trust of the community, Leo suggested that the farm operation be drastically cut back. Bede reacted: if the farm were to go, he would leave. By way of compromise, Leo proposed that Bede accompany him to Israel to observe the community there for a year. Abbot Leo made futile efforts at dialogue, but Bede was intransigent and chose to return to Missouri and his home monastery, Conception Abbey. The separation was extremely painful for both men. The Midwesterner, devoted to the foundation of Weston Priory, had invested himself in establishing the community on the soil of Vermont. Leo felt a personal friendship for his chosen prior and had tried in vain to get beyond feelings of mistrust.

The bitterness of Bede's departure further contributed to Leo's deteriorating health; he internalized the tensions and burdens of this period. In his November letter to Abbot Stephen Schappler of Conception Abbey, Leo put in plain words the reasons for Bede's departure from Weston:

> Now briefly to the main difficulties. We all like Father Bede as a person. He is lovable in many ways, and has very good qualities. We also appreciate the tremendous job he has done here. I know that it was sometimes very difficult, and I could not give him the help I should have liked.... The main thing is double: First there was a terrible chasm between him and the community. Every time I returned here, I had to put up with that almost unbearable tension.... Here I come to perhaps the most serious difficulty: He acted against my intentions. He claims that he never did that consciously. Well, I cannot explain it. He actually did. For one thing, he never liked the tie-up with the Dormition and spoke openly against it to the postulants and novices. He complained before them about me and conveyed the impression that there was a difference of policies between him and me.

Before returning to Israel for the winter of 1958–59, Abbot Leo named Stephen Fronckewicz prior-administrator of the Weston community. Ordained just one year earlier, and only in his mid-thirties, Stephen was the lone Weston monk in solemn vows. He was also a diabetic. To assist the new prior and to serve as novice master, Leo enlisted Father Bernard Crepeaux, a seasoned monk of Saint-Benoît-du-Lac monastery in Quebec and recently a hermit in the community of Jacques Winandy in British Columbia. After making the latest changes, Leo once again chose to trust in God's help in a still precarious situation.

A highlight of the Congress of the Abbots of the Benedictine Confederation in 1959, greeting Pope John XXIII at Sant'Anselmo in Rome.

9
Mapping Uncharted Waters

During his stay in Israel in 1959, Abbot Leo had an experience that would profoundly affect his life. Explaining how it came about, he wrote:

> I found it more and more necessary to learn at least some elementary Hebrew, the language of the country in which we live at the Dormition. Knowing that I could never find the necessary time to do it while at the Abbey (I had tried for almost ten years), I went to school again at one of those adult Hebrew schools called *Ulpan*. Purposely, for the reasons given, I went to one away from Jerusalem, among the citrus groves near the seaside town of Nathania. It was Ulpan Akiva....[1]
>
> Hebrew is the language of the Scriptures of the Old Testament. We learned a little while studying theology, but we were barely able to read it, even with great effort. So I went to this school to learn it as a spoken language. In my four weeks of study, I acquired at least a basic knowledge on which I can build, enabling me to understand

> and carry on a simple conversation and to read and write simple letters.

For Shulamith Katznelson, founder of Ulpan Akiva and its directress for forty-seven years, Leo's application in 1959 was an unprecedented event. At her center of Hebrew language and culture on the Mediterranean coast near Tel Aviv, men, women, and children practiced the spoken language, shared meals, sang traditional songs, and danced the Hora and other Israeli round dances. That a Benedictine abbot would enter this environment was unheard of.

The Ulpan welcomed Abbot Leo warmly, bestowing on him the affectionate name *Arieh* (lion), Hebrew for Leo. He responded by joining with zest in all the school's activities, "going in those days always in my khaki habit (when I came to the Holy Land it was unheard of to go in civilian clothes)." He found the spirit of hope and joy at the Ulpan contagious. He loved the folk music and dancing and the friendly conversations. He established personal friendships with Israelis, whom he always found very warm-hearted. "It was there to a great extent that I conceived my love for the Jewish people." At the Ulpan, he was with ordinary Jewish folk—the people of Israel. These encounters were far removed from the politicians, government officials, and scholars he met most frequently. On his part, he felt accepted, not for a role that he played, but for who he was.

> It was a human experience of a very deep nature. My old professor, who gave us high school students the elements of English about forty years ago, had told us: "When you learn a language, you learn to know the soul of a people." Learning a language is alone a deep human experience, but it became more so because of the circumstances. My Benedictine habit was an exceptional sight among all

> those people. They came from many countries: most of them were Jewish immigrants—many from Romania and Poland; some were tourists, also mostly Jewish; there was a sprinkling of Christians—even three or four Baptist and other Protestant ministers; and one Arab from a village in Galilee. As a priest and monk, I was the only Catholic.

At the Ulpan Leo had an opportunity to represent Christianity in the Holy Land in the manner he had long tried to instill as a key purpose of the Dormition Abbey.

> Here it was given to us, through the grace of God, to do what we consider our mission at Dormition Abbey: to build bridges of mutual understanding and sympathy. It is necessary that we know one another on this our small planet, where we have to live with one another, but we make it so difficult by closing our hearts to our fellow men. If we open our hearts, we will also find open hearts—it is always mutual.
>
> That was the deep and delightful experience of those weeks: that there was an atmosphere of love and understanding, of readiness to learn from one another—to be enriched by the mutual experience. All of us did learn, not only Hebrew, but much about human nature, much about the thirst of the human heart for understanding, much of the enrichment that flows from trying to give and to receive such mutual understanding.[2]

He concluded the report of his first Ulpan experience with this message to readers of Weston's bulletin:

> "Ask the Lord of the Universe to make grow that spirit of love and understanding, so that all of us may contribute towards the fulfillment of the petition: 'Thy Kingdom Come!'"[3]

Through his studies of Hebrew language and culture at Ulpan Akiva on that first visit and subsequent ones, Leo came to a deeper understanding of Judaism. What he referred to as his first "little experience" there, was actually a turning point that gave direction and energy to the remaining years of his life.

Bold Steps for Monastic Renewal

Following his stay at the Ulpan that year, Leo spent little time in Israel. He was anxious to see how the Weston community was progressing under its new, young leadership. He took ship again from Haifa to the United States to be with the community in Weston for Pentecost of 1959.

On his arrival in Weston, he was reassured as he witnessed the joyful spirit of the Priory community. After most of the dairy cows were sold, community work had become diversified among several crafts and was therefore less burdensome. The tension had lifted, and the brothers were experiencing a more harmonious balance of prayer, work and recreation. In that atmosphere Abbot Leo was freer to further his hopes for the Dormition Abbey and monastic renewal.

The matter of non-priest choir-monks was an issue confronting the Weston Priory community. Existing church legislation declared that, to be fully a monk, it was necessary to be ordained a priest. In order to participate in the monastic choir and have a voice in community decisions in the monastic chapter, the aspiring monk had to spend years in study at a seminary, so that he would eventually receive the sacrament of Holy Orders. Non-ordained members of the community could only be lay brothers, who had a second-class form of membership inside the community.

Most of the young men who were applying for admission to the Priory community desired monastic life, but did not feel called to priesthood. Attracted especially by Benedictine spirituality, they were influenced by contemporary monastic writers—Trappist Thomas Merton, Jean Leclerc, Benedictine of Clerveaux Abbey in Luxemburg, Oratorian Louis Bouyer, and the English Benedictine, Bede Griffiths, who spent much of his monastic life in India. These authors proposed a return to the original inspiration of monasticism as a lay movement, dedicated to communal life, rooted in the spirit of the Gospel, and unattached to clerical or pastoral apostolates. Among Benedictines, Abbot Leo and Prior Damasus of Mount Saviour were the leading American proponents of the movement to return to a more pristine and simple form of monastic life.

Soon after Abbot Leo's arrival in the U.S. in 1959, Damasus, accompanied by one of the monks of Mount Saviour, visited Weston. Their purpose was to address the issue of choir-monks that was as critical to the Elmira monastery as it was to the Vermont priory. Together both founders wanted broad acceptance of the concept that, within a Benedictine monastic community, there would be equality between ordained and non-ordained monks. Damasus wanted the American precept "Equal opportunity for all" to be the guide for a new type of monastery "where all monks would be given equal rights and equal voices."[4]

Leo shared his friend's hope for this important change, though he approached it with less daring.

> "Father Damasus proved to be more consistent and far-sighted than I was. We both wanted to abolish the distinction between the choir-monk and the lay brother but I, always more timid and hesitant than Father Damasus, wanted to retain the canonical difference while uniting all

> the monks in daily life. Father Damasus wanted to go all the way and simply disregard the canonical situation. Of course, he was right."[5]

The two founders were not far apart in their hopes for monastic renewal, and as the Abbots' Congress scheduled for the fall of 1959 approached, they saw the opportunity to gain wide backing for what was an urgent need in their home communities—and a change that would be a Benedictine milestone.

Together they worked out a strategy for the Abbots' Congress. Their objective was to secure canonical approval for the equal status of all monks, ordained or not. They conceived a plan to enlist the support of as many abbots as possible prior to the Congress. Leo would visit the monasteries of England and much of continental Europe. Damasus would go to a number of German monasteries. Reuniting in France, they would move on to finish the task together.

At the same time, Abbot Leo was eager to engage the Weston community more actively in the process of bridging the gap between the Dormition Abbey and the Priory and addressing the future relationship of the two communities. To this end, he decided that Robert Hammond, who had made his first monastic profession the previous year, would accompany him on his forthcoming journey to Rome and Israel. With Bernard Crepeaux at Weston to support Prior Stephen, Leo and Robert set out in midsummer for Rome and the Abbots' Congress, embarking in New York for England aboard the SS Ryndam.

During their weeklong voyage, there was much to discuss. For relaxation, Leo gave basic instructions in the German language to his companion. In more serious conversation, he confided that, beyond the immediate issue of choir-monks, he faced a matter of grave concern. The See of the Latin Patriarch of Jerusalem had become vacant due to the recent death of the occupant. To fill that position, the Israeli Ministry of Religion had proposed Abbot Leo's name to the Vatican. If that appointment were to come about, he mused, the prestige of his position as Latin Patriarch would enhance his authority for work in Jewish-Christian relations. On the other hand, as Bishop of Jerusalem and Latin Patriarch, he would no longer be Abbot of the Dormition Abbey—and he would not return to Weston. In that eventuality, what would be the fate of the Weston community? That was a troubling question, for which he had no ready answer.

On landing in England, Leo shifted his attention to more proximate matters. The Benedictine community at Farnborough Abbey provided hospitality and a home base for the travelers. It was the place where Leo, whenever he passed through England, would meet a group of Oblates of the Dormition Abbey to give a conference and spiritual direction. They were military men, with their wives, who had served in the Holy Land during the British Mandate, prior to Israeli independence. On this trip, the English oblates, in turn, were helpful in arranging transportation for the itinerant American monks.

For Leo and Robert, successive days were filled with visits to numerous English Benedictine monasteries. Most of those communities were actively engaged in education or parish work. A few, like Prinknash and Quarr Abbeys, were more contemplative, supporting themselves with craftwork and agriculture. Without exception, the English abbots received Abbot Leo cordially and indicated that they were not opposed to the idea of non-ordained choir-monks and their basic equality with ordained monks. At the more contemplative monasteries, the proposal was received with enthusiasm and the pledge of positive support at the impending Congress.

The mission to garner abbatial support continued on the Continent after a short and uneventful boat ride across the English Channel. The two Americans lobbied intensely, canvassing several countries, before they could relax for a few days at Abbot Leo's home monastery of Gerleve. The European abbots, they were pleased to find, reacted in even more heartening fashion than their English counterparts.

It was then time to meet up with Damasus to complete the planned round of visits in France, Germany, and Switzerland. They rented a small Renault car in France. It had a defective ignition switch, and Robert was persuaded to push the vehicle until the motor turned over while the two senior monks applauded his efforts from within. The threesome enjoyed stimulating conversation, enlivened by the buoyant spirit of Damasus, who slyly urged Robert to replace Leo as driver. The accelerator under Leo's dancing foot caused Damasus to get seasick even on land!

When the group arrived in Paris, Damasus suggested that he and Leo take a side trip to Africa for a conference entitled "Mission and Contemplation," to be held at the monastery of Toumliline in Morocco. Besides the opportunity to address highly relevant monastic issues, the trip would also provide an opportunity to witness firsthand a monastic experiment in a Muslim country. The Americans found the monks at Toumliline living a very simple monastic life. They prayed the Liturgy of the Hours, tended their plot of land, and offered hospitality. To serve the medical needs of their poor neighbors, they also provided a small clinic. There were no efforts to convert or to preach to the surrounding Muslim population. Their "mission" was one of monastic presence rooted in hospitality and prayer—a vision close to Abbot Leo's heart. The example in Morocco of radiating the Christian life through prayer, dialogue, and neighborly care strengthened the resolve and broadened the vision of the two monastic pioneers.

After their inspiring trip to Africa, they rejoined Robert in Paris and continued their European enterprise. A visit to the monastery of Chevetogne in Belgium had special meaning for the three North American Benedictines. For the two German expatriates, it was a return to the source of their monastic vision. For the last time, they met the monk who had inspired them to question creatively the meaning of monastic life in the modern world. In his company they recalled their time as students together in Rome, hearing Lambert Beauduin[6] challenge them to return to the living source of their vocation, the Rule of St. Benedict and its spirit.

At 86 years of age, nearing the end of his long life as a pioneer in ecumenism and liturgical and monastic renewal, Lambert was confined to a wheel chair. Nonetheless, he was alert and delighted. For the teacher, it was a joyous reunion with his two protégés who, following in his spirit of monastic renewal, had made foundations in the New World. For Robert, the younger monk sitting beside the elderly man in the wheel chair in the monastery garden, the encounter made a lasting impression—one that melded the human and the historic. Joy and simplicity radiated from Lambert Beauduin as he praised the ecumenical work of his brother monks and as he expressed gratitude that the Church was beginning to undertake the revolutionary task of renewing the Liturgy.

On their return to Paris, Damasus parted company with his confreres for business matters. Leo and Robert continued for a brief visit to Abbot Leo's sister-in-law and for a concluding visit to the Benedictine Abbey of Einsiedeln in Switzerland. From there it was a short trip to Rome for the opening of the Abbots' Congress on September 16.

The Pope, the Benedictine Congress, and the Curia

The audience with Pope John XXIII was a highlight of the Abbots' Congress of 1959. In a typical gesture, Pope John announced that contrary to the established custom, he would travel across the city from the Vatican to Sant'Anselmo on the Aventine Hill to meet with the assembled abbots and priors. He reasoned that it was easier for the Pope to travel across the city than to transport more than three hundred Benedictines to St. Peter's!

When the Pope arrived at the entrance of the ample monastery church, no one had thought to bring the customary holy water for an initial blessing. Brother Avelino, the blustery porter of Sant'Anselmo and monk from Maria Laach, raced down the middle aisle of the church muttering, "aqua benedicta, aqua benedicta" (holy water, holy water)! His anxiety was in vain, for as the story goes, Pope John made a sign of the cross over the large fountain in the atrium of the church, saying that there was plenty of holy water—no problem! The peaceful and joyful presence of the Pope was remembered long after his words. He proceeded to the Abbot Primate's throne behind the altar at the far end of the church. When he was seated, he began to swing his short legs as he could not reach the floor. With a jovial smile, he joked as an assistant placed a large pillow under his feet. He remarked that Benedictine Abbots' Primate should always be tall men—taller than the popes if they were to be comfortable on that throne.

On the third day of the Congress, in response to the request of the Abbot Primate, Bernard Kaelin, Abbot Leo presented a *votum* or petition to the assembled abbots and priors of the

above: Abbot Primate Benno Gut addressed the Pope in the chapel of Sant'Anselmo. Abbot Leo is the first on the left in the second row. *below left:* Prior Damasus Winzen of Mt. Saviour Monastery in Elmira, New York, supported Abbot Leo's *votum* requesting full monastic rights for non-ordained monks at the 1959 Congress. *below right:* Laurentius Klein, abbot of Trier Abbey in Germany, third Abbot of Dormition Abbey, with Leo and Father Lambert Dunne, secretary to the Abbot Primate.

world confederation of Benedictines. He proposed that "superiors of monasteries" be granted the freedom "to accept candidates for full monastic life that includes praying the Monastic Office in choir, chapter rights, etc. without the need to seek a special indult."

Speaking "not as the Abbot of Dormition Abbey, but as the superior of Weston Priory," the sponsor argued that canon law made provision only for religious congregations, clerics, and the laity, ignoring the fact that the monastic life was a different vocation. Before calling for a vote, Father Damasus and several abbots offered *relationes,* or statements, supporting and developing the proposal presented by Abbot Leo. The Congress voiced its approval and requested that the Primate present the petition to the Vatican Congregation of Religious.

The Congress proceeded to the election of a new Abbot Primate. The popular Archabbot of Einsiedeln, Benno Gut, who had just recently warmly received Leo and Robert, was elected. It was the same Benno Gut who carried the petition for the admission of choir-monks to the Congregation of Religious.

The Secretary of the Congregation of Religious was in basic agreement, but with the condition of two amendments. The Vatican office wanted the number of non-ordained monks limited to two-thirds of the members of any community. The other requirement: that the major offices of the monastery—abbot, prior, and novice master—be held only by priests. In plenary session, the Congress accepted the Vatican's changes. The efforts of Father Damasus and Abbot Leo had largely met with success. Well ahead of the convocation of Vatican Council II, Abbot Leo's *votum* was a significant step in the realization of Benedictine monastic renewal in the twentieth century.

Another matter demanding Leo's attention while he was in Rome was the question of the successor to the Latin Patriarch and Bishop of Jerusalem. The endorsement of Abbot Leo by the Israeli Ministry of Religious Affairs by no means assured that he would be named to the position. Still, there was a possibility and, if chosen, he was inclined to acquiesce.

Between sessions of the Congress, he was ushered back and forth between congregations of the Roman Curia—the Congregation of the Holy Office, the Congregation for Religious, and the Oriental Congregation. He was questioned thoroughly on his support for Israel. While his work on Christian-Jewish relations was appreciated, his pro-Israel views and his concerns about the Palestinians were deemed insufficiently nuanced by the Vatican Curia. A crucial error, in the view of his examiners, was Leo's signature on a document urging support for the State of Israel. By the end of the Congress, he was certain he would not be chosen Latin Patriarch of Jerusalem.

One encounter during the Congress had overriding significance for Abbot Leo—a meeting with Pope John XXIII. In a private audience, he was assured that Pope John was in full accord with his own hopes for the reconciliation of Christians and Jews, as well as for the Benedictine presence in the Holy Land. This confirmation of his endeavors was enough to buoy his spirits.

A delightful voyage across the Mediterranean from Bari to Haifa brought the two travelers from Weston to their farthest destination, the Holy Land. The dour black-bearded Father Paul, bursar of the Dormition community, met them at the pier in Haifa. He drove them with sparse and unsympathetic comments past the still visible roadside wreckage of the Israeli war of Independence to the city of Jerusalem.

Holy Order Within Monastery Walls

Thus, in the fall of 1959, Father Robert joined brother Bernard at the abbey on Mount Zion. The process of integrating these two young monks from Vermont with their German counterparts at the Dormition Abbey was soon underway. The presence of the two young American monks served as a 'trial run' for Leo's projected hope of internationalizing the Dormition community.

In the monastery on Mt. Zion, distinctions determined order—absolutely. Solemnly professed, simply professed, novices (if any), postulants (if any), followed by lay brothers, stayed resolutely in rank on all occasions. In work assignments, "humble obedience" was not merely encouraged, but enforced.

Robert was placed under the watchful eye of Father Willibrord, an ancient member of the Dormition community. Lean, lanky, with hollow cheeks and long scraggly graying beard, Willibrord had a fearsome look. He prowled about the monastery with silent, lengthy, cat-like strides. Perhaps as a test or more likely because of many pressing matters elsewhere, Abbot Leo left the young American and the elderly German to their own devices.

The instructions on monastic prayer given by the elder monk to his charge were indicative of the rigid hierarchic observance of the Jerusalem community. In the procession to Mass, for example, solemnly professed monks made a deep bow to the altar, while those in first profession as well as lay brothers were required to genuflect. Robert, at the side of Father Willibrord, was told to genuflect while Willibrord made his profound and graceful bow.

Private masses with only the priest celebrant were a common practice before the Second Vatican Council. Robert, as a priest-monk, had the privilege of celebrating a private Mass in the lovely crypt of the monastery church each day. Willibrord beckoned him into the sacristy where he had laid out the vestments and other necessities for Mass. On a large table in the center of the room was a magnificent display of the ornate chalices from the monastery treasury. Robert was instructed to choose the five chalices that he found most attractive. It was a tough decision. Obediently, he selected five outstanding pieces. A task well done! Willibrord sternly declared that none of those chalices would be available for Robert's celebrations of Mass.

Humility had always been a priority in Abbot Leo's teaching on Benedictine spirituality at Weston. The same virtue had a decidedly distinctive flavor at the Dormition. Willibrord did not hesitate to inculcate that flavor early into the diet of Robert's spirituality. On a warm September afternoon, he led Robert to the roof of the monastery that was exposed to the blazing Jerusalem sun. Out of a compartment, he dragged several wooden boxes of broken glass—the shards of windows shattered in the shelling of the church during the war of Independence. The pieces of glass were to be stacked into neat piles according to color, shape and size.

After these instructions, Willibrord departed for other activities. When he returned at the end of the work period, he expressed satisfaction at the accomplishment of the junior monk; another task well done. Willibrord proceeded to deliberately dump the segregated piles of glass back into the wooden boxes from which they were taken. With the broken fragments safely restored to their compartment, the two monks retired in silence to the choir for Vespers.

Meanwhile, Bernard, the other North American monk, remained hunkered down with the lay brothers in the basement kitchen of the awesome monastery. His peaceful routine of preparing the daily entrée of sauerkraut was interrupted only when he timidly sallied forth to the monastery church to join the ordained monks chanting the monastic office.

Engagement in meaningless work coupled with rigid regulations of monastic observance, and divergent spiritualities loomed as a formidable barrier to integrating North Americans into the daily life of the Jerusalem monastic community.

Another World Beyond the Walls

But experience beyond the confining walls of the monastery provided the Weston monks with another perspective on life in Israel. On a rare occasion, Leo dispatched Robert on an errand to a nearby settlement. Clad in his khaki monastic habit, the young monk boarded an ancient lumbering bus—the usual public transport for the common folk in Israel. Initially, there were vacant seats for everyone. After a few stops, there was standing room only. When an elderly Israeli woman stepped aboard, laden with heavy shopping bags, Robert rose and gestured for the woman to take his seat. With a grateful sigh, she accepted. The surrounding passengers looked on approvingly and tried to engage the North American in friendly conversation in their contemporary Hebrew tongue, Ivrit. Totally at a loss for words, Robert stammered that he only spoke English. A pall of silence descended on the passengers and noses turned up as though a foul smell had entered the bus. Flustered, the monk realized he had uttered an embarrassing word—"English." It brought back to his fellow passengers memories of the British mandate and the feelings of betrayal when the English left Palestine at the time of political and national crisis.

He made a stab at repairing the damage and pointed at himself with the word "American, American." The amicable atmosphere quickly returned as the passengers made friendly gestures, pointing and repeating to one another, "American, American." The lesson graphically taught: when in Israel, learn Ivrit.

Another touching incident gave further insight into the spirit of the people of this newly born State. The flock of chickens tended by the lay brothers provided an occasional enhancement to the usually frugal menu for community meals. A fresh boiled egg or chicken soup was an occasion for festivity. The chickens roamed freely from the garden plot outside the open kitchen door and frequently found their way into the kitchen as they hunted for scraps on the floor. They also needed grain.

One of Robert's assignments was to assist the lay brothers to pick up the chicken grain delivered to the foot of Mt. Zion. The road from the Gehenna Valley up to the monastery at the top of Mt. Zion had been destroyed during the War of Independence. The only access to the Dormition was by a winding path up the steep incline. All deliveries were left in the valley at the entry to the footpath.

Robert joined three friendly but aging brothers on their mission to fetch the chicken grain that was left in the valley below. They brought along a kind of stretcher for carrying the grain that consisted of two long poles with a canvass in between. At the base of the Mount, they laid the device on the ground and proceeded to roll the heavy sacks of grain onto it. A trio of young Orthodox Israelis in long black smocks and curly sidelocks happened by. The tall, pale youths, gently and without a word, brushed the elderly brothers aside. The three each took one end of the poles and motioned to Robert to grab the remaining end. In silence, with the brothers falling in behind, they hauled the burden to the summit of the Mount, dropped their burden, and just as quietly continued on their way.

Fashioning a Dream at the Sea of Galilee

To provide a break for both himself and Father Robert, Abbot Leo suggested some days at the mission monastery at Tabgha on the shore of the Sea of Galilee. The mood of the little community there was markedly different from the one at Mount Zion. So was the climate. The Lake of Tiberias, as the Sea of Galilee is also known, is nearly 700 feet below sea level, the lowest elevation of any fresh water lake in the world. Temperatures at Tabgha regularly rise above 100 degrees Fahrenheit, a far cry from the cooler climate on Mt. Zion where mid-80s are the peak.

The lake community consisted of three monks. The superior, Father Jerome, managed the farm and directed the tasks of the hired Arab workers. He was affable and efficient, and he respected Abbot Leo's efforts to renew the Dormition community. The two elderly and bearded German lay brothers, Englebert and Cletus, did the household chores and cooked meals on a primitive outdoor fireplace. There was no monastic office or common prayer. Life was unregimented and tranquil.

On the way to Tabgha, Leo had business to tend to in Haifa. He left Robert on his own for lunch at a hostel managed by a community of German nuns. An irresistible glass of clear cold water was served with the meal. The result was disastrous! By arrival time in Tabgha, Robert had contracted a fever of 103° and all that went with it. The body temperature matched the air temperature.

Still, picking up stones and chopping firewood was a welcome change from the frustrating tasks assigned in Jerusalem. Walks on quiet days at the monastery in Tabgha gave occasion for reflection and discussion of the complexity and possibilities surrounding Leo's dream for a new form of Benedictine presence in the Holy Land. Already there were palpable indications of the difficulties that lay ahead, but the full scope of obstacles to integrating the American and German monastic communities were unimaginable.

The brief attempts to mix the North American monks with their Dormition counterparts so far presented more questions than answers. The peaceful setting of the Tabgha monastery provided the needed atmosphere to assess the situation and to plan for the future.

Fresh ideas began to emerge. Perhaps a small group of Weston brothers could be brought to Tabgha within the next few years. Centered there, they might serve as the core of a new community, modeled on the life at Weston, and formed under the personal guidance of Abbot Leo. Prayer, work, and study would provide the framework for a simple monastic life. The monks would work the land and receive guests. All members would study Hebrew and eventually the monastic office would be prayed in that language. Cultural and religious exchange would be fostered with groups of interested Israelis. Ecumenical encounters would be encouraged. On the major feast-days the Tabgha community would journey to Jerusalem for solemn celebrations of the liturgy at the Dormition Abbey.

Eventually a center for biblical and liturgical studies would be established at the Abbey. As the community in Weston continued to grow, more brothers would be attracted to join the Holy Land venture for more or less extended periods of time.

The older German monks would be encouraged to take part in the spirit of renewal to the extent they were able.

The lovely setting of the Tabgha monastery at the base of the Mount of Beatitudes, the daily early morning dip in the fresh waters of the lake, and his customary brisk walk south to the ruins of Capernaum lifted Abbot Leo's spirits. His outlook became much brighter. It was almost time to return to the Dormition when news arrived that Father Maurus, the subprior there, had become seriously ill. A hasty departure ensued. On arriving in Jerusalem, Leo saw that Maurus's condition was critical. Summoning the community's physician, he administered the Last Sacraments. Within a day, Father Maurus was dead. The following morning the community celebrated Mass and buried their confrere in the garden beside the church. All was starkly simple: no guests or relatives in attendance.

Shortly before Christmas, word arrived from Weston that Father Bernard Crepeaux, who was helping Father Stephen, had decided to return to Saint-Benoît-du-Lac. At the same time, Stephen was experiencing further problems with his health. Suddenly it became necessary for Robert to return to Weston.

MANSUETUDO — POTENTIA

September, 1959. Pope John assured Abbot Leo that he was in full accord with his hopes for the reconciliation of Christians and Jews, as well as for the Benedictine presence in the Holy Land.

10

Expanding the Vision

The situation in Weston proved not to be critical. Although Father Stephen's diabetic condition was worsening, he was still able to perform his duties as prior. Vocations continued to be abundant. Father Robert resettled in Weston, assisting in the construction of added housing for the growing community.

Abbot Leo returned to Weston in 1960, optimistic about his latest plans for reconciling his two disparate communities. He took a playful step in that direction and began basic classes for the Weston brothers in Hebrew. The community embarked on the new studies with enthusiasm. "Shalom" soon equaled the customary Benedictine greeting of "Pax" among the brothers. At the same time, Leo expanded his earlier teaching on the Rule and Benedictine spirituality. In the Pentecost edition of the Weston Priory Bulletin, he emphasized the expression that became the hallmark of his teaching: 'give room to the Holy Spirit':

> Ever since Saint Gregory the Great said, "[St. Benedict] wrote a rule for monks that is remarkable for its discretion,"

> that quality of the Rule of Saint Benedict has been praised as its outstanding characteristic. What exactly is that "discretion" of the Holy Rule? One may say it is its mildness, its consideration of human nature and life. All that is true, but it does not yet touch on the very heart of the matter. I should like to express it in this way. Saint Benedict, in his Holy Rule, gives room to the Holy Spirit.

For Leo, "giving room to the Holy Spirit" was the pervasive and underlying theme of Benedict's Rule:

> The same spirit is observed in Saint Benedict's attitude towards silence and prayer. No one could put more stress on the importance and greatness of silence than does Saint Benedict in his chapter 6.
>
> Instead of enforcing a hard and fast rule that no one may ever speak, he has a sentence so typical of his spirit: "Monks should always be given to silence"—they should be striving for silence (chap. 42). Is it not evident from these facts that Saint Benedict wants to give room to the Holy Spirit? This he says expressly at the end of the seventh chapter of the Holy Rule—"On Humility": "May the Lord be pleased to manifest all this by His Holy Spirit."

In these texts, Leo presented a Benedictine spirituality that he hoped would nourish and bond his two far-flung communities:

> One could also apply this to the question so frequently posed nowadays: "Is the Benedictine life contemplative or active?" I would say that this distinction really does not apply. The Rule of Saint Benedict antedates such sharp distinctions. What Saint Benedict wants is to create con-

> ditions favorable to contemplation and seeking God. The rest is up to God. In that sense he really meant it when, in the last chapter, he calls his Rule one for beginners, because perfection is up to God's calling and guidance. No rule can be written for that....
>
> The main thing is this: We should always try to create favorable conditions in our lives—and then rely on God. Benedictine spirituality does not overemphasize the psychological effort in striving for perfection. When rightly understood, the Benedictine attitude of "waiting for God" leads to true greatness. It makes for an unhurried growth towards God.

Consistent in his style of teaching, he evoked an image from the sea to illustrate his point:

> This point can be further illustrated by the simple image of two men on a ship—the nervous type who stands in the bow and who is on constant lookout for the harbor, trying to speed the vessel in his concern, and the more relaxed type who, while not completely at home on the boat and keeping his suitcases packed, is nevertheless at ease in the conviction that the ship will reach port in due time. Give room to the Holy Spirit![1]

Feeding the Fire of Renewal: John XXIII and Vatican II

Even as he instructed the young Vermont community on openness to the Holy Spirit, a revolutionary event was taking place in Rome that confirmed irreversibly Leo's vision for Christian-Jewish reconciliation. In October 1960, a delegation of one hundred thirty leaders of the United Jewish Appeal on a study mission to Europe and Israel stopped in Rome to pay their respects to Pope John. The purpose of the visit was to express gratitude for all he had done as Apostolic Delegate in Turkey to save the lives of Jews fleeing Nazi persecution.

With his typical warmth, the Pope walked toward the Jewish leaders with extended arms and greeted them—and through them all Jews—echoing the familiar words of the fourth patriarch: "I am Joseph, your brother" (Gen. 45:4). This symbolic gesture by Pope John reinforced the driving force of Abbot Leo's life: his engagement with the Jewish people and his emerging view of a new mode of Benedictine life in the Holy Land.

The vivid image of Pope John's arms outstretched to welcome his Jewish brothers and the memory of his own personal audience with the Pope in the previous year reinforced Leo's resolve to dedicate his energies to the reconciliation of Christians and Jews. He returned to Israel in the fall of 1960 with the conviction that his dream for a Benedictine presence in Israel were understood and shared in Rome.

The year 1961 was one of expanding vision and change in the Catholic Church. The elderly new pope infused the church with youthful vigor. He threw open windows to "give room to the Holy Spirit." On January 21, 1961, soon after he announced that he would convene the Second Vatican Council, Pope John appointed Abbot Leo to the Secretariat for Promoting Christian Unity. The sub-commission of the Secretariat to which Leo was assigned was assigned the task of preparing the document on Catholic-Jewish relations to be discussed on the floor of the Council.

For Leo, this was an exciting and invigorating charge. Energized by his appointment, he plunged into the work of the

above: Pope John XXIII meeting with the Vatican *Secretariat for Promoting Christian Unity* in preparation for the Second Vatican Council. Abbot Leo, right side center. *below:* Tabgha monastery of the Loaves and Fishes with Sea of Galilee and Golan Heights in background. "It became a favored place for me."

commission, giving it his highest priority. Meetings in Rome demanded his presence and preparation. Study and discussions with scholars at the top level of ecclesial authority consumed his time and ability.

Tilling the Soil and Planting Seeds

On his return to Weston in the late spring of 1961, Leo intensified his efforts to prepare the Weston monks to carry out his dream for Dormition Abbey and the Holy Land. He utilized every opportunity to bring his message to the community still in its early stages of growth. The visits of his distinguished Jewish friends and colleagues were especially helpful in this task. In these guests the young community encountered the Jewish reality not just in words and abstract teaching, but in living persons.

He introduced the Weston community to Rabbi Arthur Gilbert of the National Council of Christians and Jews, who graciously responded to an invitation to journey to Weston for a weekend. Meeting in the bright recreation room of the Priory with the brothers, Rabbi Gilbert recited in Hebrew a text from Genesis and then responded to a barrage of questions on the Jewish understanding of the text. Members of the community sang two psalms that they had learned in Hebrew. The Rabbi reciprocated with a song in Hebrew, and soon all were singing in unison. The visitor with his expansive personality and wide-ranging experience furthered the interest and enthusiasm of the community for Leo's project.

Abbot Leo continued to personally instruct the community. He searched for images to plant the seeds of his dream among the Weston brothers. He imagined the Benedictine monastery as the locus of a new path of hospitality, welcome, forgiveness, compassion—and ultimately reconciliation. Drawing on his early experience in Israel, he first came up with the example of a consulate.

> I try sometimes to explain this peculiar position of a monastery (according to ancient monastic ideals) by using the analogy of a consulate in a foreign country. The consul is especially obligated to care for the interests of his co-nationals in a foreign country. Take for example the American Consulate in Paris. Naturally it is a house like any other house in Paris, probably built by Frenchmen. It has relations to the Parisian surroundings. The porter or receptionist is probably a Frenchman who speaks English with a foreign accent. Yet, when you put your foot into that consulate you come under the laws of the United States of America. It is an extra-territorial place in a foreign country. In private life the consul himself may do many things according to the French way, but in his official capacity he acts, representing his country in France, according to the laws of the United States of America.[2]

Later, acknowledging the limitations of this image, he sought a replacement. As he explained, "The consulate is preoccupied with the rights and privileges of its own citizens in a foreign land. It lends an air of exclusivity and self-concern." Ultimately, to conjure up the type of monastery that was his goal, he preferred a more embracing, outgoing, and inclusive image that he would locate in another arm of the diplomatic service:

> The embassy is a place of good will, of mutual hospitality with the host country, of dialogue, welcome, and acceptance. While not excluding the interests of its own citizens, it focuses on healthy relations with the host

> country, respectful of its customs and culture and learning its language. In a limited way, it speaks of reconciliation, shalom, peace.[3]

In a journal interview published in 1961, he described the projected community in Israel as having an "indirect apostolate." In his previous instructions to the Weston community, he assiduously avoided the expression "apostolate." He attempted to clarify his meaning:

> I am convinced that the apostolate to Arabs and Jews cannot be a direct apostolate. It must be an indirect one and precisely this kind of apostolate of just being the presence of the Church, an apostolate, not of activity—not of doing—but of being. I consider this apostolate most important. You can already see the reactions in Israel. While missionaries are somewhat looked down upon and are, well, unpopular, we have a certain respect among the people. Why? Exactly because of this peaceful Benedictine existence which builds a bridge of understanding, not ostentatiously, not obtrusively.

He confessed the novelty of his approach and noted that he was still in the process of exploration:

> This is the apostolate we consider our task: to build bridges of understanding—by being—by letting people see us, not to begin by insisting that they become one of us. We want them to glimpse this Christian existence.... It would be absolutely the wrong approach to try to convert Moslems or Jews. We do not want that. We want to work for mutual understanding, and we will do this by just being there, making the Church present.... We are philosophical and theological pioneers.[4]

Leo's spontaneous gestures of welcome and expressions of openness were seeds that he hoped would germinate and flower in his future community. Still not explicitly articulated or fully thought out, his ideas hinted at a concept of monastery, not as an efficient, regimented institution, but as a community of the heart. His vision evoked rather the image of the community of the Beloved Disciple, where the spirit of love was both hidden and revealed in the weakness and strength of human beings, falling and rising as they groped for wholeness and peace.

> [W]e monks build our lives in the monastery according to the laws of heaven, not of earth. Our fraternal love imitates the love of the saints in heaven. Our obedience is not functional as it is in an army, nor temporary as it is in a family, where the children outgrow it. Rather it is a fulfillment of the petition, "Thy will be done on earth as it is in heaven." Naturally we are men, still living on earth. We do things according to the laws of this earth—we sleep and eat, etc.—but in our official capacity we represent heaven on earth. We create an extraterritorial place of heaven on earth.[5]

Teach Us to Pray

The spirituality of the Hebrew prophets was at the heart of Leo's attachment to Israel, the land, and the Jewish people. Among his dearest friends was the distinguished rabbi and theologian, Abraham Joshua Heschel. The visit of Rabbi Heschel to the Priory in the summer of 1962 was an awe-inspiring moment for the monastic community.

The fourteen young Benedictine monks gathered in the pine-paneled recreation room of the Priory. They sat wordlessly in a semicircle around the illustrious rabbi. He broke the awed silence affably with a question: "Now, what do we want to talk about?" Hesitantly a brother ventured, "Rabbi, teach us how you pray." There followed no lecture, no scholarly discourse on theories of prayer. The rabbi closed his eyes, folded his hands, and began to rock gently back and forth to the rhythm of a Hebrew psalm. There was no sense of self-consciousness, no artifice. In utter simplicity, there was in the room a palpable experience of presence to the holy and a holy presence. In that all too brief afternoon, the Weston brothers witnessed prayer not as a technique, not as a ritual, but as a joyful, profound experience of being present to the presence of God. They were graced to have a prophet, a holy man of Israel, in their midst.

While many of Leo's Jewish friends were scholars and rabbis who hailed from a great distance, he reached out to neighboring Jewish communities in Vermont as well. Rabbi Solomon Goldberg of Rutland was an especially close friend, who identified with Leo's desire for closer Christian-Jewish relations. Responding to a request from the Weston community, Rabbi Goldberg generously drove weekly to the monastery to present a fascinating series of conferences on Jewish feast days, ceremonies, and customs. The friendly Rabbi invited Leo and a group of brothers to the bar mitzvah of his son, and later the whole Weston community was invited to sing at a service in the Rutland synagogue. In small steps, and with the help of friends, Leo's hopes began to take root in the Weston community.

As Abbot Leo prepared to depart again for Israel, he observed an encouraging sign. The community began publication of a series of articles on Jewish feasts and customs in the Priory bulletin. The series, titled "Joseph Your Brother," beginning with the Lent-Easter issue in 1962, opened on a note of inclusion from Pope John: "We are all sons of the same heavenly Father, among us all there must ever be the brightness of love and its practice."

When Leo arrived at the Dormition Abbey after his sojourn in Weston for the summer of 1962, brother Bernard, the lone monk from Weston at the Abbey, had long since left the Benedictine community and relocated on his own elsewhere in the United States. As elder monks at the Dormition became increasingly discouraged, Abbot Leo reassured them that relief was close at hand.

The crucial work of preparing a document on Christian-Jewish relations for discussion on the floor of the Council was in the hands of Abbot Leo and his colleagues in the Secretariat for Christian Unity. With the opening of Vatican Council II in Rome on October 11, 1962, Leo's highest priority was his work with the Council sub-commission for Jewish-Christian relations. His stay in Jerusalem was interrupted intermittently with calls for critical meetings with commission members in Rome. His time and attention at the Abbey were consumed with study, correspondence, reflection, and meetings relative to his passionate commitment to this concern. Little time was left for building a spirit of trust and welcome, still lacking but so needed, among the German monks in anticipation of the contingent of monks expected in the near future from America. Time passed too quickly, and it was already time for him to return to North America.

An Unquenchable Light

En route from Israel to the United States in high spirits, on June 3, 1963, Abbot Leo was saddened with news of the death of Pope John XXIII. He was moved to write of the significance of that great man:

> Good Pope John has been taken from us. Hardly any pope has been so generally loved as Pope John was. What was the secret that made this pope leave so deep an impression on the world? In one word: He was a man of the heart. Make no mistake. Pope John had a brilliant mind. (The Holy Father could also be strict and very decisive.) Anyone who ever had the great privilege of speaking with him face to face (as this writer did several times) was impressed by his quick grasp and understanding, by the—I may almost say—shark edge of his penetrating eyes which seemed to look into your innermost heart. Still, there have been other popes with brilliant minds. The real greatness of Pope John was that he was a man of the heart.

Leo went on to expand on a cherished theme, the human heart:

> What is the heart of man? It is that inner core where mind and body—spirit and matter—meet. Out of the two elements that make up human nature and so often wage war against each other comes a wholesome center. It is the heart that makes for what we call personality in the sense of a harmonious Oneness that we encounter when we meet such a person.
>
> The heart of man is also the seat of the Holy Spirit, whom we may call, with much less exactness of expression, the heart of the Holy Trinity. Even if we have misgivings about the latter expression, there is no doubt there is a relationship, a kinship between the Holy Spirit and the heart of man. The heart is not mere emotion. It is too

> spiritual for that. A sentimental man is not really a man of the heart. Neither is the heart mere intelligence. An intellectual is not necessarily a man of the heart. The heart is where the mind and spirit enter the body to become flesh and blood. And it is where the flesh is lifted up into the spirit. Furthermore, the heart is the power and energy of man which makes him simple and helps him to simplify (not over-simplify) things and events. That is the key to the fact that Pope John could do things no one would have thought could have been done. He did them simply.

Adding a light touch, Abbot Leo illustrated his point from the life of Pope John:

> A little story I read not long ago in a German weekly is an anecdote about the Pope which bears the marks of truth. It is said that once a bishop of a large diocese had a papal audience. At the end of the audience, the bishop asked a special blessing and a word of encouragement because, he said, he was often oppressed by the heavy burden his duties laid upon him. Then, so goes the story, the Pope said, "Oh, I know that feeling, my dear bishop. I, too, have many burdens. My diocese is the world. If such feelings of inadequacy befall me, I go into my chapel and pray. Recently on such an occasion, it was as if the Lord spoke to me, saying, "Oh Johnny, don't take yourself so seriously. I am still here." There you have the man who was John XXIII—humble, simple, pious. I think he was a saint. It was shown to the world again that it is really the man of the heart, not so much of the high intelligence, who leaves the deepest impression on the world.

Pope John reflected a new face of the church to the world. It was the kind face of a mother and the wise face of a teacher, words he used to describe the church in his 1961 encyclical, *Mater et Magistra*. He was a pope who listened deeply, responding with few words, but with generous symbolic gestures.

The Summer of 1963: Ten Years of Weston Priory

The summer of 1963 was a season of high hopes and expectations for Leo. His stay in the United States began with a short drive from Weston to the University of Vermont in Burlington. The University awarded him an honorary degree of Doctor of Divinity in recognition of his "outstanding contribution to Christian-Jewish relations." On the same occasion he was invited to deliver the baccalaureate address to the graduating students in the beautiful Ira Allen Chapel on the university campus.

Later in the summer he traveled to Santa Fe, New Mexico, where he addressed the 26th annual convention of the Catholic Art Association. The theme of the nine conferences was "The Ecumenical Approach to Non-Christian Cultures." Abbot Leo's address was aptly titled "The Emergence of an Indigenous Culture in Israel—Problems and Hopes."

In the midst of a very busy summer, Leo welcomed a steady stream of monastic guests and distinguished visitors. Guest monks came from far-flung places: Montserrat Abbey in Spain, St. Vincent's Abbey in Pennsylvania, Conception Abbey in Missouri, the Eremetical Foundation of Father Jacques Winandy on Martinique, St. Joseph Abbey in Louisiana, and Mount Saviour in New York.

Among the distinguished visitors, Dr. Zvi Werblosky, a cherished friend of Abbot Leo and professor of Comparative Religion at the Hebrew University in Jerusalem, arrived in September. He fascinated the community with a recounting of a ten-day sojourn at a Buddhist monastery in Japan. During his stay, he presented two stimulating conferences on Saint John of the Cross, whose works he was at that time translating into Hebrew.

There hardly seemed space in such a short time for a momentous event in the life of the Weston community—the first official "Visitation" of the community as a Benedictine monastery. Abbot Primate Benno Gut arrived in Weston from Sant'Anselmo in Rome in August. He was no stranger to Abbot Leo. From the time of their first meeting in the Abbey of Einsiedeln in Switzerland, prior to the Abbots' Congress of 1959 and the election of Abbot Benno as Abbot Primate of the Benedictine Confederation, he had championed Abbot Leo's causes. Now, on his first official visit to Weston, he came as a friend and collaborator.

Abbot Benno conducted the visitation with sensitivity. He was perceptive and personal as he interviewed each member of the community. In his final report of the weeklong visit, he encouraged the community, but soberly called attention to the role of the prior in the dependent Benedictine monastery:

> The Abbot is the major superior of the house and in his presence no one takes precedence.... The Abbot is the superior and the Prior executes the Abbot's will in his absence. Nothing of consequence may be undertaken without the permission of the Abbot. We are sorry for the poor health of the Prior and that he is overburdened with work. He must have more time especially to spend with the novices. It has been suggested that he divide his responsibility with others and give a certain independence to individuals so that some do not get the impression that they are being treated like children.

He commended the community for its monastic observance and spirit:

> I have been greatly edified by the manifest good spirit I find especially in obedience to superiors and the charity that marks the relationship of monks with each other. For this wonderful fraternal charity, I wish to commend you especially and encourage you to nourish it.[6]

After the successful visitation and the departure of the Abbot Primate, Leo was ready to announce a new moment for his two communities. Leo's dream had crystallized into a plan, and he concluded that it was time to launch his experiment of internationalizing the community in the Holy Land. The Weston community was firmly established and promising; the monastery buildings were more ample and comfortable; the work, better balanced; the economy, more secure. In 1953, he had been quoted in an interview in the *Boston Globe,* "It is expected it will take ten years to fully organize the monastery and by then the monks might number as many as 50." The prophecy was at least partially realized!

At the conclusion of his stay in Weston in the autumn of 1963, a decade after the founding of Weston Priory, Abbot Leo had reason to give thanks:

> Ten years of Weston Priory! If we draw the balance, what do we have to show? Well, it is as it is with all those matters. Very little on our part and very much on God's part. We must and can be very, very grateful for all the loving kindness God has shown us. First of all, we exist. And Weston has now a community, not a very big one, but nevertheless a community, and one (we may say) united in spirit, in love and zeal for our monastic ideals.

At last he could rejoice that his labors had born fruit:

> As a symbol of our coming of age, we are sending out this year for the first time a contingent of three young monks to the mother abbey in Jerusalem with its dependency in Tabgha at the shore of the Sea of Galilee. This may be said to be a sign of life and a confirmation of the belief that the founding of Weston was also a means of reviving the Abbey in the Holy Land.... Thus, with confidence we look into the future, a confidence that does not rely on our own abilities, but solely on the goodness and omnipotence of the Lord whom we try to serve. It is especially the great sanctuary of His Mother on Mount Zion which we serve for His Honor."[7]

The time had come to select a small group of Weston monks to serve as the core of a revitalized Benedictine community in the Holy Land.

above: The new monastery at Tabgha in1953 with the Mount of Beatitudes in the background. "I had hoped we could build up a good monastic life there." *below:* Brothers David and Ambrose with Dr. Leon Smith and Abbot Leo in Tabgha. "As a symbol of our coming of age, we are sending a contingent of three young monks to the mother abbey in Jerusalem with its dependency in Tabgha at the shore of the Sea of Galilee."

11

New Horizon on the Sea of Galilee

Before he returned to Jerusalem in the late summer of 1963, Abbot Leo interviewed prospective candidates among the professed brothers for the forthcoming adventure in the Holy Land. The pool of available monks was limited. The full Weston community numbered fourteen members, including Father Stephen, the prior. Three brothers were away from the monastery and involved in studies. Three other brothers were still novices and not eligible for the mission. Of the remaining few available, not all were anxious to leave their Vermont location.

Abbot Leo was concerned not to weaken the Weston community, yet he desperately needed men whom he could reply upon. In consultation with Stephen, he chose three monks whom he felt especially qualified to carry out his experiment. Brother David, a native of Worcester, Massachusetts, was a non-ordained choir-monk. He made his solemn monastic profession in Weston in July of 1963, shortly before departure time for Israel. Leo prized David's personal loyalty and practical skills. Brother Renat was a solemnly professed monk of the

Olivetan Congregation before he transferred to Weston in 1957. He was ordained to priesthood in August of 1963. Fond of studies, he enjoyed intellectual circles and the monastic choir. Brother Ambrose, a non-ordained choir-monk in temporary profession, hailed from the Bronx. A gifted linguist eager to learn Hebrew, he was looking forward to celebrating his solemn monastic profession at the Dormition in the following year.[1]

The animated group of three young monks set off for Israel with Abbot Leo in the early fall of 1963. After a gala sendoff by oblates and friends in New Jersey, the little group embarked from New York Harbor for Europe and the Middle East. They purchased a small car in France, toured Europe, spent some days in Rome, and finally went on to Israel. Their journey from Weston to Jerusalem was not a short one: it was November before the group reached their destination.

The community at the Dormition Abbey welcomed the Weston brothers with mixed feelings. The aged and frail lay brothers who looked forward to returning home to Germany were jubilant. The ordained monks remained skeptical. They questioned if the North Americans had the capacity to adapt to the monastic way of life practiced at the abbey.

The first letter from the Weston monks in Israel, written after Christmas to their brothers at home in Vermont, was almost euphoric:

> We are finally in the Holy Land, and you can imagine what a joy it is for us.... The Dormition is one of the loveliest churches in the Holy Land.... How we wish you could experience our joy in being here Christmas night under the moonlit, starlit Jerusalem sky, and the new geographical closeness to the one great event in human history. We walked out on the terrace that magnificent night

> before offering the midnight Mass, and thought we could hear angels singing and shepherds snoring and kicking their wine skins.... The journey here and every moment that we have been in the Holy Land have been terribly exciting...[2]

Though they arrived in Israel in high spirits, the small band of monks from Weston were hardly formed into a cohesive group. All three of the brothers admired Abbot Leo and held him in high esteem. They did not, however, share an equally deep understanding or conviction of their common purpose. Lacking, too, was a bond of mutual trust between them that would make deep interpersonal communication and support possible in times of hardship. Were these factors but another version of the seeds of division, dissension, and ultimately, disaster that flawed Leo's earlier life experience at Keyport?

The three youthful North American monks were ill prepared to cope with the aging community of German monks in Jerusalem. In this situation, Leo's appointment to the Preparatory Commission on Jewish-Christian Relations for the Vatican Council proved to be a serious drawback. He relished the meetings and study required for that prestigious assignment. Yet, his attention and presence were sorely needed to meld the North American and the German monks into his design for a new Dormition community. With meetings in Rome and time set aside for intensive study and consultation, he was not able to give undivided attention to the formation of the new community in the Holy Land as he had envisioned it.

Frictions developed between the older ordained monks of the Dormition community and the group of young monks from the United States. Their cultural, spiritual, and monastic backgrounds could hardly have been more diverse. The newcomers were far from fluent in German. Monastic life in Weston had not prepared them for the rigid discipline familiar to monks trained in the Beuronese tradition. The two-class system that separated lay brothers from ordained monks at the Dormition was repugnant to the North Americans. Obstacles to communication between the Weston monks and their Dormition counterparts soon became insuperable.

In a short time, as he had planned, Leo removed the North American monks from the hostile situation in Jerusalem to Tabgha on the tranquil Sea of Galilee. Their reception at the small monastery was more friendly and welcoming. The newly arrived monks began to pray the monastic office and celebrate Eucharist in the temporary monastic church, joined occasionally by Father Jerome, the local superior, but not by the two lay brothers. Leo remembered these beginnings with guarded hope:

> We spent much time in Tabgha. We had fixed the church and also a side-chapel for choir services and Conventual Mass. We held the office rather regularly.... Father Jerome joined us as often as he could.

Soon after their arrival at Tabgha, Abbot Leo sent Ambrose and Renat to Ulpan Akiva to study Hebrew. He hoped that this training would prepare them to integrate the Hebrew language into the monastic liturgy. It would make it possible for them to converse with Jewish visitors to the monastery as well. Reflecting on his own experience, Leo saw the Ulpan as an opportunity to imbibe the warmth of the Jewish people and to be exposed to Israeli culture. At the same time, he trusted that the experience would further a bond of friendship and communication between the two monks. Unable to join them, David went separately at a later time.

Troubles on Both Fronts

Meetings with the Council Preparatory Commission drew Abbot Leo away from Tabgha. At the same time, the community at the Dormition Abbey was a constant source of anxiety, calling for his presence. Within a year, while Leo was distracted elsewhere, issues dividing the Weston brothers from the Dormition community and from one another reached a critical stage.

It was with misgivings that Leo departed Israel to return to Weston for his annual visit in May, 1964. On his arrival, ominous news awaited him. In the winter, Father Stephen had spent several weeks in the hospital. After that, his diabetic condition deteriorated. All the while, bearing the responsibilities for the community and the reception and training of postulants and novices, he was involved with plans for a new chapel at the Priory. An architect had been engaged, a design approved. Leo protested that he had not been sufficiently consulted in the process. He wanted advice from Oblate friends in New Jersey concerning finances and on the choice of an architect before going ahead with the building project.

In weakened physical condition, feeling overwhelmed and sensing a lack of confidence, Stephen submitted his resignation as prior to Abbot Leo. Seeing no other option, Leo accepted it, and he gave Stephen permission to take a position as chaplain to a community of Sisters in Connecticut.

After the departure of the three brothers for the Holy Land and the exit of Father Stephen, only ten members of the Weston community remained. Four of these were solemnly professed monks, three were in temporary vows, and there were two novices and a postulant. Two of the brothers in temporary vows were in the seminary preparing for priesthood. Of the entire Weston community, just one member met the canonical requirements of priestly ordination and solemn monastic profession to succeed Father Stephen as prior.

Father Robert, who had accompanied Abbot Leo on the trip to Rome and Israel in 1959, had made his solemn monastic profession in 1961 and at that time his name was changed to John.[3] He was pursuing studies in psychology at the University of Ottawa from 1962 until the spring of 1964.

When John returned from Ottawa in early June, the decision had been made that Father Stephen would leave to become chaplain for the Brigittine Nuns in Darien, Connecticut. On June 24, 1964, the feast of Saint John the Baptist, Abbot Leo named John prior to succeed Father Stephen.

Some ten years, later Leo summed up his appreciation for the contribution of the early priors to the life of the Weston Community:

> I would also like to put in here a memorial page for the first priors of Weston, who held the fort while I was in Jerusalem. I had to leave a lot of responsibility to them, and I am truly grateful to all of them and for all they did towards the existence of Weston.

After this reference to Hugh Duffy, Michael Ducey, Bede Scholz, and Stephen Fronckewicz, he alluded to the pain of their exit from Weston, "The changes of priors always came about under pressure of the whole community, not through incompatibility with my person." Of the new transition in 1964, Leo had a positive assessment, "The present Prior, John Hammond, is a true God-sent for this Priory." At a later date, he penned a personal note into the typewritten text, "I like to call him 'the second founder' of Weston."

Even as Leo pondered where he could find assistance for his new prior solemnly professed only three years earlier, Vincent Martin arrived on the scene and asked to be received at Weston for a limited period. A Benedictine monk of the monastery of Valyermo, California, Father Vincent had served in China for many years. Subsequently, he earned a doctorate in sociology at Harvard. Because of differences with the prior at Valyermo, Vincent needed to remove himself from his home community temporarily.

With the fortuitous arrival of Vincent Martin and the prospects of new applicants to the community coming in the summer and fall, Leo navigated another difficult transition. Almost immediately Vincent took up the duties of novice master for the Weston community. Amid all his problems and anxieties, Leo interpreted the events at Weston as signs of God's providence. He encouraged the community to support one another and to become a distinctly North American monastery. His confidence was confirmed as the community began to share responsibilities, strengthen fraternal relationships, and construct the new monastery chapel.

Reassured that the Weston community was in good hands and would flourish, Leo set out again for Rome and the Holy Land. His time in Rome on this trip was a high point among his many visits there. He reported a "wonderful meeting with Archbishop Philippe, Secretary of the Congregation for Religious...absolutely in favor of monks-non-priests."

As a member of the Secretariat for Promoting Christian Unity, Abbot Leo was privileged to attend a session of the Second Vatican Council.

Bitter Disappointment in Israel and in Rome

After his stimulating experience in Rome and a visit with relatives in Germany, Leo pushed on to Israel, impatient to continue the process of renewing the monastic community there. On his arrival at the Dormition, he was greeted with shocking news. Father Renat informed him that he no longer wished to be a part of the Holy Land project. A stunned Abbot Leo reported to brother John without further explanation, "Father Renat is a huge worry. The worst is my disappointment in him as a man."[4]

Leo had invested high hopes in Renat as the senior and ordained member of the trio brought from Weston. During the following weeks, Leo remonstrated with him, striving to dissuade him from leaving. Leo protested that he had trusted the Weston monks to carry out his dream for Benedictine life in the Holy Land. For a time it seemed he had succeeded; Renat agreed to rethink his decision.

It was a time of bitter anxiety for Leo. Instead of a period of constructive implementation of his plan for the renewal of Benedictine life in the Holy Land, he found himself beleaguered by the basic problem of holding the fragile group together. He gave vent to his feelings in a letter to brother John on February 11, 1965, "Sometimes I don't know how to go on. Father Renat is reconsidering again. Where will it lead? This was such a terrible blow to me. I saw all my work collapse right around me.... I was really at the end of my rope in every respect."

In the midst of his personal distress, he was summoned again to Rome for additional work on the preparatory working paper for the Council. Writing from Sant'Anselmo, he said, "I arrived here last Tuesday. I expect to return to Jerusalem next Saturday, March 6. The work is important, sometimes quite hard and difficult, and at any rate strenuous. Thank God I am feeling much better now, and I do get my diet fairly well."[5]

Back in Israel, he confided, "I returned from Rome whole and in one piece.... I was glad I went. It was very important, and I could really contribute." Then, addressing his most nettlesome problem in Jerusalem, "Father Renat, changing his mind several times, is just unable to take it. We have decided to let him go to study in Europe.... Maybe it is good for him to get away from it for a while."[6]

Leo would later recall these early months of 1965 as "the most difficult period of my life":

> I personally thought things were going all right. Was it a case of my usual naiveté? It was a slow beginning, but it seemed to me a beginning that had promise. Then the things happened that pulled the rug completely from under my feet. First, Father Renat, only a few weeks later, let me know that he had no intention of staying. He rejected everything I tried to do. The thing that really made me mad is that (as Brother Thomas told me in Weston afterwards) Father Renat had said before he left that he went only because he wanted to see the Holy Land, not intending to stay. That was real treachery. If he had never come to Jerusalem, no great harm would have been done. His leaving proved to the monks of the Dormition that Americans had no staying power. It was disastrous. It was the beginning of the end for me. It really finished everything.

This was not Leo's final word on his relationship to Renat. Ten years later he had this to say in his Reminiscences: "When I love, I love forever. I cannot simply drop someone whom I once loved. Love is eternal and cannot die, even after the greatest hurt. If I may say so, with all my limitations, loyalty is one of my good qualities. Although Brother Renat has hurt me and damaged my cause beyond repair, I still love him."

Disheartened and distraught, Leo's already fragile health rapidly deteriorated. He began to suffer debilitating pain from

above: 1963. Abbot Leo at Ecumenical meeting with Orthodox, Armenian, and Roman representatives in Jerusalem. *below:* Leo with novice and guest about to ice skate in front of the "novitiate" that housed classroom, recreation room, dormitory, and garage at Weston Priory.

stomach ulcers. Unable to eat or sleep, he entered the hospital in Nazareth. Treatment and rest there afforded him some relief, but his doctors recommended surgery as soon as possible.

Because of his implicit trust in his devoted friend Dr. Leon Smith, he decided to go to New Jersey for the necessary surgery. He set out in early May, 1965, for the United States. On his way he stopped in Hamburg to visit his brother, the bishop. By that time, Leo's condition had reached the acute stage. It was necessary for him to undergo an operation immediately. Two serious ulcers were removed, one attached to the pancreas, which had been the source for several years of excruciating pain. The doctors ordered a period of complete rest and recuperation. The most favorable place for such a period was at the Priory in Weston. For the first time, Leo would spend the winter and the better part of the year with the community there.

The brothers at Weston received him with welcoming arms and were heartened by his presence. He was in a weakened condition and extremely concerned for the community in Israel. Vincent Martin, who had been helping the Weston community as novice master for the past year, was captivated by the question of Christian-Jewish relations and Abbot Leo's plans for the Dormition Abbey. He offered to go to Israel while Leo recuperated at Weston.

Since the Weston community was progressing smoothly, Leo accepted Vincent's offer to lend a hand at the Dormition Abbey. Leo settled in comfortably at Weston for several months of convalescence. While he was getting his strength back, he kept in touch with developments at the ongoing Council sessions in Rome.

Together with the other commission members—Monsignor John Oesterreicher, specialist in Judaic-Christian studies, and

Cardinal Augustine Bea, eminent German Jesuit Scripture scholar—Abbot Leo had hammered out the working paper, *De Judaeis,* the text presented on the Council floor for discussion.

Abbot Leo deferred to Monsignor Oesterreicher as the principal author of the document they prepared, casting himself as a "hod carrier or bricklayer" in the endeavor he considered so important.[7] Nonetheless, Paulist Father Tom Stransky, past rector of the Tantur Ecumenical Institute in Jerusalem, who was recording secretary for the small working paper group, remembers the strong feelings and convictions with which Abbot Leo contributed to the construction of *De Judaeis.*

The working paper was subject to numerous interventions by the curial offices and was finally discussed on the floor of the Council. On October 28, 1965, at the conclusion of the Council, it was promulgated in modified form by Pope Paul VI as the groundbreaking document, *Nostra Aetate.*

In early fall of 1965, someone in Rome sent Leo a secret copy of the latest version of the document he was most directly involved with. A few days after receiving the text—and less than three weeks before *Nostra Aetate* was promulgated at the Vatican—Abbot Leo addressed a letter to Cardinal Bea, his fellow subcommission member, venting his feelings of disappointment and frustration at changes to the working document their group had presented for debate by the Council Fathers. The copy found among Leo's letters is marked "not sent":

> I have been studying this last draft of our schema very carefully. I have come to the following conclusions, which I would like to communicate to you, more to lighten my conscience than in the hope of gaining any influence on the final form of the schema. True, many essentials have been preserved. One might even say, that if this had been the very first draft of the schema, it might have been

> received with pleasure, though mixed with misgivings. But, coming as it does after other redactions, which have all been widely discussed in the press, I cannot help saying that it is disappointing. All the warmth—all the spontaneous expression of love—which we tried to instill in the original drafts, has been suppressed...
>
> Let me, at the end, express my conviction that Your Eminence has done all in your power to have a really satisfactory schema passed, for which I thank you.... And I am sure you will forgive these lines coming from an anguished heart.[8]

Recalling, in his later years, his work on the commission and the results in Vatican II, Leo still grieved over the final outcome:

> I cooperated in the document on Jewish-Christian relations that was published during the Council—unfortunately in a watered-down version. Much of the warmth and clarity with which our commission had tried to write it was lost. I remember many of the preparatory commission's sessions—often so frustrating—in which other bodies, like the Secretariat of State, interfered. The enmity from the Arab hierarchy was felt strongly.

A Stab in the Back

Even at Weston, Leo did not completely escape the burdens associated with the Dormition Abbey. As the time approached for his return to Israel in the spring of 1966, he received a disturbing letter from Jerusalem written by Luke Joerg. He was among the group of Dormition monks who fled Israel during the war of Israeli Independence in 1948. In the meantime, he had settled at St. Joseph's Abbey in Louisiana.

Leo tried for several years to persuade Father Luke and the other exiled monks of the Dormition to either return to Israel or go to Weston and assist the community there. Luke made two attempts to re-enter the community in Israel. His first visit lasted only two weeks. In 1965–1966, he was again in the Holy Land.

From Tabgha he wrote a blistering condemnation of all that Leo had done on behalf of the Dormition Abbey community. He accused Leo of abandoning the German monks in favor of his "little American monklets." He wrote that this view was not just his own opinion, but what other German members of the community confided to him:

> We old fathers and brothers consider ourselves now as before as belonging to the Beuronese Congregation, and we have no interest in your personal innovations, which you have introduced in Weston. We are Beuronese and not Westonians, and we do not want to become Westonians. Therefore, a mixing between the old community and the Westonians is not only undesirable, it is impossible....
>
> It is easy to see that the discontent of the community has a great deal of justification. The advice has already been given us, to demand an Apostolic Visitation from Rome, and perhaps it is the only means to bring order into these confused conditions. Dormitio is Dormitio, and Weston is Weston. Be you the abbot of either one! We have become the laughing stock of everybody, especially the American Benedictines and the secular and regular clergy here, on account of our abbot with the triple crown: Dormition, Tabgha, Weston.

> Do not take this letter amiss! You must know what the mood is at the Dormition and in Tabgha. Do reunite us with the Beuronese Congregation and keep your Americans for yourself. Nobody wants them, we the least.[9]

Leo responded, point by point, to Father Luke's allegations and sent the letter by diplomatic courier from France. Stung by the offensive tone and claim that the accusations represented the "justified discontent of the community, "Leo presented the historical facts of his relationship with the Dormition Abbey and avoided polemic argumentation. Still, he could not resist pointing out the irony of Luke's protestation of courtesy, "At the end of your letter you remark: 'Do not take this letter amiss.' That is as if somebody who has just thrust a dagger into the back, says: 'Please, excuse me!' In spite of this, I shall try not to take offense. I can excuse your letter on ignorance...."

Frustrated and nearing the end of his patience with the recalcitrant community in Israel, Abbot Leo promised a "show-down":

> Final remark: Be assured of one thing: At the latest, upon my return, I shall force a showdown with the community. It is impossible to let me build the machine, get it going, and then throw a monkey wrench into the works. If our ways must part, all right I must resign. This way I shall not continue. I have already ruined my health on account of the Dormition. Some day there must be an end to it. If you want to bring the odium of an Apostolic Visitation down on us, go ahead. A canonical visitation will be next year (spring?) anyway. Then a decision must come. For me there is only this: Either the community stands behind

> me or I resign. As I have said in my short previous letter: May God forgive you and them all. I greet you as your abbot always ready for love.[10]

In the spring of 1966, after a period of rest and relaxation in Weston, Leo, rejuvenated, prepared to return to Israel, though still with raw feelings. Before taking ship for another Atlantic crossing, he made a ten day visit to Mount Saviour monastery in Elmira to consult with his friend Damasus, and to express his gratitude for the assistance the community there had been offering to Weston. Upon his arrival at Mt. Saviour on April 19, he wrote back to the Weston brothers, "I am already missing you dreadfully. I haven't felt such pangs of homesickness in a long while. I wish I were back in Weston and had never to leave it. Well, it cannot be, God knows. Therefore He will help...."

Expressing the sentiments of the Weston brothers after the prolonged stay of Abbot Leo with the community, brother John replied to Abbot Leo, who was still in Mt. Saviour on the 24th of April, "I think this has been our most joyful year for inner growth in the community, and I know that both I and all the brothers have found you as our real Father in a way we had never experienced before...."

1966. Abbot Leo, Abbot Primate Benno Gut, a guest, and Prior Benedict Stolz of Dormition Abbey. The Abbot Primate assured Leo that he would conduct a visitation of the Dormition Abbey after the Abbots' Congress in the fall of 1966.

12

Storm Tossed and Engulfed

After a long and strenuous trip visiting relatives in Europe, meetings in Rome with Abbot Primate Benno Gut, Cardinal Bea, and the Secretariat for Christian Unity, and finally representing the Abbot Primate as Visitator for a group of nuns in Athens, Leo arrived back in Israel. Renat had departed for Europe. Brother Ambrose, no longer in residence at the Abbey, was enjoying studies at the Hebrew University. Of the three Weston monks, only brother David remained at the Abbey carrying out practical tasks for the community and for Abbot Leo.

Leo's first letter back to the community in Weston expressed his frustration, "Well, here I am, with problems and tasks coming over me like a Niagara. For a couple of days I also went to Tabgha. But at present I am staying in Jerusalem. I liked Tabgha very much."[1]

Abbot Leo was disappointed with Father Vincent's proposals to resolve the problems at the Abbey. His series of suggestions only further confused and bewildered Leo, who wrote in a dispirited vein a feast day letter to brother John:

> Often I wish I could have you here with me. As I promise you my prayers, I most earnestly ask you for yours. Life is not easy. So far, whenever I talked with Father Vincent, he did not much beyond rubbing in all the problems and difficulties I have always known to exist. With much pushing up of his sleeves he overwhelms me with many thoughts and suggestions, which he himself admits are not yet ordered in his own mind. You know how fertile his mind often is.... Well, I am at present very much in the dumps and quite discouraged. This is not a nice way of writing a name's day letter. But it is, you see, a sign of my confidence in you and love for you.[2]

Abbot Primate Benno Gut assured Leo that he would conduct a visitation of the Dormition Abbey after the Abbots' Congress in the fall of 1966. He also proposed to make official visitations at Mount Saviour and Weston Priory in the summer. Since his previous visitation at Weston in 1963 was a friendly and positive experience, the Weston community looked forward to his coming.

A Heartening Visitation at Weston Priory

A fatherly figure, Abbot Benno arrived in Weston in July of 1966, accompanied by his secretary and canon lawyer, Lambert Dunne, the monk of Morristown, New Jersey, who had assisted Leo in financial matters when he first became abbot of Dormition Abbey. The Weston visitation was a festive and joyful occasion and lacked the legalistic formality sometimes associated with such events. The Abbot Primate was relaxed and enjoyed a hamburger cookout and evening recreations with the brothers. He set a leisurely pace and interviewed each brother personally. The spirit of unity and contentment in the community impressed him, and he learned that at least three of the brothers were open to going to Israel if they were needed. In the official report of the visitation sent to Leo, Benno presented an encouraging picture:

> To report on this visitation is at the same time an easy task and at the same time a difficult one. It is easy because we find little or nothing to condemn or correct in the life of the monks; it is difficult because visitators are expected to find faults and discrepancies, to offer solutions and corrections. Yet we are happy to say that we are much pleased with this visitation and extremely gratified that we find little to criticize. We asked the Father Prior if there was something he thought should be stressed in this visitation. His only response was: tell the monks to continue being brothers....
>
> We are most edified to learn that everyone in the community is content with his life here at Weston. Little improvements here and there are desirable, but in general everyone is content.... It is equally edifying to hear of the love and respect the individuals have for the Rt. Rev. Father Abbot and the Father Prior. Perhaps the most outstanding characteristic of the members of the community, in our opinion, is the manifest charity toward all and the love of the brethren.

Benno commented on improvements that he noticed in the monastery buildings and expressed his appreciation for the Liturgy and monastic prayer of the community:

> We feel that your beautiful chapel is a miniature rustic gem, worthy of the house of the Lord, and that your plans for future building will carry out the theme of this characteristic Vermont architecture....

above: Abbot Leo with the Weston Priory community in 1966.
center: The renovated chapel at Weston. "…your beautiful chapel is a miniature rustic gem, worthy of the house of the Lord."
below: Eucharist on the lawn for an overflow congregation at Weston.

> The singing of Holy Mass and Divine Office are most edifying and, we are sure, an inspiration to all the people who can come here.... We sincerely beseech you to persevere in this.
>
> It has been inspiring to hear the laments of the community for the absence from Weston for their Father in Christ, the Abbot. All likewise understand why he is absent.... Every community that has two houses always has the problem of their relationships. You are all aware of the difficulties which at the present time seem insoluble....

He summed up his visit with praise and gratitude:

> In conclusion, there remains for us to say that we note progress in the spirit of the community in the last three years and see great hopes for the future. We feel that the love of Christ rules in this monastery.... From our hearts, we thank you for your genuine Benedictine hospitality, your extreme charity and priceless friendliness, and the magnificent spirit of cooperation in this visitation....[3]

With a genial sense of humor, he assured the community that Father Lambert would find the necessary canonical loopholes to justify the continued use of English in the monastic office that had been early implemented by the Weston community. He was also sympathetic to Abbot Leo's plans for the Dormition Abbey in Israel. At the completion of the visitation, the brothers celebrated with a joyful send-off for their Roman visitors.[4]

The Signs of the Times

The years 1965 to 1969 were excruciating for Leo. Even as he labored to heal the wounds of Christian-Jewish relationships, he witnessed the dissolution of his dream for a transformed Benedictine presence in the Holy Land. In the midst of such pain, his gratefulness and longing for the Weston community increased. The intensity of his anxiety is reflected in a letter written before the beginning of the Abbots' Congress in September of 1966:

> I fled to Tabgha for a few days. I simply could no longer sleep in Jerusalem. Even double doses of sleeping pills sometimes did not do the trick. Please, pray for me very hard. I am now doubly glad I stayed in Weston for a year after my operation. In Jerusalem, the healing process would have been badly impaired. How I feel the difference between Weston and Jerusalem! Weston kind of spoiled me. Here in Tabgha it is much better, thank God...[5]

He continued to offer affirmation, support, and advice as the Weston community reached beyond the need for survival, now seeking its identity as a monastic community rooted in Benedictine tradition and engaged in living dialog with North American culture.

In the waning years of the 1960s, the climate of change and experiment was alive in the United States. The Vatican Council, harkening to the spirit of John XXIII, issued the call to read the signs of the times. Leo repeatedly admonished the brothers in Weston to stay open to the Holy Spirit and to be mindful of the prophetic origins of monastic life. Often at a distance, separated by oceans and cultures, he resisted the temptation to control the innovative choices of the community that he referred to as "my baby." Rather than making authoritarian decisions from afar, his reaction to the many questions and suggestions addressed to him by brother John was usually, "Well, I would be a little cautious. But why not give it a try?" With a word of caution and confidence Leo made room for the brothers to grow in a consensual way of living a contemporary monastic life.

A Hard Press for Monastic Renewal

Urgent questions rising from Vatican II beset the Congress of Benedictine Abbots in the fall of 1966. Of special concern was a papal directive ordering monasteries to use only Latin for the monastic office and the liturgy. This decree sparked tension and division among the assembled abbots. Some favored change and renewal; others desired the status quo or the restoration of medieval forms.

The ruling on Latin for monasteries seemed to contradict the Council's call for a renewal of religious life based on the "return to the Sources"—the very project Leo and Damasus had undertaken long before in implementing their monastic vision. Damasus succinctly formulated the principle for their shared vision, "Renewal or rebirth of the monastic life is guided by two basic considerations, which in their actual operation really join each other and become indistinguishable. The first is to return to the sources, the second, to express the spirit of the beginnings in forms that speak to the present."[6]

In advance of the Congress, Abbot Gabriel Braso of Montserrat, the coordinator and secretary of the Abbots' Preparatory Commission for the Congress, invited Abbot Leo to deliver a paper entitled in English, "Monasteries of a Simpler Way of Life." In his text, Leo utilized the vocational material of Weston Priory and articles from the Priory Bulletin.

He prefaced his remarks calling attention to a rising tendency among monastic foundations of the times toward greater simplicity:

> There is no doubt that we live in a time when Christians, in fact, all people look to a more simple way of life as the Vatican Council reminds us. For us monks, there is a tendency to look more deeply into the Rule of Benedict to find the true norms for such a return. In practice, many Benedictine monasteries are looking toward such adaptations that take us away from a more mediaeval approach and return to the spirit of the Holy Rule.

Leo went on to enumerate characteristics of monasteries of a more simple observance:

> 1. Small number of monks. To preserve a family spirit in the community, the number should be small. Small numbers promote personal relations both among the members and with the Abbot as a true father and such can be sustained....
>
> 2. A simple oratory, not too large. Abbatial or quasi-Cathedral monastic churches are a thing of the past.... Adaptation for participation is called for in liturgical renewal of the times.
>
> 3. The monastery itself should be less institutional, not so large as to take away from simplicity and poverty.
>
> 4. The form of life and observance should be more simple. Priests and non-ordained monks should share equally in manual and spiritual work and activity. Full participation in the divine office and all chapter rights should be shared by all as in one family. Even strenuous manual labor is necessary for monastic life and pertains to a simple observance. All should cultivate spiritual and intellectual pursuits in accord with their capacities.

5. The Abbot is the father of the monastic family. He is consecrated (blessed) as a spiritual father, not a prelate. The use of episcopal insignia should be very restricted if not totally excluded.

6. Poverty is applicable to the simplicity of life in clothing, food, and manner of life—all without ostentation. It is also to be evident in the monastery buildings and oratory.

Leo could not resist adding a vulnerable personal note highlighting to the assembled Abbots that his observations were based on experience and not on theory:

> All the above are based, not on theory but rather on practice. These elements exist in monasteries today. One of the first has been the Abbey of Le Bouveret that has existed for forty years. There are also the Conventual priory in Cuernavaca, the Conventual priory of Mount Saviour, and the Claustral priory of St. Gabriel the Archangel in Weston, Vt.
>
> My personal experience has been with Weston and Mt. Saviour. Weston is 'my baby' and therefore better known by me. Thanks be to God I am able to say that Weston is flourishing in the number of vocations as well as in monastic spirit and its economy.[7]

He made his presentation to the divided assembly of abbots at an early session in Latin and reported with relief that it was 'generally well received.'

After heated discussions and unresolved issues, the Congress adjourned until the fall of 1967. The Abbot Primate, weary and discouraged from lengthy debates and some rancor among dissenting abbots, postponed the visitation that he had scheduled for the Dormition Abbey. Leo could not hide his disappointment. Stressing the urgency provoked by Luke Joerg's visit to the Abbey, he pressed for the visitation. At length, Abbot Benno agreed to delegate the responsibility to a visitator recommended by Abbot Leo.

The Dormition Abbey Visitation : A Revival of Hope

Prior Nicolaus Egender of Chevetogne Priory in Belgium agreed to conduct the visitation before Christmas in 1966. As prior of the monastic community created by Lambert Beauduin, Nicolaus was actively engaged in ecumenical work as well as monastic and liturgical renewal. He was in full agreement with Leo's designs for the Jerusalem abbey.[8]

True to his word, he undertook the daunting task of visitator to the Dormition Abbey before the end of the year. While he was of a cheerful and friendly disposition, he did not mince words either in personal or community encounters.

At the conclusion of the visitation, the Belgian visitator challenged the Dormition community in his official report in no uncertain terms, "Everybody should take it to heart, that he is responsible for the existence and development of this monastic community."

The official report of the Visitation left few stones unturned:

> Since the brothers (lay-brothers) have no longer an office in common, it would be desirable that they take part, as far as possible, in some of the offices of the choir.... I am surprised that the brothers do not receive the chalice. This is probably the only Benedictine monastery in which the brothers do not share in the chalice; this is the more unintelligible as we stand here at the place where the

> Lord Jesus has left to us the sacred meal under the form of bread and wine....

Prior Nicolaus forcefully called on the community to embrace a Pentecostal spirit:

> On the whole, it would be rewarding to emphasize the proper character of the local "Zion's piety": to live out of Pentecost, to come closer to the early Christian community, to emphasize the cult of prophets and apostles.... We are indeed here near to the event of Pentecost and the First Council. To live out the spirit of the unity of the Council is easier, and at the same time more important, here than elsewhere!

He did not hesitate to criticize the recalcitrance of the resistant members:

> Community spirit is lacking, and so is the will for renewal, which the Ecumenical Council has brought. Should this retarding diffidence with regard to the further development persist, the monastery would be left to die. Therefore, I wish to appeal urgently to behave constructively, to avoid everything that is destructive, as hasty criticism, idle talk, and discordant words.... All should help each other, and especially they should support Father Abbot, so that he may not lose courage, a thing which would affect the whole community.

The visitator underlined the need to internationalize the community:

> In every one of the reports of visitations since 1949, the international character of the monastery was emphasized. This should be done here again. It is not so much

> a question of being a German or an American monastery, but much more to have an openness and width, that it will be possible, that the monastery adapt itself more and more to the conditions prevailing in Israel. International character and embedding the monastery in Israel go hand in hand.... The community should find out whether something could be done in Hebrew....

Emphasizing monastic hospitality he took on the sensitive issue of the shrine mentality:

> Our Benedictine monasteries favor the hospitality of the gospel. To be able to receive our neighbors is a virtue for us, which we cultivate especially. How appropriate that is in the Holy Land! The pilgrims to Mount Zion have increased very much, Christians and Jews. This problem deserves special attention, so that the monks not be overburdened and depressed, but can also give a truly monastic witness to pilgrims.... Monasticism has here a special mission (to help in the encounter of Christianity with Judaism). May the whole community of the monastery on Zion, with the help of the guests, contribute to it.

He concluded with a resounding affirmation of Abbot Leo's efforts and vision:

> The only project which exists is the one which Father Abbot has realized with Weston for more than fifteen years...it should be continued with the help of everybody.... It would be, therefore, unintelligible and undignified, if now, in the midst of that difficult road, the community would not support it any longer.

Every point in the visitation report emphasized Leo's vision. Prior Nicolaus confirmed in detail Leo's initiatives over the previous twenty years. He insisted that the community required a newer, more open understanding of monastic life. He refuted the negative critique that Luke Joerg had set forth so offensively.

Leo was both relieved and grateful. Writing to brother John on the day after Christmas 1966, he said: "The visitation gives me ground under my feet. Many decisions had waited on it. I can now act more decisively." On January 31, 1967, his sixty-fifth birthday, he reported, "I have seldom felt better than I do at present. I go to class again three afternoons a week to learn Hebrew. Am really making progress now, I think."

For a time, it seemed that the chastened Dormition community took the visitation challenge to heart. Brother David was elected to the senior council of the community. Community meetings were introduced to stimulate responsibility and cooperation for carrying out Leo's objectives. In that context, Leo confidently resumed his place at meetings of the Secretariat for Christian Unity in Rome in April of 1967.

The Six-Day War of 1967

As was his custom, at the conclusion of the meetings in Rome, he visited relatives and friends in Germany. He then continued on to the United States. No sooner had he arrived in Weston, than the Six-Day War between Israel and the neighboring Arab States broke out. The Israelis drove the Egyptians from the Sinai Peninsula. The Syrians were dislodged from the Golan Heights, overlooking the Sea of Galilee and the little monastery at Tabgha.

Jordan held the Old City of Jerusalem, its walls just in the shadow of the towering Dormition Abbey Church. Yet again,

Dormition Abbey became a strategic outpost for the Israeli army. While heavy shelling rocked the buildings, the monks huddled together in the basement of the monastery. When the short war was over, Jerusalem was reunited as one city under Israeli rule. Though the abbey was now no longer under military occupation, the roof of the church had again been destroyed.

Leo hurriedly made plans to return from Weston to the Holy Land. This time he skipped the luxury of a crossing by ship; he left by plane as soon as possible. In Rome he conferred with Cardinal Dell'Acqua of the Secretariat of State, "who had talked to the Pope that very morning—and the Pope had asked about the Dormition." Abbot Leo then spoke with the Israeli Ambassador to Rome. Following that meeting, he communicated to Vatican officials Israel's "very generous plans for the Arabs and the refugees." In his letter to brother John, he appended a disquieting note: "To my surprise I have found in Rome that my name is mentioned as a candidate for Abbot Primate. But I have no idea how many would think of me. Oremus. But still, what should I do? A great question of conscience!"[9]

Once back in Israel, Leo entered into negotiations with Israeli officials for damages to the monastery property, estimated at a hundred thousand dollars. The work of restoration began at once but there were still further negotiations to be conducted with the German Association for the Holy Land in Cologne. Despite the added work, Leo was optimistic. "The changed situation is still like a dream to us," he reported. As a result of the Visitation and in spite of the trauma of the war, from all appearances, the community had recovered to good spirits.

A Sudden Reversal

With barely a hint that all was not well with the Dormition community, Abbot Leo announced that brother David would return to Weston for a year in the fall. On August 14, 1967, the day before the patronal feast of Dormition Abbey, brother John received a short note from Abbot Leo: "I am enclosing a letter to Father Damasus, which I hope will not upset you too much. But the time comes to face certain facts. Weston, with Thetford,[10] is more and more inviting as the place that I can retire to, resigning as Abbot."

In the enclosed letter he had written to his friend at Mount Saviour:

> Thank you for your lovely August 7 letter from Weston. I am so glad you find some pleasant and resting days in my "dear little baby".... The one thing in which it does not fulfill my hopes is to help re-vivify Dormition. It is not altogether Weston's fault. There are many reasons that contribute to it. But the fact remains, my original plan with Weston—to be also a backing and help for the Dormition—has failed....
>
> This poses for me personally a very grave question, and I come to you as a brother and friend, proven over many years—sometimes in fire. There is a real question of conscience for me. I am the Abbot of Dormition Abbey, and I cannot just quit that—at least not yet. So it seems to me there is in conscience no other alternative for me: I should as soon as possible make Weston an independent Priory. That would mean that my official relation with Weston will come to an end. I still hope that the time of my resignation may come fairly soon, and then I shall humbly ask Weston to receive me there, in the hope that

> I can spend most of my time in Thetford all by myself, but be at the disposal for help in Weston whenever needed....

He spelled out the full measure of his desolation in his concluding paragraphs:

> I am a spent and tired man. I cannot take great responsibilities, at least not before I've had prolonged rest and recollection. I am exhausted and empty.... As soon as something can be established (at the Dormition Abbey), I shall resign.... I am at the end of my rope. I don't know in and out anymore. That is a fact.
>
> Well, Dear Brother in Christ, please give me some good advice. Of course, we shall meet in Rome soon. So perhaps it can be done better by word of mouth.

He signed the letter to his onetime German compatriot, "Your somewhat melancholy old Kampf-Genosse" (comrade in battle). Abbot Leo's letter to brother John offered no explanation for the abrupt change from the optimism expressed in a letter to Weston on July 12 and what, a month later, seemed close to despair.

St. Peter's Square, Rome, September 1967. Leo followed by Nicolas Egender, fourth abbot of Dormition Abbey, and at far right, Damasus Winzen. "I am a spent and tired man. I am exhausted and empty."

13
Journey's End

In September, Leo was again in Rome for the 1967 resumption of the Abbots' Congress. Archabbot Rembert Weakland of Latrobe, Pennsylvania, was elected to succeed Abbot Primate Benno Gut. In the election, Leo received only one vote—probably that of his friend Damasus Winzen. With that, a last glimmer of hope harbored by Leo to save his project in the Holy Land vanished. In a photo of a group of abbots walking away from St. Peter's, Leo's face appears strained, drawn, and haggard. The only consolation he took from the Congress was the assurance from Abbot Primate Rembert that he would assist him in the difficult period of transition.

From the Congress, Abbot Leo traveled through Europe with brother David, eventually reaching Weston in the month of October. It was again a short visit for Leo: before Christmas he was back in Jerusalem, reporting:

> I am feeling well, but I miss all of you terribly. I truly hope that the Abbot Primate will come and help us come to a

> decision.... Father Vincent thinks I should not rush into resigning my office. He thinks it might be possible to arrange my being Abbot here and Prior in Weston, i.e., Conventual Prior of an independent Priory. We will find out whether that is possible....

The months of indecision were trying for Abbot Leo as well as for the Weston community. Father Vincent tried to enlist the aid of the Weston brothers to dissuade Abbot Leo from retiring. On a visit to the U.S. in January of 1968, he spent a few days at the Priory. His agenda generated strong reactions within the community that took the form of a deluge of letters to Abbot Leo. Summarizing the community's feeling in early February, brother John wrote:

> Father Vincent made it quite clear that he cannot see how you can retire very soon without a certain lack of faithfulness. He based this on the comparison of a captain on a sinking ship.... As far as we are concerned, no matter how much you may like the sea, and no matter how much you may enjoy sailing, you are not nor have you been the captain of a ship.... I do not think that it is an oversimplification...to see that you have given beyond the point of natural human endurance, and that, like all human beings, you do not have the forces you had when you were younger.

Replacing Father Vincent's functional image of a ship's captain with a familial figure, he continued:

> The father of a family is not expected to carry the weight of his grown sons; they allow him to age gracefully and to live his declining years with dignity and with tasks that are proportionate to his strength.

With an expression that Abbot Leo had employed while at Weston, brother John wrote for the community:

> It is true that monks of Dormition Abbey are your sons, but it simply is not true that they are helpless children.... We too are your sons, but we are not infants either.... We ask that you come to live quietly and peacefully among your young adult sons. Enrich them with your prayer, your presence, your love; read, write, and teach as you still can—these are magnificent gifts.

The strong emotions of the community at Weston are evident in the sardonic tone of the letter:

> We do not feel, as Father Vincent put it, that you can say to the monks at the Dormition, "Bye, bye, it was nice to know you fellas." Neither do we believe that you are the captain of a sinking ship and that you must go down with it. The community here is neither a bunch of sailors nor a brood of infants....
>
> Father Vincent said that the plan you proposed was simply impractical. He mentioned that he intended to submit the objective report of a sociologist to the Abbot Primate. He further stated that he was ready to take over the project of the organization of the Dormition, if the Primate put it in his hands. What Father Vincent expressed here left a great deal of foreboding in the brethren....

The letter concludes with a clear and resolute request:

> The second point I wanted to mention in this letter, Abbot Leo, is the reaffirmation of our desire for independence as a conventual priory. This was the unanimous desire of the chapter....[1]

One Heart, Three Compelling Loves

The decision to retire to Weston was painful and difficult to the extreme for Leo. His heart pulled him in three directions. His first love had been for the Abbey of Saint Joseph in Gerleve. There he had celebrated his monastic profession. Throughout his adult life the monks of Gerleve had supported him with their love. They welcomed him warmly on his frequent visits as he stopped for a respite from traveling between far-flung places where demanding duties engaged him. The monks of Gerleve, and especially his friend and classmate, Abbot Pius Buddenborg, entreated him to retire there and become a respected senior monk of that community.

His second love was Israel. When he first landed in the Holy Land, his experience was one of falling in love. His love for the land, for the people of Israel, for Jews everywhere, became the passion of his life.

> The first thing that comes to my mind, thinking of the time in Jerusalem is the awakening of my love for Israel, the Jewish people, Judaism. "Awakening" is perhaps not totally correct.... But in Israel this blossomed into a strong and lasting love. It was as if a smoldering flame had been blown into a roaring fire.

In his heart he embraced the language, the culture, and the faith of the Jewish people. Laurentius Klein, his successor as abbot of the Dormition, assured him that there would be a place for him in the community and that he would be free to continue his work there for the reconciliation of Jews and Christians.

His third love was the community of Weston Priory which, in the context of his monastic commitment and his passion for

Israel, Abbot Leo had conceived and brought to birth. In his own words, he nourished it "more as a mother than a founder." Deep in his heart, it was his baby. In the experience of many a parent, the grown-up child is not quite what was anticipated. Still, the bond of love is just as strong. Abbot Leo had that kind of bond with Weston Priory.

Leo's choice was both an act of love and of courage. Of his life he said on more than one occasion, "There is no going back." Gerleve, the home of his monastic beginnings had changed with time. He too had changed. Dormition Abbey had received all that he felt that he could give to the Jerusalem community. In Weston he could continue his 'mission of reconciliation' and move forward in the brotherhood that he brought into existence. At sixty-six years of age, he still chose to move forward.

Abbot Primate Rembert cautioned the Weston community that Leo's retirement there could present problems. He advised that it was difficult for someone who had held the position of superior for a protracted period to be integrated as an equal into the community where he had exercised that ministry and authority. The Weston community was mindful of the Primate's advice and still determined to welcome Abbot Leo permanently to their home as a brother.

On February 15, 1968, Leo replied to the entreaties of the Weston monks with a letter confirming his resolve to see to the independence of Weston Priory, to resign as abbot of the Dormition, and to retire to Weston as a member of the community.

For the first time, the abbot addressed the prior with the fraternal salutation, "Dear Father John, *my brother*." With that expression he welcomed the process of relinquishing the abbatial role and embracing more fully the fraternal relationships that were the distinguishing characteristic of the community at Weston Priory. In his letter he expressed the resolve to take leave of the Dormition Abbey and his long cherished hopes for renewed Benedictine life in Israel:

> On the whole, I should like to hear from you. My heart is a little heavy. But my resolve is firm.... Let us hope and pray. Father Vincent did not even try to change my mind, and I think he himself has abandoned the idea of myself being both Abbot of Dormition and Conventual Prior of Weston (which would never do).... He thinks of Father Jerome as the next abbot of Dormition. I cannot quite yet see him as such. But then the whole matter depends on what we plan with the Abbot Primate. Perhaps there will be no abbot anymore—what I rather think.

He made no effort to hide the pain in this transition and the simple faith that gave him the strength to bear it:

> This is all quite difficult. But God will help us through. As I have written in my letter to the Brothers, my canonical status will not be too important. Love will find the right way. And thank God, I feel so much one with you.
>
> Let us keep praying together. And I hope to be with you before too long....

He concluded on a plaintive note:

> You see, we must really-unselfishly-find what the will of God is. That is not always easy.... I know you helped me last fall in this dilemma. Keep doing so. Pray for me and give me a 'verbum bonum'....[2]

With the sympathetic and efficient assistance of Abbot Primate Rembert, Leo moved forward with the transition. His first urgent task was to secure the independence of Weston Priory. The Priory community qualified for the status of a conventual priory since it had the required number of solemnly professed members, was self-sufficient, and had a record of affirming visitations by the Abbots Primate. As a claustral Benedictine priory, Weston was subject to the monastic Chapter at Dormition Abbey. It was not difficult to obtain the approval of the community in Jerusalem for separation from the North American community.

The Abbot Primate then graciously accepted the fledgling community within his jurisdiction, retaining the privilege of the monastery to be independent of other Benedictine Congregations. Bishop Robert Joyce of Burlington wrote approvingly for the Priory's change of status.

In spring of 1968, Leo sailed to the U.S. to formalize Weston's status as an independent conventual priory.[3] After consultation with the professed monks and polling all the members of the Weston Community, Abbot Leo named brother John the first conventual prior of Weston on June 24. In this process, he exercised his canonical prerogative as founding abbot to name the first conventual prior of the monastery he founded.

In a simple ceremony with only the community present in the new chapter room of the monastery at Weston, Abbot Leo led brother John to the prior's chair in the circle of the brothers. Without fanfare and in the absence of external dignitaries, Weston Priory became an independent monastery within the Benedictine Confederation. Leo then departed once more to wind up affairs at the Dormition Abbey and in the Holy Land.

Looking back, as he descended Mount Zion for the last time as abbot, Leo could only see the stark fortress of the basilica and monastic edifice as immovable as on the day he arrived.

A Sad Farewell to Jerusalem

The continuity of the Dormition community was assured when Leo enlisted Abbot Laurentius Klein of Trier Abbey in Germany as his successor. Laurentius was young and vigorous. He was familiar with the ecumenical movement in Germany and had a particular interest in Christian-Jewish relations. A German, by birth and citizenship, he was acceptable to the members of the community in Jerusalem who clung to the hope that the Abbey would be received back into the Beuronese Congregation. Although that result did not come about, Laurentius did manage to draw vocations from Germany to reinforce the community in Israel.

The process of transition required Leo to remain officially at his post in Jerusalem until November 25, 1968. As he recalled it, he actually stayed on until early in the following year. To take leave of the Dormition community and Israel was a wrenching personal experience. He described his parting with a lay brother who had been a faithful companion since his arrival in Jerusalem in 1948:

> I had conceived a real love for Brother Jordan. I am afraid he never really knew that. I tried to show it with little signs, but I fear he did not quite recognize them. Only when we took final leave, before I left in 1969, it came out.... I told him that it was really difficult for me [to take leave from him] because I really had loved him. He looked at me almost in surprise. Then I gave him the kiss of peace. I went to the door of his room, looked back, went back to him and really kissed him. He then wept, still quite speechless and somewhat overtaken by surprise. Tears were also in my eyes. Then I left quickly....

With the exception of that single intimate exchange with a humble lay brother, the departure of Abbot Leo from the community of Dormition Abbey in 1969 had a solitary and lonesome quality redolent of his arrival twenty years earlier. There were no public expressions of gratitude for the endless toil, the heartaches, the physical, spiritual, and psychological investment of Leo's life and person in the work of recreating, sustaining, persuading, and encouraging the abandoned Dormition community. There was no suggestion of any intimate expression of appreciation on the part of the community for his exhausting efforts to bring the scattered members together, for his years of patient pleading not to give up hope, his exhortations to join in realizing a new type of monastic presence in an alien land. There was no display, no banquet, no community gathering to express emotion or sentiment for the spent man who was departing with a broken heart. There was no sign of recognition that he had poured out twenty years of his life so that the monastic community on Mount Zion might have life and become a living sign of love and reconciliation between Christians and the Jewish people. Looking back, as he descended Mount Zion for the last time as abbot, he could only see the stark fortress of the basilica and monastic edifice as immovable as on the day he arrived.

Almost single handedly, he had pulled the ravaged community from the ashes of death in the aftermath of the Israeli war of independence. The restoration of the monastery buildings, the establishment of relationships with the government of Israel, the reuniting of scattered members, the return of monastic prayer and observance to Mount Zion—all were the work of his hands and his heart. He could point to only one internal change in the Dormition community: "a less anti-Jewish attitude" among the members.

In Tabgha, the priceless ancient mosaics were secure. An unpretentious monastic dwelling blended into the gentle hill-side of the Mount of Beatitudes on the shore of the Sea of Galilee. It stood as a silent monument to Abbot Leo's sensitivity to the land and to the culture and spirituality of the people of Israel.

On a hike in the Weston forest with the Weston brothers. "I have at long last found what I have been looking for all my life: a true monastic life."

14

Setting Aside the Captain's Role

Abbot Leo embraced America and Weston as his final 'homeland' upon his retirement as Abbot of Jerusalem in December, 1968. The Weston Community welcomed him warmly amidst the January snows of the Vermont winter. He arrived at the Priory with mixed feelings. The sense of failure, rejection, and betrayal once again weighed him down as it had when he departed from Keyport and the United States in 1946:

> When I left the Dormition, I was in a deplorable mental condition. The fatigue and the disappointments told on me during the last months in Jerusalem. I tried to keep my mental balance by doing little things, taking short walks for example.... My main trouble was my almost constant insomnia. I simply could not sleep....

While he sensed the relief of the lifting of responsibilities he had carried as abbot for twenty years, he had to summon up all his courage and spiritual resources to ward off depression and a loss of meaning.

For his retirement years, Abbot Leo proposed a simple project: "to finally be able to live what I have taught." He devoted his remaining years to integrating himself as a monk and brother into the simple, contemporary monastic community of Weston Priory. It was with this hope that he began his years as a member of the community he had founded, "I feel deeply united with the brothers here, in a sense that is unique, almost inexpressible, but simply true—a fact of my life. I have at long last found what I have been looking for all my life: a true monastic life...."

In the complexity of changing times and Abbot Leo's weakened physical condition, to walk the road ahead would be difficult. His journey from father-abbot to brother monk was demanding and arduous, marked with both joy and pain—for Abbot Leo and the community.

A Culture in Crisis; Entering the Fray

The waning 1960s and early 1970s was an era of upheaval in both the church and society in the United States, a time of questioning, exploring, and experimentation—one that necessarily affected the Benedictine community at Weston.

The Abbots' Congress of 1967 had petitioned a period of experimentation with the celebration of the monastic office, and Rome approved. At Weston, the monks integrated the Eucharist into the monastic office of Vigils, celebrated at four o'clock in the morning. The monastic office and liturgy were chanted in the vernacular. A consensual mode of leadership was in the process of developing with the participation of all members in decision-making. Hierarchic roles were challenged. Creativity in work, forms of prayer, study, and education were encouraged.

The civil rights movement had ushered in a decade that brought to the fore issues long smoldering beneath the surface of societal life. War and peace, drugs, gender discrimination, and experimental communities were topics of discussion. The phenomenon of communes or experimental secular communities spread in the rural state of Vermont where the Priory is located.

Within the Priory community and in open meetings with the laity, questions were being raised on subjects ranging from spirituality, community, and human rights to the exercise of authority in the church.

It was in this atmosphere of dialog, change, and uncertainty that Abbot Leo returned to Weston to begin his fourteen-year journey as a brother. No longer engaged in theoretical discussions of monasticism, he was plunged into concrete exploration of the issues in everyday monastic living.

From early on in his monastic life, Leo had advocated equality in the distribution of work among the members of the community, whether ordained or not. He saw this as an area for his own further integration as a brother in the Weston community.

Up until this point, so much of his attention had been directed to the cultivation of his intellectual, cultural, and diplomatic skills that he had limited experience in other areas of work. At Weston, many of the occupations of the monastery—forestry, farm, and garden work—were physically demanding. The Priory crafts appealed to his artistic sense but seemed immediately beyond his capacities.

Despite his weakened condition, he threw himself into lending a hand at the monastery cider mill under the guidance of a much younger monk. He contributed an enthusiastic spirit and a sense of humor that did not fail to encourage the brothers with whom he was working. He took special delight in being able to work with his hands and to be in touch with nature. But this work was seasonal and not of long duration.

Equally appealing to him was the work in the laundry. He observed that he always "enjoyed making things white and clean," and he undertook that household task with equal zeal. When the physical strain of lifting heavy baskets of wet laundry became too much for him, he expressed interest in working in the bookbindery. Once again, under the supervision of a younger brother, he entered with zest into the adventure of exploring and learning a craft that was new to him. With a sense of accomplishment, he was pleased to create handmade journals for sale in the Priory Gift Shop.

However, it was in the context of the monastic chapter meetings that brother Leo entered the fray as a brother. In the daily assembly of the community, the brothers were accustomed to open and egalitarian discussion of matters important to their monastic life—the values and spirit embodied in the Rule of Benedict and their application to the growth and life of the community. Authority was exercised as a ministry rather than a power over others. All members of the community shared in decision-making. Taken out of the safe realm of abstraction and idealism, this process involved the honest expression of thought and feeling to make it a reality in North American life in the 1960s and 70s. Leo immersed himself into this process.

Some time before Leo's final move to Weston, the Weston monks had adopted the custom of addressing and referring to one another as "brother." This decision came out of reflection on the Rule of St. Benedict that says, "Let no one call another by the mere name." In this injunction they saw the call to affirm their relationship as brothers. It was a constant reminder of the bond that united the community. To them, the expression brother was neither a title nor a formality. Leo readily agreed to this new designation for himself as it corroborated his hope for integration into the community.

This change was not so easily accepted by some outside the Weston community, especially among those not in favor of innovations stemming from the Second Vatican Council. A Benedictine nun, who had been acquainted with brother Leo for many years, voiced her dismay in a letter of March 3, 1969, "[I]t is so obvious, without you saying a word, that you have been and are being crucified."

She spelled out her grievance in no uncertain terms:

> [T]hat the Monks of Weston can accept to have their founding Father as "just a member of the community" is to me outrageous!! You are not the superior?!!...the founding Father certainly by all the laws of human dignity and mature understanding is by his very calling from God as founding Father above any "superior" named by man. You appointed the prior, but your sons, if they are worthy sons of St. Benedict, can and should name you Father with ruling rights over the prior.

In a parting salvo she expressed doubt that the practice was in conformity with the Rule of St. Benedict, "Frankly, I don't know any of your sons or their spirit, but if this is an example of their spirit, then I can't quite believe your intense statement that 'they study the Rule and base their decisions on it.'"

On March 12, brother Leo responded, trying to assure the sister that she had misunderstood his situation, "What you write betrayed a gross misunderstanding.... My brothers here honour me very much as the founding father." Once again he groped for an illustration to make his point:

> There is a beautiful relationship in mutual understanding. I may compare it to the following situation: In some (titled) families of Germany there prevails a very patriarchal concept. When the head of the family thinks it is time to let his married son take over...he commits it to him. Of course, he remains the "patriarch" of the family. But the real administration of the family...is given to his son, whom he loves, who continues and carries on the family tradition. In about the same way, I have entrusted this, my foundation, to my beloved son John, in whom I have full confidence and who has to me a son-father relationship....
>
> But it is entirely wrong to say that I am "crucified," and if, then certainly not by anyone here in Weston. I haven't been as happy as I am now in a long time. I have finally found what I have been looking for all my life.

He unassumingly acknowledged that he still had a contribution to make as an elder in the community:

> I feel that my task remains. I inspire the community with things that only I can give, I think: Experience in monastic life, knowledge of the Holy Rule, of tradition. But to lead a young community into the future, I feel that younger men, like Father John, who has a true charisma, are called by God. I think it is wisdom to acknowledge one's limitations....

Troubled by Leo's reply, his perceptive if somewhat bitter, correspondent delighted to underscore a contradiction she found in his self-defense:

> I was sorry to read that you classify yourself as a brother among brothers, but was delighted that in the same letter you could contradict yourself by saying that Fr. John and you have a true son-father relationship.

> You say, "I haven't been as happy as I am now in a long time." Oh, my Father, if only your face and eyes had said that I would believe you and be happier about you.... I am happy that you can say that your sons at Weston do not participate in your crucifixion.
>
> However, you make Weston sound so ideally a Paradise that you are right in saying I don't quite believe it....

Frustrated by the failure in communication, brother Leo requested a termination of the correspondence, "Thank you for your letter of Laetare Sunday. But let us herewith close the exchange <u>in writing</u> and hope for a chance to talk about those matters by word of mouth (in a dialogue and not in a one-sided lecture)...."

A North American Monastery

Early on, Leo had initiated the idea of embedding the monastic life in the soil and the culture in which the community found itself. Practically, he had thought of this process taking place in Israel. He had visualized his new community in dialog with the language, the culture, the values, and institutions of that foreign land. With the collapse of his dream for the Dormition Abbey, he was denied the opportunity to experience that insight in practice in the Holy Land.

As he sat in the midst of his North American brothers in the Weston community, he sensed the enormity of that task. The community had taken his teaching to heart and monastic life was in fruitful if contentious dialog with North American culture and values. The closing question of the nun who challenged him in her letter of Laetare Sunday in 1969 touched on the issue:

> By the way, after much thinking, I've decided that I am a Benedictine American, not an American Benedictine. There is quite a difference. What do you think?

In the nitty-gritty of heated discussion over monastic practices, exercise of authority, liturgical celebrations, protest and witness on behalf of human rights, and the balance of contemplative life and prayer, the neat distinctions of either-or, black or white, Benedictine American or American Benedictine quickly blurred. True to one of the positive values in North American culture, the Weston community had chosen the way of consensus in decision-making. Each voice had an equal hearing. All opinions were to be respected. It was a tedious, demanding, and often emotional process—and not always ready with an either-or answer.

The voice of moderation and experience could be heard alongside the voice of exploration, risk, adventure, and youthfulness. At times, the impetuosity and daring of the young came into conflict with the caution and fears of the elder. All of this took place with an exchange of feeling that was new to brother Leo. That no one voice would prevail in the end, but that consensus would be achieved, was the fruit of hard work and fidelity—a willingness to stay together in the face of contradiction and disagreement.

At daily chapter meetings, the brothers discussed matters critical to their monastic life and identity: commitment to Benedictine stability, obedience, and conversatio morum (variously understood as "conversation about the things that matter" or simply, "sharing monastic life"). Brother Leo described his feelings in those heated exchanges in his "Reminiscences":

> My life in Weston has not been without problems, nor without pain and heartache. Sometimes I feel as if the

> younger Weston brothers and I operate on different wavelengths. After all, we are so different, not only in age (although fortunately we've never experienced a real "generation gap"), but also in upbringing.

He made every effort to enter the reality of the developing North American Benedictine community: "On both sides, however, the brothers and I are constantly trying to tune in to one another. That is how it should be. It is something of the challenge of my life in Weston."

Leo's love for Jewish spirituality was a sustaining factor in this difficult period of his life. His interaction with Jewish scholars and friends had a profound impact on his own spirituality. Papers found in his files after his death give ample evidence of these influences. One article, liberally marked and showing signs of repeated use, is entitled "After Itzik: Toward a Theology of Jewish Spirituality." The writer is Rabbi Arthur Green. A passage brother Leo found significant illuminates his life experience and his role in the community at this time:

> We see spiritual ebb and flow, moments of absence and moments of presence, as central to the human religious situation. Our desire is neither to deny nor to escape it, but rather to learn to live as religious human beings in our moments of spiritual ebb. What else can be done with the moment of disbelief in our cycle?

This spirituality, with its emphasis on the natural rhythms of the world and nature and with reference to the Spirit, strengthened his resolve to grow in engagement with the community he had founded:

> If we are not to deny the cycle altogether, must we allow ourselves to ever be torn apart by shallow cynicisms that

we should like to have transcended long ago? Can there be spiritual growth if there has to be constant return to such a coarse moment of ebb? Most basically: in viewing the ebb and flow of the Spirit's presence within us, can we step beyond conflict and see the thing as rhythm, as a rhythmic movement that brings some *excitement* to the spiritual life and inspiration to the "downs" as well as the "ups"?[1]

A Near-Death Experience

Construction of the monastery buildings at Weston were largely completed by the time brother Leo arrived in 1968. Large numbers of laity were increasingly attracted to the celebration of the liturgy at the monastery. Responding to the interests expressed by the expanding group of friends, the Weston community hosted a loosely organized group called Concerned Catholics of Vermont. Meeting weekly at the Priory after the Sunday Eucharist, the group addressed contemporary questions facing the Church: youth and drugs, the election of a bishop, the diocesan newspaper, politicians and religion, peace and war.

Mindful of his own pioneering interest in promoting lay-participation in the church with the publication of *A Layman's Theology* in the 1930s, brother Leo actively engaged in the discussions and activities of this new venture of the community.

Positions expressed by the group, which included all the brothers of the Priory community, ranged from radical to conservative. Brother Leo's voice was one of diplomacy and moderation. He related to all the members with warmth and dignity and did not hesitate to affix his name with the prestige of his previous title as abbot to statements issued by the organization. His presence and contribution lent an air of respectability and credibility to the youthful association.

But the pace of life, conflict, and change at Weston took its toll on brother Leo, who had hardly recovered from the ordeal of his departure from Israel. He was intent on being involved in all aspects of the communal life. By 1970, it became evident that he needed respite from the day-to-day stress of life with brothers much younger than himself. The opportunity presented itself with an invitation to attend the celebration of his brother Hans's 25th anniversary as Bishop of Hamburg in Germany. He headed for Germany by plane in mid-June. The flight was delayed and the trip was exhausting.

The time in Germany did not have its desired effect. Instead of reviving brother Leo's spirit, he found the travel and the time away to be a further drain on his energy. In the two letters he wrote to the brothers from Germany, he made a weak attempt at levity and humor. He characterized the anniversary celebrations as drawn out and expressed no joy at seeing the few remaining members of his German family. In place of his usual affectionate expression in signing his letters, he wrote simply, "always and 'till soon". He returned to Weston in an out-of-character lethargic spirit.

Personal sorrow and loss soon added to brother Leo's melancholy. Damasus Winzen, founder of Mt. Saviour Monastery in Elmira, New York, Leo's friend and confidant since their student days at Sant'Anselmo, suffered a heart attack and died on June 26, 1971. All the Weston community of brothers accompanied brother Leo to Mt. Saviour to take part in the funeral of this monk so significant and influential in Leo's monastic journey. When the community then returned to Weston, the brothers were engaged in the demanding work of recording their second album of liturgical music, *Wherever You Go*.

With Dorothea and Dr. Leon Smith in Weston. "Leon and Dorothea are to me like brother and sister. In them I have found my family in America, a home away from home."

Brother Leo, in his turn, began to experience heart problems within a few months after the death of his friend, Father Damasus. On Christmas day, 1971, he suffered a mild angina attack that took him to the neighboring Springfield Hospital. He was cautioned by the doctor to be careful and to take extra rest. The brothers suggested that a few weeks of relaxed time with his friends Dr. Leon and Dorothea Smith in Clifton, New Jersey, might be the best environment for him.

January of 1972 found Leo with his "adopted brother and sister" at 69 Edgewood Avenue in Clifton. On January 6, shortly after his arrival, he had his first serious heart attack and was rushed by Dr. Smith to St. Mary's Hospital and placed in intensive care. He seemed to be recovering quickly and was removed from the ICU only to suffer a severe cardiac infarct on January 10. A group of brothers hurried from Weston to his bedside.

The experience of his heart attack was still vivid in his mind when brother Leo began writing his "Reminiscences" in 1973:

> One event has particularly stuck in my mind. It was on the day of the heart infarct. I was back in Intensive Care and sleeping, heavily drugged, after supper. Suddenly I felt rather than saw that there was someone standing at my bed.... Then I opened my eyes fully and saw Brother John. It made me very happy, indeed.

The impact of Leo's bout with death was crucial in his journey of faith for the remaining years of his life.

> You may ask, Did you think of death? Yes and no. It is hard to tell. When the attack actually happens you are just a bundle of pain and nausea, ready to spit your life out. But I did think of death, in a strangely matter-of-fact way—without fear, really.

In prayer and in the struggle with depression, he had prepared himself for the crucial moment of facing his own death:

> Two things had prepared me months before the attack. First, a conviction that life after death and resurrection are such mysterious things that only the last, and probably supreme, act of faith can help there. No imagination, no conceptual thought, just blind trust and faith. Secondly, I had struggled with myself during those months, fighting through a depressing conviction of having done nothing worthwhile in life, to the quiet and relaxed acceptance of being ready to stand before my eternal judge with empty hands, but full of confidence in surrendering into his loving hands. "Here I am, take me as I am." In that, a true awareness of being redeemed grew lively—being redeemed by Christ who takes our life as he took water in Cana and changed it into wine. So he will change our poor lives into something greater and eternal. And so I am ready to wait for that greater future which God has in store for me. *Nunc dimittis....*

Leo remained in New Jersey with the Smiths for a period of convalescence. Under Leon's watchful eye and Dorothea's attentive care, he made a successful recovery from his near-death ordeal. When he rejoined the Weston community in the late spring of 1972, he had an air of serenity. Gradually, he entered again into the rhythm of monastic life. Among the many get-well wishes that contributed to the revival of his spirit was a warm letter from his treasured friend, Rabbi Abraham Heschel, who wrote from Los Angeles, "It would be wonderful to meet you again. I hope soon." At the same time his correspondent assured him, "I pray with all my heart for your complete and speedy recovery."

With the release of the musical recordings *Locusts and Wild Honey* and *Wherever You Go* in 1971 and 1972, Weston Priory became widely known in the English-speaking world.

15

A New Adventure: Time to Mend

As early as the late 1960s, Weston Priory had begun to receive significant attention in the press for both its contemporary liturgies and its outspoken stands on social issues. With the release of the record albums *Locusts and Wild Honey* and *Wherever You Go* in 1971 and 1972, the Priory became widely known in the English-speaking world. Up to that time, invitations from parishes and religious communities for workshops on liturgy and music had been numerous; now they poured in. Increased involvement with the "outside world" disturbed the more tranquil cycle and spirit of monastic observance that had marked the first decades of the Priory. Working through many heated discussions, the brothers agreed to respond to several of the requests—from parishes in the Vermont diocese. Brother Leo willingly took part in this period of transition and was deeply moved when the community honored him in the dedication of its third recording *Listen*.

When the community was invited to accompany a workshop at the Franciscan Renewal Center in Scottsdale, Arizona, in June 1972, brother Leo, inveterate traveler, was ready to go.

With the other Weston brothers, he enjoyed the opportunity to meet new friends and liturgical experts at the workshop and, no less, the warm western welcome extended by the Retreat Center. On their arrival at the Phoenix airport, the brothers heard the lively music of a mariachi band. Looking around to see what celebrity was being greeted, they discovered it was all part of the festivities in their honor.

From Phoenix, the community went to Christ in the Desert Monastery in Abiquiu, New Mexico, then on to the Anglican monastery of St. Gregory in Three Rivers, Michigan. Brother Leo reveled in the brothers' first extended journey beyond the New England states. It seemed that his passion for travel had been caught by the Weston community. The intricate weaving of monastic stability with modern mobility was underway.

Taking a Happy Initiative

In quiet time back at Weston, brother Leo recalled his departure from Israel and was struck by how abruptly he left the people and the land he had come to love so deeply. While the period of his leave-taking—seemingly endless—had been agonizing for him, he now realized how sudden, unexplained, and painful it must have been for those left behind. For twenty years he'd kindled friendships with the Jewish people he met in civic, social, and religious settings. There were also the colleagues of different Christian churches who had so valued his presence and contribution to dialogue. He had labored with all those people, and they with him. In his despondency at the time of his departure, he was hardly able to say goodbye, much less to help them understand why he must leave. The only farewell he remembered was the profoundly sad one he exchanged with brother Jordan, who had remained loyal to him throughout his years as abbot.

He confided to the Weston brothers his desire to return to Israel to participate in his own healing as well as that of his friends. The trip would also offer the opportunity to reassure his monastic brothers in Gerleve and his family in Germany that all was well with him. He feared that his visit the previous year, when his health and spirit were at a low ebb, left a worrisome impression that might well have given them concern for his well-being. He wanted them to know first-hand that he was now happy and in good health.

All concurred with brother Leo's initiative to embark on a journey to heal the wounds of his heart. He began planning for his 1973 visit to Israel and Germany. Anticipating the proposed trip, he entered enthusiastically into the busy life of the Weston community for the rest of the year.

With fresh energy, he began the next year with a flight to Washington, D.C., in January for his first meeting with the Israel Study Group,[1] an association of Christian theologians of all denominations who had a special interest in Israel and Judaism. As a member of this group that held annual meetings in a variety of locations in the Northeast, he contributed the unique perspective of his lived experience of twenty years as abbot in Jerusalem. The intellectual stimulation and warm friendships enjoyed among the members expanded his interests and sustained his spirit as he continued to deepen his knowledge and love for Israel and Judaism even in his elder years.

No sooner had he returned to Weston from Washington, than a friend who'd retired to Miami urged him to take a few days of relaxation in Florida. From there he went on to Nassau to spend a few months with the Benedictine community there. The hospitality of the monks in the Bahamas included visits to their missions in the out-islands as well as opportunities for brother Leo's favorite sport, sailing. He took special pleasure in getting up close to the big ships at the harbor docks. Time passed quickly, and he returned to Weston at the beginning of March.

Now he was ready for what would be an emotional return to Israel. He set out from Weston on April 25, 1973, and was not back in Vermont before the end of July. In contrast to his last European trip, brother Leo began this voyage in an animated spirit. "The flight went perfectly," he reported. "My brother [Bishop Johannes], Angela Meiners, Mr. Hufschmidt, the [bishop's] chaplain and the driver—and to my surprise my niece from South Africa—were at the airport.... That niece of mine...is a very nice girl and all of us had a lot of fun."[2]

The next leg of the journey to Israel also went easily. Even security measures did not disturb brother Leo's elated spirit:

> I had to pass through some stringent security measures at the El-Al office. The baggage was searched, I was frisked, etc. But all was done very courteously.... Abbot Laurence and Mr. Ilsar were at the airport. Everything went very smoothly and quickly.

Leo's first impressions on arriving at the Dormition Abbey were positive. He was upbeat:

> Here everybody received me very charitably. Abbot Laurence yielded to me my old rooms. Many things are entirely unchanged, others are changed...
>
> I am feeling well.... My feelings are quite mixed. Partly very joyful and partly somewhat—well—strange. It is so strange to be in my old rooms and look out of the window on the familiar scene. Many people are glad to see me, that is sure, and I shall be glad to see them....

Within a few days he was in Tabgha in the small monastery on the shore of the Sea of Galilee, his favorite spot in all of Israel. Briefly commenting from there on the military situation he wrote, "I did not go to the military parade [in Jerusalem on Independence Day], but saw some of it from the roof of the Dormition. This [Tabgha] is a very secure place. People here have never felt more secure."

By the middle of May, brother Leo was ecstatic about his reception in Israel:

> So far, my stay is almost triumphal. I am greeted everywhere with great love and joy.... At a big symposium of the Interfaith Committee Research Fraternity...the chair was yielded to me in the morning, and I was greeted with great cheer. Many old friends were there, Jewish and Christian, among them Dr. [Zvi] Werblosky [of the Hebrew University], who wants to be remembered to you.[3]

His schedule became increasingly full. Following the Symposium, he called on the Latin Patriarch Beltritti who "greeted me cordially." Then he was driven to the Ecumenical Institute of Tantur, "the Large Ecumenical Institute. A tremendous thing, interesting, scholarly, but an 'Institution'" where he "met some of the scholars, among them Professor Cullman." There followed visits to friends and acquaintances. He concluded his letter with affectionate words, "Don't forget me. Always your Bro. Leo"

The extended time in Israel without special responsibilities afforded brother Leo the opportunity to get to places he was not able to visit when he was abbot of the Dormition. Abbot Laurence, Weston brother Ambrose, or one of the Dormition monks accompanied him on these jaunts. He remarked in a letter describing his travels around the country, "The days go by very fast and are quite filled. But I also put some days of rest in, in between."

In June, toward the end of his stay, he spent some days at Ulpan Akiva in Natanya and renewed his friendship with the directress, Shulamith Katz Nelson. After a visit with another friend on the West Bank, he made a rare reference to the political situation, mentioning the announcement of demonstrations to take place on the anniversary of the Six-Day War. "In the Old City where I took a walk just now, there was little to see, except somewhat strengthened security patrols." The next day he was scheduled to meet with Jerusalem mayor Teddy Kollek ("he answered the telephone himself and asked me to come...").[4]

His former colleagues in ecumenism honored Leo at a fraternal reception:

> Next Tuesday, there will be a reception for me here sponsored by the Dormition and the Theological Ecumenical Research Fraternity: about forty are invited. That will give me a chance to see many people whom I cannot visit. It is impossible to visit all the friends.

In his last two letters to the Weston Community from Jerusalem, brother Leo described a confusion of expectations over his impending departure:

> There seems to have been some little misunderstanding. I myself really never seriously considered staying much longer. I had always said July 2nd is the very last date of my departure. Now it is fixed for June 28. When I arrived and said that to Abbot Laurence, he said, "What? I thought you came for at least six months!" And he keeps saying, "It is much too short." But I really don't feel I should stay longer. There comes a moment when one

> feels "mission accomplished," even if a thousand little things remain which still could be done.[5]

As he summed up his visit to Ulpan Akiva, he left an opening for the future:

> I still had some very fine and inspiring days. I was a few days in Ulpan Akiva in Natania and was most cordially received.... I attended a few classes and many were surprised how much Hebrew I could talk.... Shulamith wanted me to stay for a two-month course—free. But I couldn't do that. Maybe I'll be back here some day. I feel how deep I have sunk my roots in Israel. Cannot get away from it. 'Till soon.
>
> Lovingly,
> Bro. Leo

Equally joyous receptions awaited brother Leo in Germany. The community at Gerleve and his relatives greeted him warmly. Overall, the trip was refreshing for his body and healing for his spirit. He returned to Weston renewed. As he had written from Jerusalem, he sensed that his mission was accomplished. Though the sense of failure over his Holy Land project would never be totally eradicated, the gestures of friendship and heartfelt appreciation went far to heal the wounds of the past. This Jerusalem visit was wholly the reverse of his experience at the end of his term as abbot.

Recognition, Friendship, and Reconciliation

Brother Leo's spirits lifted further the same year when Seton Hall University honored him with a doctorate. The degree was awarded in recognition of his contributions to Christian-Jewish

above: Brother Leo, an enthusiastic participant in dialogue. Some Israel Study Group members: *below left:* Rufus Cornelson and brother Leo, at a 1980 meeting. *below right:* Rev. Dr. William Harter, brother Leo, and Rev. Dr. Robert Everett, at a 1981 meeting. *Photos courtesy of Dr. Alice Eckhardt*

relations and in particular for his work on the conciliar document *Nostra Aetate*. This was the third honorary degree he received for his inter-faith work. Previously, he had been honored by the University of Vermont in 1963 and St. Michael's College in 1971.

At every opportunity, brother Leo invited his Jewish friends into the circle of his brothers at the Priory. On one occasion in 1974, two affable young rabbis from the Boston area traveled to Weston to see brother Leo and to meet with the community. Their generous sharing of their learning and faith made an enduring impression on the Weston brothers. Some thirty years later, the two visitors recalled their memories of brother Leo.

When asked to share his memories of Leo, Rabbi Arthur Green, former president of the Reconstructionist Rabbinical College in Philadelphia and now Lown Professor of Jewish Thought at Brandeis University, had this to say:

> I was touched to find in Abbot Leo a real fellow-lover of Jerusalem and also a true friend of Israel and the Jewish people. That was very clear in all our conversations. Because of it, we did not have to engage in the usual pussy-footing ('Is he really an anti-Semite? 'Is he really anti-Catholic?') that so often creates obstacles before real dialogue of the heart.... There is only the glow of having known him to be a true religious spirit and a warm friend."

Rabbi Green's companion on that trip to Weston was Rabbi Zalmon Schachter-Shalomi, now at the Naropa Institute in Boulder, Colorado, and widely recognized as the primary inspiration behind the Jewish Renewal movement. In 2003, Reb Zalman discussed their visit to the Priory in a letter to brother John:

> I had heard warm things about Dom Leo, having in 1959 visited the Abbey of the Dormition in Jerusalem. (This was before the rest of Jerusalem was accessible to us.) I was impressed then and had chanted some psalms in the rotunda. When you published your 1972 recording *Wherever You Go,* I was greatly moved by the intent and content of your singing, so I wanted to visit and worship with you.
>
> You did some fine pottery, and the sacred vessels were of humble earthenware. Art and I stood below the altar steps and "assisted" in the concelebrated Mass as you stood in an open circle which we below completed. If I remember correctly, the bread to be consecrated was whole wheat and scored like a cross. At the point when it was broken, Dom Leo looked at each person as he broke his piece of bread and, as he came to our place, he looked at us also and with a loving nod broke some for us. Then the plate was passed—counter-clockwise—and came to the edge, and the prior (Was it you?) took it, bypassed us, and passed to the person on the altar to the right of me to complete the communion circle. I saw a moment of sadness on Dom Leo's face when that happened, and when we smiled at him with both understanding and relief that we were not placed in a predicament, his face relaxed and he smiled back. More than any words we shared, this was our hearts' communion.

With exquisite sensitivity for brother Leo's Christian faith, Reb Zalman closed his letter with this touching prayer, "May he enjoy the love and light in which his Savior holds him." Personal friendships like these fed his affection for Israel and the Jewish people.

Watching and Waving in Israel

His prolonged stay in Israel that year only fueled brother Leo's desire for closer contact with his Jewish friends. When Shulamith Katz Nelson, directress of Ulpan Akiva, reiterated her invitation to continue his studies in Hebrew there, he found it hard to resist. And when Abbot Laurence of the Dormition requested that he come to conduct the annual retreats for the community at both the Abbey and Tabgha, he was fully persuaded to return.

With the encouragement of the Priory community, brother Leo set out for Israel once again in April 1974. This time he planned to follow a seven-week course in Hebrew at the Ulpan and to offer spiritual support to the community he had served as abbot for so many years. With pleasant memories of his visit the previous year, he had no misgivings as he boarded the ship in New York harbor.

His first auspicious letter from Israel reported an unexpected link between the Ulpan and the Priory. The brothers, who had recently introduced communal folk dancing into their liturgical prayer, did one dance that originated in Israel and was sung to Hebrew words. Brother Leo knew that the brothers were intent on finding the translation. In May he wrote:

> How happy I was when, in a dancing class here (myself watching and "waving"), I suddenly heard "Ma Navu"! I'll soon have the exact text in both Hebrew and English. It is, on the whole, in Isaiah: "How lovely are the feet of those who bring glad tidings to Zion."

When the brothers began their folk dancing at Weston, brother Leo had excused himself from the exercise because it was too much exertion for his weakened heart. Playfully, the community reminded him of the Shaker tradition in which elders unable to do the dance steps were invited to watch and wave from the sidelines to indicate their participation. (This explains Leo's parenthetical note.)

The diversity of the Ulpan—especially the presence of Arab youth studying Hebrew and joining in the communal experience—was a marvel to Leo.

> There are ten Arabs (mostly from Gaza) in the Ulpan. In my class there are two Arabs, one from Hebron (a Moslem), one from Bethlehem...one boy from London (a rather crazy hippy, but otherwise pleasant and cheerful, only often disturbing the class)...two from Berlin (one of them originally Protestant but the whole family was converted to Judaism), one girl from Argentina, one from Paraguay, one from Toronto, one from Switzerland, one from Philadelphia, one from Paris, one from Morocco....[6]

He concluded his first letter with a non-committal observation, "They want me to talk on television," along with his fond signature, "Always with love, Bro. Leo *(Arieh)*." Ten days later, he mentioned that on the previous Sunday he had "preached, first a few words in Hebrew" during a mass for Hebrew-speaking Christians in Jaffa. Always reticent about taking part in public demonstrations, he went on to describe his unusual participation in a public protest:

> Have you heard about it? A most despicable act of murder of innocent children. And they made it clear that they want the State of Israel destroyed! I went with the whole Ulpan to the funeral in Safad yesterday. It turned out to be a most emotional demonstration of about ten thousand people. I came back early last night, but I wanted to give a witness.[7]

In the same letter he continued in a lighter vein:

> Studies go quite well. I am surprised how elastic my old brain still is. I am one of the better ones in our class, although about forty years older than most of them. I hope to get more fluency in speaking these last weeks. After that, the retreats.

Writing his last letter from the Ulpan, brother Leo announced that the school graduation would be on June 14. But first there were the final exams. "I am now getting just a little tired. It is quite strenuous. But it will be over soon."

At the same time, he was anxious about an anticipated request by Abbot Laurence and the Dormition community. "When, on June 16, the retreat on Mt. Zion begins, there is a possibility that I shall be asked for something. While I am at present quite resolved to deny any request, I would appreciate your reaction...." As he laid out the expected request, Leo described the situation at the Dormition:

> The *inner* condition of the Abbey is not good. Outwardly—programme of studies, etc.,—goes very well. But there is no unity in the community.... Now it is possible that they—and that includes Abbot Laurentius—will ask me to act as novice master at least for a time (say until September). They need something of our Weston spirit of mutual cooperation and consensus. It would be a delicate and difficult job and, as I said, I am not inclined to accept it.[8]

The Weston brothers posed no objection to brother Leo's further involvement with the Dormition community, but cautioned him to be mindful of his physical condition:

> Our first concern is that your own health not be jeopardized...it would be important for both you and the

> community there to consider how much the schedule, the change in climate, and the tensions that are necessarily involved in that task would affect your health....
>
> Our next concern is for the community at the Dormition. We do feel that you have something of value to offer to them....
>
> If you feel that it's reasonably safe from a health point of view and that there would be a proportionate good for the community there, and that you would somehow enjoy the longer stay, I don't see any obstacle from here. We all do have a care and love for the Dormition, and if a gift from the community could be given to them, we would be happy.[9]

Before he concluded the retreat with the community at the Dormition, brother Leo communicated his decision to brother John, "Your reaction and that of the brothers were very helpful.... I am rather inclined to come back to Weston soon. I do not think I can accept the offer here."

He returned to Weston with a sense of peaceful resolution and closure to a substantial commitment in his life. His two proximate voyages to the Holy Land assured him that the friendships he had established there were lasting. Abundant appreciation had been expressed for his tireless efforts on behalf of Israel and his labors in ecumenism. The Dormition Abbey community had affirmed its respect for him and its gratitude for his contributions as abbot. His work in the Holy Land was indeed finished.

"Open your heart, and keep it open, to what comes to you from all your brothers. You come to the monastery in order to grow. You cannot grow unless you agree to be challenged by your brothers."
Bullaty-Lomeo photo

16

Wisdom Shared: Still Learning

In the final decade of his life, brother Leo still faced the daunting task of integrating three major preoccupations in his life project: his choice to enter fully as a brother into the Weston community, his passionate desire for Christian-Jewish reconciliation, and his concerns for Dormition Abbey.

At first, after his retirement as abbot, brother Leo had been inclined to be protective of the young Weston community, much as a mother might defend her growing child. A 1973 letter to an old friend who expressed dismay at the contemporary music adopted for liturgy by the community, as portrayed the year before in a *Vermont Life* article, exemplifies his spirit at that time. He mounted a feisty defense of the practices of the community:

> [W]hat utterly disappoints me is that you indulge in such a harsh judgment without evidently knowing the facts at all. Let me mention only one example: We do not have "a few guitar strummers." First of all, our two guitars are never strummed. They are played, by two artists, in a

> most beautiful way, almost like harps, suggesting the harps King David used to accompany his psalmody. They are certainly much better suited to accompany worshipful song than a blaring baroque organ.
>
> If you knew St. Benedict and the Benedictine Rule well, you would know that Benedict was a link in the uninterrupted chain of monastic evolution pushing ahead in his time from an older tradition that he could no longer follow. We do consider the monastic life—in the spirit of St. Benedict—not a petrified fossil but a living thing, which, like any living thing, grows and develops, changing some outside appearance while retaining the identity of the essence....[1]

At the same time, brother Leo's prevailing attitude was open and affirming within the community. His "Reflections on the Rule of Benedict," written during that period, reveal a deepening personal appreciation for the monastic life that he shared with the Weston brothers. The wisdom of his early teaching as abbot is blended here with the experience of his five years living as a brother among brothers:

> Listen, brother. Open your heart, and keep it open, to what comes to you from all your brothers. You come to the monastery in order to grow. You cannot grow unless you agree to be challenged by your brothers. Obedience to God is essentially obedience (that is, listening and taking to heart) to everything that life will bring, in a special way through your brothers, but also through other circumstances in your life. God speaks to you by these means.

Consistent with his earliest insights, he affirmed Benedictine spirituality as a "matter of the heart":

> Open your *heart*. Your happiness as a monk, your progress toward becoming a whole human being, is a matter of the *heart*. It is not so much a matter of an intellectual decision of your will (though that is also involved), as it is a matter of your heart. Be a monk with both heart and soul. Be a loving, feeling person. The heart is the living core of a person....

Giving prayer primacy in monastic practice, he emphasized that it cannot be divorced from joy, "Enjoy your prayer, be silent before God, empty before Him, opening up more and more to His inspiration...."

No longer in his role as teacher, but rather as a disciple among disciples, brother Leo wrote of the monastic calling with intense personal conviction and feeling:

> Let us open the ear of our heart to the voice of God, being thunderstruck by it—today—now. The present moment is the one in which you should respond. Do not fantasize a tomorrow; do not be nostalgic about the past. Respond to the moment: "O that today you would listen to God's voice! Harden not your heart" (Ps. 95: 8). The psalmist asks: "Who is the one who longs for life and wants to see good days? Then keep your tongue from evil, and your lips from speaking deceit. Turn aside from evil and do good. Seek and strive after peace" (Ps. 34:13–15). Then God's eyes will be lovingly upon you, and even before you call, God says: "I am already here!" God cares for us, and loves us. God wants to live with us and in us. In the words of Rabbi Abraham Heschel, God is "in search of us."

As if anticipating the needs of his own impending period of struggle, he wrote:

> So let us be brave. Bravery is essentially the willingness and readiness to "let go," to give up the securities we have built around us. Building securities around us really stems from insecurity. A secure person is also courageous. And letting go means, in the last analysis, giving oneself into the loving hands of God. "It is by the grace of God that I am who I am" (I Cor. 15:10). By letting go, we shall gain that higher security that rests in God, and of which the Lord Jesus speaks in the Sermon on the Mount: "Such a one will be like a wise person who built a house on rock; floods will come, storms will blow. The house will not tumble, because it is built on solid rock" (Mt. 7:24–25).

Mingling a paraphrase of the *Rule* with his personal insights, brother Leo concluded the "Reflections" with a final plea and an expression of hope:

> Remember that God is patient. God knows that we grow in steps and in time, and God waits. God desires that we become more and more whole in the course of our lives.
>
> All this is matter for the *entire* human being. We must prepare heart and body; both body and spirit are involved. Let God's life penetrate the last fibers of our being, our bodily being.
>
> Thus the monastery becomes a school for truly serving God. While it is never harsh or bitter, it does require a willingness to give up, to let go, to serve. This is understandably more difficult at the beginning. Yet as we progress in our endeavor as monks, the heart is enlarged and widened. We run with inexpressible joy in pursuing this way of life in and for God. We are truly "in Christ": partakers of his life and heirs of his kingdom of freedom and happiness, to which his life, death, and resurrection lead us.[2]

Brother Leo, center front row, with the Weston Priory community on an outing in 1977. "So let us be brave. Bravery is essentially the willingness and readiness to 'let go,' to give up the securities we have built around us."

A Brother Among Brothers

In the years that followed the writing of the "Reflections on the Rule of Benedict," brother Leo put his heart into making them a concrete reality in his own life and in the life of his brothers. He accepted humble tasks with a sense of humor; he greeted guests with warmth and simplicity; he shared rich spiritual insights with clarity. The give and take of discussions and decision-making were trying for him, but he did not withdraw from the community process of consensus.

In Weston for the summer and fall months, brother Leo accepted responsibilities as groundskeeper at Bethany, the Priory guesthouse. He relished driving the riding mower around the spacious lawns. A portion of his work time was devoted to writing his "Reminiscences" and to correspondence. He also took his turn presiding at Eucharist and, on occasion, commented eloquently on the scripture readings. But it was mostly his warm and welcoming simplicity that endeared him to the many friends and visitors to the Priory.

With the passing of time, it became more difficult for him to join the brothers in their travels. It was particularly painful for him when his doctor counseled him not to travel to Mexico with the community in 1976. The community journey to Mexico was in support of a young couple who were exercising lay-ministry in the diocese of Cuernavaca, Mexico. Ray Plankey, a native of Vergennes, Vermont, and his Chillean-born wife Gabriella, had visited the Priory in 1974, and, on that occasion, asked the Weston community to sponsor their ministry to the poor under the direction of Bishop Sergio Arceo-Mendes. Raymond and Gabriella were eager to share their experience with the Weston brothers in the hope of raising consciousness of North Americans concerning the plight of impoverished people in Mexico. While the community engaged in this and other strenuous journeys, brother Leo gratefully accepted the opportunity to spend time with the Benedictine Monks and his friend Prior Elias Achatz at St. Gregory's Priory in the Bahamas.

It was in 1979 that he made his last extensive trip with the brothers. A community of Franciscan sisters had invited the brothers to visit the homes of poor people in the "hollers" of Kentucky and Tennessee. Although the trip promised to be difficult, brother Leo was eager to take part. Events lived up to direst expectations. Sisters led the community into the poorest sections of their mission to visit the families to whom they ministered. The simple rustic homes of the area were in constant danger from mudslides. Poverty and illness were the common lot of the marginalized people. In one of the hollers, the brothers sang "Happy Birthday" to the shy mother on the threshold of her simple dwelling, with little children clinging to her apron. With tears in her eyes, she said it was the first time in her life that anyone had sung for her on her birthday. A little later, a visit with a group of women gathered at the Friendship Center in Williamsburg, Kentucky, marked the beginning of an enduring Priory friendship. The women proudly displayed their sewing and handcrafts, which largely supported their families during the debilitating strikes in the coal mines.

The dramatic high point of the trip was a visit to the Jericol mines in Harlan County, Kentucky, where the coal miners were on strike. Bullet-ridden structures and signs of violence lined the roadside. Brothers stood with their guitars beside the striking miners and sang Priory songs. State Police approached the group and singled out the Weston brothers. The police proceeded to take their names and issue a warning that they were committing illegal trespass. Before the brothers were dispersed, a caravan of buses carrying scab workers passed by led by an armored vehicle, described by one brother as "looking like something out of Star Wars." The tense moments were especially uncomfortable for brother Leo. A story with photos of the event subsequently appeared in the *National Catholic Reporter.*

In the evenings, the brothers retired to the mission church for prayer and their accommodations. At bedtime, blankets were rolled out in the aisles and between the pews. Brother Leo found his needed privacy after a demanding day, rooming in the sacristy.

By the time the Appalachian excursion was over, it was clear that such an experience was not well suited to brother Leo's physical condition. The emotional strain and sparse accommodations took a toll on his energies. His travels to Israel, under less severe conditions, proved to be an exception.

An Ardent Love For Israel

Of equal significance to his involvement as a brother in the Weston community, was brother Leo's ardent love for Israel and the Jewish people. The challenge to integrate that factor into his new situation as monastic brother in Weston was uppermost in his mind.

Subsequent to his visit to Israel in the spring of 1974, he explored avenues to continue his involvement with Israel and the Jewish people, now as a brother of Weston Priory. An early attempt was the publication of a pamphlet entitled "Israel's Right to Exist."[3] In the opening paragraph of the short brochure, he stated his purpose:

> The following is unashamedly written in defense of Israel. But I hope that my readers will notice that in analyzing the tragic struggle between Israel and the Arabs, I have tried to be fair to the Arab cause.

In this booklet of twenty-three pages, brother Leo confessed that he might not be abreast of the complexity of the situation. "I do not intend to defend every single action of the Israeli Government in regard to the Arab Israelis. I am uneasy, particularly, over the treatment of the Arabs of the two loyal villages of Biram and Ikrit in Upper Galilee...."

In an effort to show Israel's serious interest in the plight of the Arab people, he cited his friend Professor Zvi Werblowsky of the Hebrew University, "The relationship to our non-Jewish population within Israel and to our Arab neighbors...creates immense social, political, and moral problems. The Zionist achievement, for all its being in the profoundest historical sense a manifestation of historic justice for the Jewish people, somehow involves an injustice to others...."

Addressing narrowly the situation of Arab residents in Israel, and not the broader Palestinian question, he again quoted Professor Werblowsky in terms that resonated with his own feelings. "'It is not enough for us to say, 'all right, we Jews in Israel can be decent to Arabs here.' Much more is needed. For these people have cultural and spiritual aspirations, not only rights as citizens.'"

In light of developments and the escalation of violence in Israel/Palestine in the 1980s and 1990s after his death, brother Leo's 1970s analysis seems limited and one-sided. What is evident in his treatment of the question is that he wrote from the fire of love he had for the people he personally encountered in Israel. As a result, Israeli authorities welcomed the publication. Brother Leo learned from John A. Brogan III,

Consul General of the United States in Hamburg, that Eliahu Kino, the Israeli Consul, greatly appreciated the copy he received.

A revised edition of the pamphlet with minor changes was published in 1977 under the new title, "Understanding Israel: A Christian View." It had an added section on "the Palestinian question" with the disclaimer, "It would be beyond the scope of this booklet to give an adequate response to the very complicated and involved questions of a Palestinian state." Following a short discussion highlighting the Israeli perspective, brother Leo tersely offered his own viewpoint: "Actually, the country where most Palestinians live and have always lived is the present kingdom of Jordan. There already is a Palestinian state." Enmeshed in the highly polarized controversy, he curtly dismissed the claims of Palestinian Arabs to any sovereign presence in the Holy Land.

As late as 1981, the year before his death, he wrote a scathing pamphlet denouncing Archbishop Hilarion Capucci, the Lebanese Melkite Archbishop of Jerusalem, who had been arrested at the Mandelbaum Gate by Israeli authorities as a promoter of terrorism.[4] One can only surmise brother Leo's disillusionment had he lived to witness the violence and terror that engulfed Israel/Palestine in the years after his death.

Brother Leo found other ways to advance his cherished cause. In response to a request from Lowell Gallin, editor of *Root and Branch*, "an international guide to Christian individuals and organizations active in support of Israel," he listed his activities in that field, including a number of talks at colleges and universities, twice-a-year meetings of the Israel Study Group, letters published in the *New York Times* and the *Christian Science Monitor*, collaboration with the Anti-Defamation League of B'nai B'rith, and attendance at pro-

Israel functions in New England cities. He concluded on a personal note, "You see that Israel and Judaism is very close to my heart, and that I use any occasion to be active in these relations...."

In the same letter, brother Leo recalled an invitation to speak at the Stephen Wise Free Synagogue in New York City on Friday, October 12, 1979. In an address of some length with a few words of introduction in Hebrew, Leo charmed the congregation:

> Now here I may make something of a personal confession. Sometimes Jewish friends of mine have said, in jest, that I am more of a Zionist than many Jews. Naturally, one has to be cautious in claiming eschatological meanings of historic events. However, I could not help but see the hand of God in the establishment of the State of Israel, arising like a phoenix after the Holocaust.... And my twenty years in Israel were some of the happiest in my life.... In the twenty years of my residence in Israel, I have become very fond of the country and its people. I have found more and more that Jews are a very warm-hearted people.

After a lengthy list of affirmative observations on questions of justice and freedom of religion in Israel, gleaned from his experience there, brother Leo concluded his talk with a resounding pledge of loyalty:

> Israel is in great danger again. Public opinion has greatly turned against it, while the PLO gains support. I, for myself, will renew my pledge of love and loyalty to Israel. May we hope and pray! that Israel will overcome all problems, relying on the One who has chosen Israel as His special people and made a solemn covenant with it.[5]

Also at this time, more characteristic of him, brother Leo responded to Rabbi Samuel Dresner's request for copies of any of brother Leo's correspondence with Rabbi Abraham Heschel, who had died in 1972. Dresner was working on a biography of the great Jewish leader. In response, Leo emphasized that his relationship with Heschel and the Jewish people was more a matter of the heart and spirit than of politics or scholarship.

> I am enclosing copies of three letters [from Rabbi Heschel]. However, I am afraid they are not so terribly significant. While we naturally also discussed matters of intellectual interest, our mutual relationship was not so much based on such intellectual exchanges. It was rather a touch of our hearts which indeed was very deep. We experienced mutually that there is deep down, at the root of beings who have a living faith in God, something which transcends dogma. He, the observant Jew, and I, the believing Christian, met on this ground where there are no barriers and boundaries....[6]

In the closing years of the 1970s, brother Leo maintained frequent and close contact with his Jewish friends in the United States. Many of these associates visited him at the Priory, and he shared the wealth of those friendships with the community of brothers.

Two More Visits to Israel

While he no longer bore responsibility for the Dormition Abbey in Jerusalem, brother Leo retained a deep feeling of love, compassion, and concern for the brothers there. He remained in frequent contact with his successor, Abbot Laurence Klein.

At the same time, a certain melancholy over Dormition Abbey never totally lost its grip on Leo. In his "Reminiscences" he recalled:

> When I think of the enthusiasm and optimism with which I began my work in Jerusalem, and the disappointment and discouragement with which I ended it, I don't know whether I should laugh or cry.... During the whole time, two things were important to me—Dormition Abbey and its restoration, and my interest in Judaism and Israel. The latter remains with me.

In reality, he never lost his interest in the Abbey either. When Abbot Laurence informed him that the Dormition was in crisis again, he was impelled to become involved. Out of concern for the Dormition community, he undertook a burdensome journey in the early winter of 1978.

Abbot Laurence, technically administrator of the community in the absence of a regular election in 1968, had continued brother Leo's ecumenical efforts, promoting dialogue among the three monotheistic religions. He also introduced an academic program at the Abbey for students from Europe. Nonetheless, ten years after brother Leo's departure, the Dormition community was still struggling for internal unity.

Lacking the support of a divided community, Abbot Laurence was unable to continue in his leadership role. Brother Leo had only a sympathetic presence and words of encouragement to offer to his erstwhile monastic associates. Little could be done. He was relieved and hopeful when the name of Prior Nicolaus Egender was proposed to succeed Abbot Laurence.

Like his two predecessors, Prior Nicolaus was a capable and enthusiastic promoter of ecumenism and Christian-Jewish relations. Moreover, it was he who had come to the support of Abbot Leo's plan for the internationalization of the Dormition community as Visitator in 1967. As a longtime member of the community of Chevetogne, he shared with brother Leo the monastic ideals of Lambert Beauduin. Sensing that the community at the Dormition was again in good hands, brother Leo moved on to visit his friends at Ulpan Akiva. Fatigued after the difficult days in Israel, he returned to Weston.

Finding it difficult to regain his energy in the cold Vermont winter, brother Leo set off from Weston again in February for a month-long sojourn in the warmer clime of St. Augustine's Priory in Nassau. There he enjoyed the relaxed pace of the community and the friendly islanders whom he met in his travels. He prayed the monastic office regularly and celebrated Eucharist with the small community. Recounted to the Weston brothers with pleasure were his journeys by motor boat with Father Henry to the out-islands, where the monks engaged in pastoral ministry along with the Mercy Sisters of Portland, Maine. He never tired of watching the ships coming and going in the Nassau Harbor, and he still exhibited a spirit of adventure, donning a deep-sea diving helmet to explore the harbor floor.

The opportunity for brother Leo to return to Jerusalem presented itself in the fall of 1979. Prior Nicolaus Egender invited—indeed, urged—brother Leo to attend his blessing as the new abbot of the Dormition. The months of October and November were ideal for the stay in Israel. First on brother Leo's agenda was the abbatial blessing.

From Jerusalem he wrote to the brothers at Weston commenting on the ceremony, "Everything went splendidly. I saw many old friends and had a great time.... The great celebration and reception is over. Of course, it was 'pomp and circumstance.' However, I must say it was very, very beautiful. Not too much pomp."[7] He also expressed hope that it was a new moment for the Dormition community. "On the whole, there is now life and creativity here at the Dormition. I am rather favorably impressed."

As the 1970s were drawing to a close, there were ample signs that brother Leo's three diverging preoccupations—Weston Priory, Israel and the Jewish People, and the Dormition Abbey—were gradually being reconciled in his spirit and integrated into his life as a brother in the Weston community. The process was well underway, but the course was not yet run.

The Weston Priory Community witnessing for Nuclear Disarmament in Washington, D.C., October 29, 1979. In his years as abbot, brother Leo raised the question, "Where was the church at the time of the Holocaust?"

17

Journey into Brotherhood

In the mid 1970s, brother Leo had described life at the Priory in endearing terms, almost as an ideal:

> I have found a true monastic life...a life of devotion, centered in community, with an intensity which I never found at Gerleve or elsewhere—a life that does not gravitate towards all kinds of activities, but rather towards the *center,* a life of intense living and growing together, and thus towards God in Christ.

As the decade of the 1970s drew to a close, the involvement of the Weston Priory community in religious, political and social issues increased dramatically.

That earlier memory remained with brother Leo and the community as a cherished value and hope. But in a short time, much had changed in the life of the community. The Benedictine monks of Weston had been concerned with liturgical renewal, civil rights, and social justice issues from as far back as the 1960s. Sporadic participation in workshops for parishes and religious congregations, dialogue with the laity, and public statements on ecclesial and civic issues were an accepted part of the monastic experience of the time. In the spirit of the Second Vatican Council, prophetic witness was considered essential to all forms of Christian life. In his years as abbot, brother Leo raised the question, "Where was the church at the time of the Holocaust?" Prophetic witness did not mar the vision of monastic life that brother Leo described in the mid-1970s.

But in the final years of that decade, the pace of life of the Priory community quickened, and the balance between the normal monastic observance and external activity shifted. More of the brothers' time and energy was consumed by activity reaching beyond the monastic enclosure, and there was, consequently, less emphasis on monastic practice and observance.

The years leading into the 1980s were fraught with challenges for the Priory community. Uncertainty and turmoil continued to sweep the church and society as a climate of fear and resistance to change followed in the wake of the Second Vatican Council and the nuclear arms race. It was in this atmosphere that the Weston monks realized that the liturgical music they were creating for their own prayer spoke not only to the prayer-needs of other religious communities far and wide, but to the broader spectrum of social issues. The Priory's new high profile brought invitations and pleas for involvement in movements for disarmament, peace, justice, and social change.

The Weston Community was drawn to more active engagement, often in situations not suitable for brother Leo's participation. In King of Prussia, Pennsylvania, the brothers sang at a gathering in support of the Plowshares Eight, on trial for civil disobedience. On another occasion they took part in a demonstration calling for nuclear disarmament in Washington, D.C.

There they joined a march, monitored by police with guard dogs on leash, to Capitol Hill, bearing a banner with a quotation from the Vatican, "Armaments kill the poor!" In the evening of the same day they led a vigil in front of the White House and, on the following morning, joined a protest at the Department of Energy against the government's nuclear policies.

In New York City, in a protest organized by the Mobilization for Survival, they sang at a Peace Convocation assembled in the Cathedral of St. John the Divine. Following the church service, they marched with a half million participants through the city streets to a huge rally in Central Park. In the park they were asked to lead a song and dance around a peace tree planted for the occasion. They circled the tree to the tune of their familiar Israeli dance, Ma Navu—"how beautiful on the mountains are the feet of those bearing the message of peace." At that weekend event, they were assigned to sing and speak out for disarmament in the small park across the street from the United Nations Plaza.

Following the deaths of four North American women missionaries in El Salvador, the community voice was raised in public confrontation with the United States government over its complicity in the carnage wreaked by U.S.-trained military officers for that region. As their awareness widened, the brothers sought a closer relationship with the people of Latin America. The Weston community entered into a covenantal relationship with a congregation of Mexican Benedictine Sisters, *Las Hermanas Benedictinas de Cristo Rey,* and began making annual visits to Mexico to support the Sisters in their ministry to the poor. These journeys took the brothers to remote sections of Mexico too perilous for an aging brother with a weakened heart. Even though he was unable to participate directly in the physically and emotionally demanding efforts that were part of the community's social-justice activity, brother Leo supported the projects and the stands taken.

While all members of the community were in agreement on the importance of the pressing issues of the day, they recognized that their involvement beyond the confines of the monastery, however laudable, disrupted normal monastic observance. Doubts about achieving a balance in community life provoked disquiet and misgivings. It was a highly problematic period; there was no desire to withdraw from the public activities, yet fundamentally all felt a diminishment of the contemplative dimension of their monastic observance. In this context, brother Leo's anxieties about the direction of the community became acute. Unwilling to broach the subject in the community, he sought out another alternative.

Words From a Mother's Heart

With confused feelings, brother Leo turned to a trusted friend for another perspective on the situation. He wrote of his misgivings to Catherine de Vinck, gifted poet and longtime friend of the community. Like brother Leo, Catherine was a member of a titled European family. Born in Belgium, she emigrated to the U.S. after World War II with her husband, Baron José de Vinck, and their two eldest children. With brother Leo, she shared the experience of being uprooted from her wider family and her native land and culture. Out of her experiences in war-torn Europe came a keen sensitivity to issues of peace and social justice.

Acknowledging the pain of the ambiguous situation at Weston, she affirmed the values of trust and commitment that bound brother Leo to the community. "I cannot judge and certainly will not take sides," she wrote. Catherine recognized that the brothers were imbued with a deep concern over suffering and injustice around the world, common ground shared by brother Leo. "In view of all the misery and pain of so many people and the urgency of so many issues (nuclear armament, etc.), it is understandable that the brothers may wish to participate more visibly in the struggle for a more just and peaceful world."

Even as she expressed uncertainty that these new goals were part of the Benedictine form of life, she nonetheless found the brothers' concerns honorable and worthwhile. "I am deeply distressed, however, about any sufferings that my friends endure," she continued. "I cannot believe that a loving community cannot solve its problems if all are of good will...." Unable to resolve the tension between those she loved unconditionally, she suggested that trust, prayer, and good will would bridge the differences. With a final appeal to compassion and gratitude, she simply offered the example of her own experience that would find echo in his.

> My love and gratitude for the brothers will never diminish or be altered. I feel certain that none of their decisions are taken lightly or without prayerful considerations. We are all imperfect instruments, so of course mistakes and misunderstanding and errors occur, but God writes straight with our crooked lines....[1]

Besides a poet, Catherine was a devoted mother. Perhaps that identity above all made it possible for her to respond to brother Leo in a way that resonated with his own maternal feelings toward the developing Weston community.

Already, writing in his "Reminiscences" some five years before, Leo had described his experience in a striking metaphor.

> I am the Father Founder (I say this facetiously). Strange as it may sound, I feel more like a mother to Weston. I conceived it (somehow). Then I gave it birth. It was almost a process of nature. Once a woman has conceived—in love—things go their way in a natural process over which she has no personal power. The same thing happened with me.

Catherine's letter was a gentle reminder to brother Leo of his deep maternal relationship with the brothers at Weston and the implied call to trust and patience. She offered no quick answers but spoke from a mother's heart.

Her letter struck a resonant chord.

Catherine did not offer a solution to brother Leo's uncertainties; she did, perhaps, help him to be in touch with his heart. Be open, trust, listen, be patient—give room to the Holy Spirit; all lessons that he had taught and now applied to his personal struggles.

The balance between the inner life and external activity of the monastic community would remain a question and a challenge without definitive answer—it was subject to the changing times, the circumstances of life, and the discernment of the whole brotherhood. The equilibrium would never be perfect; the community could only work at truing its monastic course by constant conversation, prayer, and openness to the signs of the times. It would not be until the time that the brothers declared the monastery a Sanctuary for Refugees, two years after brother Leo's death, that a new sense of balance would be restored.

The tension between monastic observance and active engagement was built into the origins of the Weston Priory community—a basic tenet of brother Leo, that the monastery was not to be in isolation from the contemporary world and society. In a constantly changing world, it is an issue that is

"I am the Father Founder (I say this facetiously). Strange as it may sound, I feel more like a mother to Weston. I conceived it (somehow). Then I gave it birth."

never definitively resolved. The critical question always remains: how to balance prophetic monastic witness with a prayerful, community-centered monastic observance.

One Last Hurdle

At least one more hurdle lingered for Leo to overcome on his journey into brotherhood as he approached his eightieth year. He still did not feel fully accepted as a brother by his brothers. The rich variety of roles that he assumed in the Weston community complicated his relationship with the community and with individual brothers. As time went on, he found himself successively in the role of founder, teacher, abbot, father, advocate, and finally, mother. Each role was associated with different shadings of relationship.

Neither brother Leo nor the other brothers found an easy formula to transform those relationships established over the years. They were engaged in the trying process of creating a new relationship without denying the gifts of the past. The wrenching changes needed for a mother to become a friend of her child were not foreign to brother Leo's experience:

> Looking at all that has developed in the life at Weston, I think I am not presumptuous when I say, I recognize in it the seed that I planted. Naturally, no one could foresee exactly the way Weston has grown and will grow. But the essential identity is recognizable, I think, just as in an oak tree, the acorn is still recognizable, and in a grown-up person, the child whom the mother bore in her womb.

It was not less challenging to pass from relating to the community as founder to that of conversation partner. While refraining from passing judgment, he did not hide a certain sense of disappointment as the founder of Weston Priory, "The original aim in founding Weston, namely to be a subsidiary to the Dormition Abbey, faded out completely. Weston took on its own life and developed according to its innate laws." Deeply human feelings were bound to accompany the difficult choices of what to retain and what to leave behind in the relationships of the past.

The brothers revered Leo in his gifted role as teacher. Much of that gift remained when he became a brother. Differing spiritual, cultural, and intellectual backgrounds were not allowed to break the deeper bonds that united brother Leo with the other members of the community. Hinting "at some of the shades of difference in our feelings and thinking," he wrote:

> I do sometimes feel that the—entirely justified—emphasis on brotherly relation, brotherly love as the way of meeting God is perhaps liable to under-emphasize the direct personal relationship to God. This is the point where my love for Saint John of the Cross enters my life. There are other divergences, but none that touch on the essence of things.

In the early period of his retirement and novice-like experience as brother, he voiced an unrealized hope more than a reality, "May I begin by saying that I am now deeply convinced, and happily so, that we brothers have really found each other. I feel fully accepted and integrated. But that was achieved not without a struggle." Sometime later he penned a qualification of that optimistic observation into the margin of his text: he added "almost!" to the words "fully accepted and integrated."

That gloss may indicate a touch of humor or even a hint of bitterness as the struggle went on. In a frankly disarming passage, brother Leo shared his insight into those years of integration, "In my opinion [the struggle] derives from two sources, one in me and one in the other brothers."

> Let me start with what I think was an obstacle in me. I confess openly and freely that I had been wearing several masks—or should I say façades?—I had built around my real, inner self. And I suppose that my brothers felt that, perhaps instinctively, perhaps also clearly. The latter may apply especially to Brother John with his deep psychological insight. That made me sometimes a little afraid of him, in the past. It was perhaps not easy to break through those masks or façades.
>
> I see especially two such façades, hiding my real deepest being. One was the difference of background and education. You simply cannot shake such things off like a coat. It is a long and sometimes painful process. After all, I was thirty-six years old when I came to America, in many aspects set in my ways. I was—and probably still am, to some extent—a European. And do not forget: in Darlington, and during the early time in Keyport, I still had the *von* before my name....
>
> Then there was the second façade, that of the abbot. In the past tradition, alive in the Benedictine Order, the abbot was a person taken out of the rest of the family and placed upon a pedestal. The concept was very paternalistic. Naturally, the Rule of St. Benedict provides well that the abbot become not a tyrant or dictator. Still, according to the Rule, as it was written around 520 A.D., the paternalistic concept is there, the monks being treated more or less like children (less so in the "Rule of St. Benedict" than in the "Rule of the Master," which shows in what direction things were developing). The abbot, as the name

> indicates, was the "father" of the family and the one who made the decisions.
>
> Things were aggravated from the Middle Ages by the status of the abbot as a mitered prelate, in a way a member of the hierarchy. I had been influenced by that. I admit I had been fond of "playing at bishops." Even the way of thinking expressed in my article, "Thoughts on the Blessing of an Abbot," while expressing some valid ideas, no longer agrees with my present way of thinking....

Leo then presented his view of the brothers' part in the struggle for his integration at Weston:

> I do believe that you brothers had me in a box. I noticed that quite often by the way you reacted to some of my remarks, interpreting them not as I meant them, but as you prejudged them.
>
> But that obstacle, too, has broken down in recent years [in margin: almost! perhaps not totally!!]. You have pierced that armor and taken me out of the box, taken me really as one of the brothers.

Again words were later added to the text, possibly at the same time as the previous interpolation. He brought the frank but ambiguous passage to a conclusion:

> [T]hat façade has fallen down and lies in ruins. No regrets! My real self seems to emerge from beyond all those masks or façades. Of course there are personal hurdles to be overcome, as with every member in our brotherhood. There seems to be no essential difference, except that I was older and more set in my ways.

Nowhere in brother Leo's writings can be found a final resolution to his struggle for full acceptance as a brother or the emergence of his "true self" from the box or boxes that seemed to hold him bound. There is however an incident that reveals that here, too, in a gifted moment of recognition, he found peace. It will happen in the midst of his brothers as they celebrate his eightieth birthday.

May 1982. Abbot Nicolas Egender with brother Leo at Dormition Abbey in Jerusalem. "Little Leo is somewhat depressed. Man proposes and God disposes. That is all I can do now. My pain does not allow more."

18

Anchor's Aweigh: Into Dawning Light

During his last years, living as a brother in the Weston Priory community, its founder continued to evolve his own thinking about monastic life. As late as 1981, only months before his death, brother Leo wrote a short monograph on the role of leadership in the monastic community, entitled "The Abbot is Dead."[1] In that essay he quoted a piece he'd written more than fifteen years earlier: "It is exactly the blessing of an abbot which makes him not just a superior but a father."[2] In light of the more recent history of Benedictine communities as well as his own experience as a monk and brother at Weston, he took issue with his earlier assertion:

> If we look, without prejudice, at recent developments in our order, concerning the position of an abbot, it seems very obvious that this "paternalistic" concept is dead. The fact that nowadays most abbots are elected for a term, that numberless abbots have resigned after serving only a few years—these are radical departures from the ideas expressed in the Rule of Benedict. These developments

> have served a deathblow to the idea of the abbot as pictured in the Rule of Benedict. They make the abbot "just a superior."

In contrast to the twentieth century, he described the era in which the Rule of St. Benedict was written:

> In Saint Benedict's time the father-son relationship made sense. It was a fact. Saint Benedict had with him a few really mature monks, like Saint Maur, and probably those from whom the deans were chosen. But everything in the Rule shows that the majority of the monks were immature, needing the guidance of a father. They were like children. (See the rules about punishments and satisfactions.)

Yet even in the Rule of Benedict, brother Leo located a shift away from the paternalistic to the brotherly:

> It is also very interesting to see that, in the Rule of Saint Benedict, a decisive step was taken towards the fraternal relationship of brothers, away from the exclusively vertical relationship (abbot to monk, monk to abbot) in the direction of a really fraternal relationship, monk to monk—a more horizontal relationship.

As the modern practice of monasticism evolved at Weston, the goal of consensus became an essential element of the community's life. Consensus in the Weston context is not majority rule. It is rather a function of the monastic chapter, in which all the monks take part, each contributing his position on an issue. A matter is discussed and worked through until *everyone* is willing to give his consent to a decision. Decidedly, this does not mean that an individual monk necessarily approves the decision, only that he is willing to embrace it, and in good conscience, able to put his heart into it. If a consensus cannot be reached, the matter is suspended. Before consensual decision-making, the brothers of Weston know, consensual living is necessary. This mode of community decision-making is not the most efficient way of reaching its goal: that is why it is so at variance with North American life. Whatever its drawbacks, the concept of consensus as practiced at Weston—a wholesale reversal of the centuries-old autocratic tradition of monasticism—was the subject of a paper, which the abbots had called for, that was presented at their 1970 Congress.

In brother Leo's 1981 mongraph, he confirmed his approval of the process of consensus as practiced at Weston, locating its roots in ancient monastic history:

> [W]hen we compare the Rule of Benedict with the Rule of the Master[,]...the horizontal relationship is totally missing. In the Benedictine Rule there is more emphasis on the council of the brothers, where the youngest will also be heard.... It seems therefore justified to say that in our praxis of living by consensus (the prior being chosen particularly for his ability to draw consensus), we only continue the historical march of monasticism in the spirit of Saint Benedict in the direction to which his Rule points. Monasticism is a living, not a dead, thing. It moves with the times, because the Rule is not a dead letter, but an inspired work, conveying the Spirit.[3]

A Birthday Gift

As brother Leo approached his eightieth birthday, he retained his vigor and alertness. He was still involved in Priory activities and ready for new adventures. On community walks he took the lead and set the pace. Reading, listening to classical music, and a solitary walk in the woods were his favored forms of relaxation. His patience was tried at times by an increased hearing impairment: he did not want to miss out on anything.

Brothers affectionately recall seeing him early in the morning, before vigils on a summer day, walking barefoot on the front lawn of the monastery, gazing in wonder at the starry Vermont sky. The sensation of cold dew on soft grass was for him a childlike delight. In another familiar picture, he could be seen typing near the window of his room in the monastery dormitory while brothers engaged in a raucous game of volleyball at a distance in the field outside. An occasional wave or smile confirmed that he was not really removed from the sporting group.

Above all, his connection with Israel and the Jewish people never waned. At an evening recreation with the community toward the end of 1981, he shyly brought out an invitation from Abbot Nicolas Egender of the Dormition to the blessing of the restored church of the Loaves and Fishes at the monastery in Tabgha on the Sea of Galilee. Brother Leo suggested that it was too soon after his recent visit to Israel to return. Yet brothers noted he was unable to disguise a certain wistfulness in his expression.

Some weeks later, the community gathered in the "Upper Room" of the monastery for a festive celebration of brother Leo's eightieth birthday. A large, gaily wrapped box bound with ribbons was placed in front of him. With sparkling eyes and a look of expectation, he unwrapped the gift and waded through piles of crumpled paper until he found a small fuzzy stuffed golden lion—a Leo, an *arieh*. With a flourish he lifted *arieh* out of the box. The lion was sitting on a large envelope:

inside was a proposal for the Tabgha trip. Playfully, brother Leo draped the golden ribbons of the wrappings around his head and shoulders and broke into spontaneous laughter.

Was this perhaps the patiently awaited moment of insight—the moment of recognition that his real self had indeed emerged as Arieh, the playful lion? Only he could take his true self from the boxes in which he felt bound. His faithful monastic life in the midst of gifting brothers had indeed born the fruit of peace and acceptance—and he was overjoyed at the prospect of returning to Israel.

In the early spring of 1982, he made preparations for his forthcoming ocean crossings. In Israel many friends eagerly awaited his return. Gatherings and celebrations were planned. There would also be the opportunity to visit his much loved community at Saint Joseph's Abbey in Gerleve and relatives and friends in Germany and Holland. His mood was one of trusting anticipation and exhilaration.

But brother Leo stayed fully present to the moving events taking place at the Priory in the weeks remaining before his journey. On Sunday, April 19, the community assembled in the summer barn chapel to celebrate a public Eucharist commemorating the anniversary of the Holocaust. For the occasion, brother Leo had invited his longtime friend and colleague Rabbi Leon Klenicki. At the large gathering, Rabbi Klenicki read a text that was close to brother Leo's heart, "The Meaning of this Hour" by Abraham Joshua Heschel.

> There is a divine dream which the Prophets and Rabbis have cherished and which fills our prayers, and permeates the acts of true piety. It is a dream of a world rid of evil by the grace of God as well as by the efforts of humanity, by their dedication to the task of establishing the kingdom of God in the world.

> God is waiting for us to redeem the world. We should not spend our life hunting for trivial satisfactions while God is waiting constantly and keenly for our effort and devotion. The Almighty has not created the universe that we may have opportunities to satisfy our greed, envy, and ambition. We have not survived that we may waste our years in vulgar vanities. The martyrdom of millions demands that we consecrate ourselves to the fulfillment of God's dream of salvation.

The other reading for the memorial service was taken from a novel also familiar to brother Leo, "The Last of the Just," by Andre Scwartz-Bart.

> (Ernie and Golda, in the novel, are two young Jews who meet in Paris during the Nazi occupation.)
>
> "Oh Ernie," Golda said, "you know them. Tell me why, why do the Christians hate us the way they do? They seem so nice when I can look at them without my star."
>
> Ernie put his arms around her shoulders solemnly. "It's very mysterious," he murmured in Yiddish. "They don't know exactly why themselves. I've been in their churches and I've read their gospel. Do you know who the Christ was? A simple Jew like your father. A kind of Hasid."
>
> Golda smiled gently. "You're kidding me."
>
> "No, believe me, and I'll bet they'd have got along fine, the two of them, because he really was a good Jew, you know—a merciful man, and gentle...."

A Grove Planted in Israel

As the time for departure drew near, Abbot Leo mentioned severe back pain, but he did not want to complain. Neither would he see a doctor, despite the brothers' urgings. As he passed through the Priory dining room on his way to the car that would take him to the airport, he stopped to whisper to brother John. With a smile, and some sadness in his eyes, he made a request: "Promise that you will see to it that I return home to Weston, even if it is only in a box!"

Brother Leo's last ocean crossings were by plane, not, as he would have preferred, by ship. From the moment he left Weston, he was in excruciating pain, yet he remained elated at what lay immediately ahead. By the time he reached Israel, he was barely able to walk. Notwithstanding, he attended the lengthy ceremonies for the consecration of the new church in Tabgha, where the beauty of the restored Sanctuary of the Loaves and Fishes surpassed his expectations.

The latest work completed the monastic buildings he had envisioned in the early 1950s when he was abbot in Jerusalem. On this celebratory occasion in Tabgha, his feelings were a mixture of joy and sadness. It was here that he had dreamed of building a new Benedictine community and creating a new style of Benedictine life in the Holy Land. It was here that he had spent so many hours of quiet prayer and reflection. It was here that a treasured hope had died. Yet the restoration of the church with its priceless mosaics he had so carefully protected together with signs of new life in the small community could not be overlooked.

His stay in Israel was brief but full. From Tabgha, brother Leo went to Ulpan Akiva, the community he valued so much for initiating him into the Hebrew culture and language. There, with many friends and distinguished guests, he attended a banquet held in his honor. Among tributes presented on the occasion was a special message of gratitude and friendship from Teddy Kolleck, mayor of Jerusalem. In a strained voice, weakened by intense pain, brother Leo thanked his extended family in Israel. Following the banquet at the Ulpan, he was driven to a nearby grove of trees planted in his honor. There he unveiled a stone monument engraved with his name.

His strength declining with each day, he took a plane for Amsterdam, arriving at the home of Dutch relatives, exhausted and approaching his limits of endurance for pain. An ambulance took him from Holland to Germany where the community of his early monastic days received him with fraternal affection and cared for him at St. Joseph's Abbey in Gerleve. He was attended by his nephew, Doctor Jürgen van de Loo, who recognized that cancer had spread throughout brother Leo's body.

'Little Leo' is Somewhat Depressed

Even as he struggled with intense pain, brother Leo's thoughts were never far from his brothers of the Weston community. His spirit was sustained with the assurance of the brothers' presence to him as they assembled several times each day in prayer in the barn chapel in far away Vermont. For the first time in fifteen years he would miss the annual community retreat that began on May 31, the day of his last overseas letter from Gerleve:

> Dear Brother John, dear brothers all!
>
> Here I am finally. Unfortunately quite ill. Pontifical Mass? Sermons? Out of the question! I am almost paralyzed and in constant pain. Tomorrow a.m. I'll go to the Medical Center of the University of Münster where—it so happens—a nephew of mine, Jürgen van de Loo, is head

of the Dept. of Inner Maladies. But about that later. Pray for me! I suffer!

In spite of that, things in Israel went rather well....

Little Leo is somewhat depressed. Man proposes and God disposes. That is all I can do now. My pain does not allow more.

Lovingly your
Br. Leo

That plaintive letter reached the Weston brothers at a tense moment. They had agreed to participate in an evening of prayer and solidarity for the Salvadoran refugees at the National Shrine of the Immaculate Conception in Washington, D.C., at the end of their first week of retreat. With anxiety at the news of brother Leo's deteriorating condition, they pressed on to fulfill their commitment to support others in their suffering with their prayer and song. The attention of the standing-room-only crowd assembled in the Basilica was riveted on the plight of the suffering refugees of El Salvador. The brothers sang and prayed in the massive Shrine, holding their suffering brother in the silence of their hearts.

The conclusion of the second week of retreat was no less challenging for the concerned community. In New York City on Friday, they played a prominent role in the Religious Convocation for Disarmament at the Cathedral of St. John the Divine and on the following day, with their banner reading "Armaments Kill the Poor," they led a section of the immense demonstration that marched through the streets of New York to the United Nations.

The brothers returned to Weston with apprehension in mid-June. There they waited in prayer for further news of their afflicted brother in Germany.

Homecoming

As soon as news of brother Leo's deteriorating condition reached Vermont, the brothers made preparations to bring him back to Weston. Brothers Robert and Elias were dispatched to Gerleve to make arrangements and to accompany brother Leo on his return to America. Still in great pain, but in anticipation of home, he arrived in Boston in good spirits, and was taken immediately by ambulance to Dartmouth-Hitchcock Hospital in New Hampshire. Doctors there recognized that it was too late to treat the cancer. Brother Leo asked that he be returned to the Priory as soon as possible. Plans were made to provide the best quality of life that could be realized for him in the time that remained.

Each day, a group of brothers traveled to the hospital bringing bread and wine and the prayer of the community. In a light spirit, brother Leo celebrated Eucharist with them from his bed. Dr. Richard Waters, a close friend of the Weston community, daily brought him the *New York Times* and cheered him with his visit. Staff members, so impressed with his simplicity, patience, and graciousness, were sorry to see him leave the hospital.

It was the playfulness of the delighted child coming to the fore in his later years that so endeared brother Leo to the many people he encountered at the Priory. That quality endured even in the pain of his final illness. From early on, a man of dignity and noble bearing, he exemplified the spirituality of the prophets of the Hebrew scriptures as Avivah Zornberg describes it:

> For the prophet, there is one requirement: to *listen* to God's voice. To listen means to speak, to bear the tiger that springs forth.... "If your Torah had not been my *plaything,* I should have perished in my poverty!" cried the Psalmist

> in a moment of burning vision.... It is precisely the play mode that generates the unique and variable idioms of relationship—to other human beings and to God.[4]

As summer was drawing to a close, brother Leo was able to leave the hospital and to again be among his brothers at the Priory, as he so ardently desired. The brothers engaged the services of hospice to assist in caring for him, and nurses and friends volunteered help. Brother Leo's room in the dormitory was remodeled and enlarged to accommodate a special bed and wheelchair. Large sliding doors gave access to a porch, overlooking the back pond and the playing field, with a view to the National Forest beyond.

On community recreation days, brother Leo watched the brothers at volleyball as he sat on the porch in a wheelchair. At other times, he quietly absorbed the natural beauty surrounding the monastery. An intercom system enabled him to listen in his room as the community celebrated the hours of the monastic office and the liturgy a short distance away in the barn chapel.

I Have a Jewish Heart

Gradually he became weaker. Soon he was no longer able to leave his bed. Brothers took turns keeping a quiet vigil, reading at his bedside. Occasionally, brother Leo broke the silence to share a thought or a memory. A few words uttered simply, peacefully: "Brother, it is quite mysterious, I have a Jewish heart." And after a long pause, "Really, I am not afraid to die!"

The community found opportunities to pray with brother Leo. While he was still alert, the brothers gathered around his bed for the sacrament of reconciliation. Each brother, in turn, approached him and asked forgiveness for any hurt or offense. Gently and humbly, brother Leo asked the same of each brother. Peace was palpable in the room. Brothers accompanied the sacramental celebration with the song, *Listen,* written some ten years earlier when brother Leo suffered his first life-threatening heart attack:

> *Listen, and gentle, be present*
> *to all you've ever kept close in your loving heart...*
>
> *Shadows appear at your doorstep,*
> *but don't you worry, life's lesson has blossomed now.*
> *This moment immense with a stillness*
> *that makes you listen and want to be listening.*[5]

A few days later, the community gathered once more for a sacramental prayer with their failing brother. A light and joyful spirit pervaded the room as brother Leo was anointed with holy oil on lips, eyes, ears, hands, feet, and chest. Again music and the voices of all the brothers accompanied the prayer and gestures of the sacrament bringing healing and peace.

After the prayer and anointing, brother Leo refused to take further nourishment and soon lapsed into a coma.

The Peace of the Oceans

Serenity characterized brother Leo's final voyage through death to new life. It was as if his frequent ocean crossings had been the practice and preparation for the last passage. As he lay quietly in his monastic cell in those final days, gone were signs of anxiety or fretfulness. The ambiguities and ambivalences, the failures and triumphs, all the struggles of his very active contemplative life, were taken up in peaceful resolution: all had become one.

Some seven years before, brother Leo had concluded his "Reminiscences" with a vision of the time when he would be called into the embrace of God. It was as though he had prepared for this moment throughout his life and prophetically pictured it in his memoir:

> I feel I should write an epilogue to my reminiscences, but then, I don't know how to write this epilogue. It should be and only could be in poetry. Let this begin with the words of Psalm 40.
>
> *I waited, I waited for Yahweh*
> *And he stooped down to me,*
> *He heard my cry.*
>
> *He drew me from the deadly pit*
> *From the slough of the marsh,*
> *He set my feet upon a rock*
> *And steadied my steps.*
>
> *He has put a new song in my mouth.*
> *A song of praise to our God.*
>
> I would like to sing a paean—a paean to my brothers in Weston—sing to what they have meant to me in the last years of my life. They have really opened my heart. Thus only (perhaps), I shall be ready to meet my God, when that hour has come.

He concluded his epilogue by quoting the spoken text that accompanies the Priory song, *Wherever You Go:*

I want to say something to all of you
who have become a part
of the fabric of my life.
The color and texture
which you have brought into my being
have become a song
and I want to sing it forever.[6]

He appended his own "AMEN" to these lines.

The usual summer crowds thronged the Priory grounds, quietly aware that brother Leo was embarking on his last ocean crossing. Word circulated that he had lapsed into a coma. Brothers thought that he might be awaiting the fifteenth of August, the patronal feast of the Dormition Abbey in Jerusalem. But that day came and went. It was two days later, August 17, when the nurse attending brother Leo stopped brother Richard as he returned to his room from the early morning Eucharist. "It is time. Call the brothers together. Brother Leo is passing."

The monastery bells summoned the community. The twelve brothers stood around brother Leo's bed. For the first time since he sank into a coma, brother Leo's eyes were open in bright recognition of his community. The words of farewell were spoken: "Receive the Bread of Life for your journey!" After he received the Eucharistic viaticum with a sip of water, he was once more anointed with holy oil and the brothers began to sing the Song of Ruth from the Hebrew Scriptures:

Wherever you go, I shall go,
Wherever you live, so shall I live.
Your people will be my people,
and your God will be my God too.

As the community sang the concluding words, brother Leo softly drew a final breath; the light of his eyes was extinguished:

Wherever you die I shall die,
and there shall I be buried beside you.
We will be together forever,
and our love will be the gift of our life.[7]

Individually, the brothers approached the bedside and kissed the forehead of their beloved brother and father, gone before them. On his last journey, brother Leo relinquished the guidance of his vessel to the navigator of his life. He gave himself and his life graciously into the hands of his God.

The monastery bell tolled far into the morning, alerting friends and neighbors to the passing of brother Leo. Brothers washed his body and clothed him in his white monastic cowl. His body was placed in a wooden casket fashioned by a local craftsman and lined with fresh, hand-sewn, cotton cloth. The coffin remained in the dormitory prayer room as brothers kept silent vigil until noon. When the bells tolled again, the community walked in procession, bearing brother Leo's body to the stone chapel where they placed it in front of the monastic choir. Friends and neighbors filed by until the Vesper Eucharist in the evening.

As friends assembled for the Eucharist in the barn chapel, the brothers gathered around brother Leo's body in the monastic oratory. Each brother held a wooden peg, marked with a cross or a Star of David, which he used to secure the lid of the coffin. The brothers then carried brother Leo's body to the barn chapel where a familial Eucharist of thanksgiving was celebrated.

At the conclusion of Eucharist, under an overcast sky and misty rain in the west, brothers, singing psalms and alleluias,

"Brother Leo tried to soften the hard lines. As Rutland's Rabbi Solomon D. Goldberg suggested, the priory's founder may have been one of the 36 'wise and saintly' men for whose sake the world is preserved." *The Rutland Herald,* August 24, 1982. *photo courtesy of Dr. Eugene J. Fisher*

bore the coffin to the knoll overlooking the pond and the monastery buildings. With prayers of farewell, brother Leo's body was lowered into the ground and all took turns filling the grave with earth. As the community walked slowly from the knoll back to the monastery, the clouds over Weston Priory parted and a rainbow appeared.

The clearing sky and arc of color overhead at the conclusion of brother Leo's burial were a picture in striking contrast to the first memory his "Reminiscences" recorded. "The Horizon is overshadowed; the air is as if filled with smoke.... The people live here as if in the grasp of a dull pain: they are either under the burden of suffering, or they themselves are the foes who inflict that suffering, hard and to be feared." Throughout his life brother Leo did indeed "walk through the valley of darkness." But, with a touch of nobility, he found his way to the light. The brothers' final memory of him is suffused with light and color and hope.

His legacy to the community of Weston Priory—ever his child—is a life nobly lived. The spirit he breathed forth was one of peace and reconciliation. That spirit was born, not of tranquility or complacency, but from the lived struggle of reconciling the faith of Sinai and the faith of the Beloved Community in his own person. His was not an abstract or theoretical faith. It was faith rooted in life, in land, and in people. An image he loved seems to convey his struggle best:

> Sinai is eternal, its demand infinite, and we want to reject both madness and flight. In learning to live with the rhythm of our inner tides there may be a path that brings some peace. Not the stillness-peace of a lake or a pond: those we strugglers can never attain (and thus we reject them)! Rather the peace of the waters of Ocean, ever churning, smashing, rising, and falling—find their peace

> in the regular breathing of tides, seeing themselves and their beauty both in ebb and in flow.[8]

Following brother Leo's death, an editorial in the *Rutland Herald* captured the meaning of his life for countless people far and near:

> A tribute to brother Leo is the image his priory carries as a place at which any visitors are welcomed. To most Vermonters, it appears to foster a feeling of acceptance regardless of creed, or the lack of a creed. That in itself is no small accomplishment in these days of moral majorities.
>
> The abbot's effort to ease the way for Catholic-Jewish communication and understanding is noteworthy because it is so necessary. It's too bad each major religious order hasn't had more like him over the years.
>
> The story of civilization shows more tears, anguish, terror and bloodshed due to religious antagonism than to any other single cause. From Agamemnon appeasing his god—he sacrificed his own daughter so the wind would start moving his becalmed ships—to the current war between Iran and Iraq, religious beliefs have left a bloody trail.
>
> Brother Leo tried to soften the hard lines. As Rutland's Rabbi Solomon D. Goldberg suggested, the priory's founder may have been one of the 36 "wise and saintly" men for whose sake the world is preserved.[9]

The "thirty-sixers" *(lamed vovniks)* of ancient Hebrew tradition are people who demonstrate extraordinary generosity and selflessness to humankind. At the same time, they never seek to be identified as do-gooders. Essential to their character is humility.

If brother Leo was a *lamed-vovnik,* it was in his own play mode that coupled "little Leo" with his divine dancing partner. The dance, always demanding, was not perfect: sometimes his steps were out of sync. But he gave himself wholly to it. And, by the end of the dance, he was in touch with the mystery of his Jewish heart.

This Christian—Benedictine monk, abbot, and brother—who walked by the sea of Galilee, stumbled along the path of a certain Jew who traveled the same shores. Even when he felt betrayed, brother Leo, a gracious man, a humble man, found it in his heart to say, "When I love, I love forever!"

Let us set out
On a pilgrimage of the heart;
Wandering in the wilderness—
Learning how to dance![10]

Brother Leo (abbot, 1952-1969), brother Richard (prior, 1998-), brother John (prior, 1964-1998). “Monasticism is a living, not a dead, thing. It moves with the times, because the Rule is not a dead letter, but an inspired work, conveying the Spirit…in [it] a decisive step was taken towards the fraternal relationship of brothers.”

Afterword
by Rabbi Arthur Green

Many years ago, my teacher and friend Rabbi Zalman Schacter taught me that a deeper dialogue between Jews and Christians, one for which we both longed, should focus around the Psalms. When we returned to conversations about this theme over the years, we both thought immediately of the beautiful psalm chanting we had heard at Weston and of some precious hours of conversation with the brothers there. It is for this reason that I turn to the Psalter as a text for these brief remarks in memory of Father/Brother Leo Rudloff, may his memory be a blessing. I choose to focus on Psalms 122 and 36 (by our count, the Catholic Bible numbers may differ slightly), for reasons that will be clear to the reader of brother John's narrative.

I rejoiced when they said to me:
Let us go to the house of the Lord.

Where, indeed, is the "House of the Lord?" This wonderful book is the life story of a man devoted to the journey to God's house, but paying a great price for having had more than one answer to the seemingly simple and obvious question. Why,

God's house is in Jerusalem, of course. The Psalmist goes on to say it quite clearly:

> *Our feet stood inside your gates, O Jerusalem.*

In this case, it was in fact "just outside your gates," the Dormition Abbey being a few steps from the Zion Gate, the way into the Old City that leads through the Jewish Quarter to the Temple Mount. It was no accident that Leo Rudloff was so devoted to a church positioned just that way. His way to "God's House" was increasingly one of gaining familiarity with those realms of his own soul and our conjoined spiritual traditions that may be called "the Jewish Quarter." His vision of a Christian house of prayer so close to the Jewish side of that great center where the three faiths meet and struggle was important and unique. Unlike so many of the Holy Land Christians, engaged in turf-battles with one another and locked in insular struggles each to preserve its own distinctive truth-claims, Brother Leo conceived of a Christian presence open to others and welcoming pilgrims and seekers of all sorts. In contrast to the rather chilly reception given to Israeli statehood by many in the Christian world, Leo Rudloff wanted his abbey to exist comfortably within the State of Israel, encouraging his brothers to learn Hebrew and incorporate it in their worship, as well as to house authentic dialogue between Jews and Christians.

But the Dormition was not the only "House of the Lord" in Brother Leo's life. In his beloved Weston, he was able to build God's house much more as he wanted it to be: simple in both architecture and liturgy, down-to-earth in its connection to physical labor and agriculture, and closer to egalitarian in the relationships between abbot and brothers, as is so well documented here. All of these were problematic in Jerusalem, perhaps overly rich in traditions and therefore hard to reshape. In

Vermont the only tradition was simplicity itself! No wonder this man, so much a person of Vatican II, was attracted to this house of God as well as the other.

He also understood that the inner peace of monastic devotion was much dependent on the surrounding environment.

> *Rebuilt Jerusalem is like a city joined together;*
> *there the tribes come as pilgrims,*
> *the tribes of the Lord.*

But Jerusalem in all the years that Leo Rudloff knew and loved it was not "like a city joined together." In the early years of his stays there, before 1967, it was indeed a physically divided city, separated by walls of concrete and barbed wire, with hostile soldiers on each side of the divide. Indeed, the Dormition was one of those rare places within Israeli Jerusalem from which on could "peer through the wall (see Cant. 2:9)" over to the Old City with its many sacred sites. It seemed both like a few feet and a thousand miles away, separated by hostility and distrust. After 1967, the physical barriers came down and Israel rightfully reclaimed the Jewish Quarter. In the early years, it seemed that indeed there might be a coming together here of Israelis and Arabs, Jews, Christians, and Muslims. Alas, that was not to be. The Israeli victors soon fell victim to the turf-war mentality, claiming and settling ever more than should have been permitted. Muslims, deeply threatened by an Israeli rule that was theologically as well as politically uncomfortable for them, remained ever hostile. Christians witnessed a rising tide of emigration by their local communicants, felt mostly helpless to mediate in what was mostly a Jewish/Muslim struggle, and so fell back upon protecting their own historical rights and mini-territorial claims. This was hardly a setting for the sort of "pilgrims" that Leo Rudloff might have had in mind. One comes to Jerusalem today for seminars on protracted violence more than for inner peace. For all that, however, his love of the Holy City did not diminish, and he continued to

pray for the peace of Jerusalem.
May those who love you find tranquility.

More than many others, Brother Leo also understood that peace, a tranquility within the heart, depended upon a family or community in which they could be properly fostered. This meant, in the monastic context, a community of true love among brothers, joined to one another by their love of God and devotion to God's service. Therefore, the Psalm concludes first with

For the sake of my brothers and friends

and only then goes on to

For the sake of the House of the Lord our God.

It is brotherhood and friendship that make a place in "the House of the Lord our God." This Leo founded and found at Weston, and it was because of this that the Weston Priory has indeed thrived over these stormy decades in the life of the church and has achieved renown as a House of God that is loved and respected by so many.

It is our Jewish custom, when donning our *tallit* or prayer-shawl for morning prayers (that should indeed take place at dawn!), to cover our face with the shawl for a moment of private devotion, during which we recite the following verses from Psalm 36:8–10:

How precious is your loving kindness, O God!
Humans find shelter in the shadow of your wings.
They are sated by the rich feast of Your house;
You give them drink from the streams of your Eden,

With you is the font of light;
In Your light we see light.
Draw Your compassion toward those who know You
And Your beneficence on the upright of heart.

These verses are chosen for this liturgical moment probably because of their second line. The Jew wrapped in a *tallit* is to feel the "shelter in the shadow of Your wings" as a real moment of divine presence. But there is much more to them as well. The reality of God's *hesed* (rendered here as "lovingkindness" and "compassion," but also translatable as "grace") is their central theme. This *hesed* is the great gift of God that sustains us through our life's journey. It is a generous and inexhaustible flow of blessing, given to us without judgment, without measure of how deserving we are to receive it. The challenge to us implicit in this gift is that we pass it on to others, that we share it in the human community and with all God's creatures in the same spirit of non-judgmental giving.

"How precious is Your lovingkindness" indeed, when we are able to give it as a gift to all those we encounter. We are sheltered in God's wings so that we can give God's love to others, allowing all to be "sated by the rich feast of Your house." Here we have another description of God's house. It is a place of rich feasting, not in the material sense, of course, but in the nurturing of the spirit. There the great gifts that mystics of all ages have known, the streams of Eden's rivers, and the rays of God's own shining light are to be found in abundance.

It is about the building of such a house, and the life and struggles of its builder, that you have read in this volume. Go forth and build as well.

Rabbi Arthur Green
Philip W. Lown Professor of Jewish Thought
Brandeis University

Notes

Chapter 1

1. Düren was named for the diets summoned by Charlemagne in the eighth century. With its Gothic Saint Anna-Kirke, it began to draw European pilgrims unable to reach Rome, Campostello, or Jerusalem as early as the 1500s. By the late 1800s, located on the main rail line to nearby Cologne, it was a thriving commercial center churning out cloth, paper, carpet, artificial wool, sugar, iron wares, and needles.

2. Winter and Linn, *Damasus Winzen, A Monk of Two Worlds,* unpublished, 1974, Mount Saviour, Pine City, N.Y., p.60.

3. Cfr. *Great Benedictines: Lambert Beauduin, O.S.B. 1873-1960,* in Crescat, Volume. 12, No. 1, Fall, 1988., Anselm C. Biggs, O.S.B., publ. Benedictine monks of Belmont Abbey. This article is the helpful source for much of the factual information on the life of Lambert Beauduin in the following section.

Chapter 2

1. *Father Damasus and the Founding of Mount Savior,* J. M. Roarke, Pine City, N.Y. 1998, pp.63–91.

2. Ibid.

3. Ibid.

4. Ibid.

Chapter 3

1. *Father Damasus and the Founding of Mount Savior,* J. M.Roarke, p. 108.

Chapter 4

1. The community of St. Joseph Abbey in Gerleve was a stalwart support to the Dormition Abbey from its earliest days. At the request of Abbot Ildefons Schober of the Archabbey of Beuron, Abbot Raphael Mollitor of Gerleve conducted a canonical visitation of Dormition Abbey in 1912. Consequently, he became administrator of the abbey and sent Mathias Breitback and Benedict Stolz to augment the staff in 1921. When the abbey accepted the task to teach at the Seminary of the Latin Patriarch in Beit Jalla in 1923, he sent Maurus Killer, Johannes Hülsmann, Willibrord Bungardt and Petrus Siffrin. In that same year, Maurus Kaufmann, a monk of Maria Laach, became the first abbot of the Dormition. (From *Die Benediktinerabtei Gerleve,* Ashendorf Münster, 1997, p. 120.)

Chapter 5

1. *An Early History of Weston Priory,* Dorothea Smith, unpublished, Weston, Vt.

Chapter 6

1. The Camerlengo of the Catholic Church is the administrator of the property and the revenues of the Holy See, and as such is successor both of the Archdeacon of Rome and of the *Vicedominus,* the former of whom administered the property of the entire Roman Church, i.e., the Diocese of Rome, while the latter was especially charged with the administration of the *mensa* of the pope and the entire personnel of the *patriarchium Lateranense* (St. John Lateran). [Note from the Catholic Encyclopedia]

2. Benedictines are not organized as a religious order or congregation in the strict sense. They are united in a confederation of independ-

ent monasteries and congregations. With the Abbot Primate functioning as liaison between the independent houses and the Holy See, abbots and conventual priors (heads of independent priories) enjoy "ordinary jurisdiction," that is, their authority derives from their office in their own monastery, rather than being delegated by an external authority.

Chapter 8

1. *Weston Priory Bulletin,* September 1957.
2. There were four stages of integration into the community: *Postulants,* for a period of three months to a year, wearing the monastic tunic and belt, lived with the community without formal commitments. *Novices,* lived in special dormitory area, wearing tunic and short scapular, with commitment for one year. *Temporarily professed,* wearing full monastic scapular and tunic, with commitment to obedience, stability, and common life for a period of three years. *Solemnly professed,* clothed with scapular, tunic, and cowl, with life commitment to obedience, stability, and conversatio morum, understood as faithfulness to the common life in accordance with the Rule of Benedict and the observance of the local monastery.
3. A tangible sign of the fraternal relationship of the two communities is the gray tunic and black scapular worn as a monastic garb. The distinctive habit originated with the Benedictine community in Cuernavaca, Mexico, founded by Gregory Lemercier. Father Damasus brought it to Mount Saviour after some months of recuperation with Lemercier's community following his illness in the 1950s.

Chapter 9

1. The Ulpan Akiva, founded in 1951, carries the name of Rabbi Akiva, a founder of rabbinic Judaism, whose life straddled the first and second centuries of the Common Era. This renowned Jewish leader is considered a master of transformation and growth. Beginning his study of Torah after the age of forty, he became one of the greatest of the Tannaim, scholars of the Mishnah, the earliest written form of the Oral Torah. Rabbi Akiva, who witnessed the

destruction of the Temple in 70 C.E., was noted for his ability to envision rebirth amid devastation.

2. *Bulletin of Weston Priory,* June, 1959.

3. Ibid.

4. Damasus Winzen, *A Monk of Two Worlds,* Winter & Linn, 1974, p.98.

5. Ibid.

6. After he left Sant'Anselmo, Beauduin consulted with Archbishop Angelo Roncalli, Apostolic Nuncio to Bulgaria. He then founded the joint Latin-Byzantine monastery at Amay in 1925. He was active in Ecumenical exchanges. His views were considered radical in Rome, and he was summoned to answer charges in 1930. In 1932, he was induced to choose self-exile from his monastery that subsequently moved to Chevetogne. After the election of Cardinal Roncalli as Pope John XXIII, Beauduin's positions were vindicated, and he was invited to return to his community at Chevetogne. [Also see above, Chapter 1, pp. 16–18]

Chapter 10

1. *Weston Priory Bulletin,* Pentecost, 1960.

2. *Weston Priory Bulletin,* Advent, 1961.

3. *Weston Priory Bulletin,* September, 1962.

4. *The American Benedictine Review,* 1961.

5. *Weston Priory Bulletin,* Advent, 1961.

6. *Recessus Visitationis,* Most Reverend Benno Gut, Abbot Primate, August 7–10, 1963, Weston Priory.

7. *Weston Priory Bulletin,* Autumn, 1963.

Chapter 11

1. As long as Weston Priory remained a canonical dependency of the Dormition Abbey, all Weston monks were technically members of that abbey and made their monastic commitment to the Dormition community.

2. Letter from brother David to Weston Community, January, 1964.

3. At his solemn monastic profession in 1961, Father Robert received, at his own request, the name John. He was addressed as brother John soon after he was named prior in 1964 when the Weston community adopted the custom of calling one another brother. Abbot Leo continued to address him as Father John until 1968. For the sake of simplicity, the text identifies him as brother John from this point on. Brother John served as prior of the Weston community from 1964 to 1998. He is the author of the present book.
4. Letter of Abbot Leo to brother John, October 10, 1964.
5. Letter of Abbot Leo to brother John, February 21, 1965.
6. Letter of Abbot Leo to brother John, March 12, 1965.
7. Speech by Abbot Leo marking the fiftieth anniversary of Monsignor Oestrerriecher's ordination.
8. Copy of letter from Abbot Leo to Cardinal Bea, October 10, 1965.
9. Letter from Father Lucas Joerg, O.S.B. to Abbot Leo, Dec. 7, 1965.
10. Letter from Abbot Leo to Father Lucas Joerg, Dec. 14, 1965.

Chapter 12

1. Travelogue from Abbot Leo to community, circa June 11, 1966.
2. Letter from Abbot Leo to brother John, June 13, 1966.
3. *Recessus* (Report) of Canonical Visitation at Weston Priory, July 7–10, 1966, Most Rev. Benno Gut, O.S.B. and his secretary, Rev. Lambert Dunne, O.S.B.
4. Soon after Abbot Benno returned to Rome and the fall assembly of the Abbots' Congress, he was appointed to the prestigious office of Cardinal Prefect of the Congregation for Worship.
5. Letter from Abbot Leo to brother John, August 20, 1966.
6. *Mount Saviour Chronicle,* Christmas, 1964.
7. *Address to Abbots' Congress,* Rome, Abbot Leo Rudloff, Sept., 1966, translated from the Latin.
8. Nicolaus Egender became the fourth abbot of the Dormition Abbey in 1979.

9. Letter to the Weston community from Abbot Leo, July 6, 1967.

10. A small property, once a Camaldolese hermitage in Vermont on the New Hampshire border. When the Camaldolese monks were no longer able to manage the property, they turned it over to the Weston community.

Chapter 13

1. Letter from brother John to Abbot Leo, Feb. 4, 1968.

2. Letter from Abbot Leo to brother John Feb. 15, 1968.

3. A *conventual priory* enjoys the same canonical status and juridical independence as an abbey. A *claustral priory* is dependent canonically upon the founding monastery. The authority of a claustral prior is delegated and dependent upon the authority of the founding abbot or prior.

Chapter 14

1. *After Itzik: Toward a Theology of Jewish Spirituality, Art Green, Worship Magazine,* April, 1971, pp. 206–213.

Chapter 15

1. Known informally as the *Israel Study Group,* at a later date it formally became the *Christian Study Group on Judaism and the Jewish People,* with a subsequent slight revision to *Christian Scholars Group on Judaism and the Jewish People.* It is currently titled the *Christian Scholars Group on Christian-Jewish Relations.* The original group consisted of 15–20 members with Franklin H. Littell, A. Roy Eckardt, and Sr. Ann Patrick Ware as the conveners. Other members at that time were Markus Barth, Roland de Corneille, Edward Flannery, Robert Handy, Walter Harrelson, William Harter, George Lindbeck, Vincent Martin, John Oesterreicher, Bernhard Olson, John Pawlikowski, Donna Purdy, J. Coert Rylaarsdam, John Sheerin, Theodore Stylianopoulos, Leonard Swidler, Rose Thering, John Townsend, and Eberhard von Waldow.

   After the *Statement to Our Fellow Christians* was issued in 1973, some members retired from the group and others were added, including: Paul van Buren, Claire Huchet Bishop, Philip Culberston, Alice Eckardt, Eugene Fisher, Eva Fleischner, Ursula Niebuhr, Cornelius Rijk, Abbot Leo Rudloff, and Franklin Sherman. (Taken from *Christian Scholars Group on Christian-Jewish Relations,* website, *Historical Sketch,* Alice Eckardt and Franklin Sherman)

2. Letter to brother John and community, May 7, 1973.
3. Letter from brother Leo to community, May 18, 1973.
4. Letter from brother Leo to community, June 6, 1973.
5. Letter from brother Leo to community, June 13, 1973.
6. Ibid.
7. Letter from brother Leo to brothers, June 17, 1974.
8. Letter from brother Leo to brother John, April 6, 1974.
9. Letter from brother John to brother Leo, June 12, 1974.

Chapter 16

1. Letter from brother Leo to friend, October 12, 1973.
2. *Reflections on the Rule of Benedict,* Leo Rudloff, unpublished manuscript, written in the early1970s.
3. *Israel's Right to Exist,* Abbot Leo Rudloff, Anti-Defamation League of B'ni B'rith, New York, N.Y., 1974.
4. *Archbishop Capucci and Terrorism,* Abbot Leo Rudloff, Anti-Defamation League of B'nai B'rith, 1981.
5. *A Christian Looks at Israel,* Address by Rt. Rev. Leo Rudloff, O.S.B. at Stephen Wise Synagogue, New York City, October 12, 1979.
6. Letter from brother Leo to Rabbi Samuel Dresner, December 18, 1978.
7. Letter from brother Leo to Weston brothers, November 7, 1979.

Chapter 17

1. Letter from Catherine de Vinck to brother Leo, September 29, 1981.

Chapter 18

1. *The Abbot is Dead,* by brother Leo, monograph, unpublished, April, 1981.

2. Abbot Leo Rudloff, *American Benedictine Review,* December, 1965.
3. Ibid.
4. *The Particulars of Rapture, Reflections on Exodus,* Avivah Zornberg, Doubleday, New York, N.Y., p. 276.
5. *Listen,* ©Benedictine Foundation of the State of Vermont, Inc., 1973.
6. *Wherever You Go,* ©Benedictine Foundation of the State of Vermont, Inc., 1972.
7. Ibid.
8. *After Itzik,* Rabbi Arthur Green, *Worship,* April, 1971.
9. *Rutland Herald,* August 24, 1982.
10. *Pilgrimage of the Heart,* ©Benedictine Foundation of the State of Vermont, Inc. 2001.